I0802200

Old English Liturgical Verse

Old English Liturgical Verse

A student edition

edited by Sarah Larratt Keefer

broadview press

© 2010 Sarah Larratt Keefer

All rights reserved. The use of any part of this publication reproduced, transmitted in any form or by any means, electronic, mechanical, photocopying, recording, or otherwise, or stored in a retrieval system, without prior written consent of the publisher—or in the case of photocopying, a licence from Access Copyright (Canadian Copyright Licensing Agency), One Yonge Street, Suite 1900, Toronto, Ontario M5E 1E5—is an infringement of the copyright law.

Library and Archives Canada Cataloguing in Publication

Old English liturgical verse : a student edition / edited by Sarah Larratt Keefer.

Includes bibliographical references.
ISBN 978-1-55111-788-1

1. English poetry—Old English, ca. 450-1100.
2. Religious poetry, English. I. Keefer, Sarah Larratt

PR1505.O44 2010 829'.1008 C2010-901597-5

Broadview Press is an independent, international publishing house, incorporated in 1985. Broadview believes in shared ownership, both with its employees and with the general public; since the year 2000 Broadview shares have traded publicly on the Toronto Venture Exchange under the symbol BDP.

We welcome comments and suggestions regarding any aspect of our publications—please feel free to contact us at the addresses below or at broadview@broadviewpress.com.

North America
Post Office Box 1243, Peterborough, Ontario, Canada K9J 7H5
2215 Kenmore Avenue, Buffalo, NY, USA 14207
Tel: (705) 743-8990; Fax: (705) 743-8353
email: customerservice@broadviewpress.com

UK, Europe, Central Asia, Middle East, Africa, India, and Southeast Asia
Eurospan Group, 3 Henrietta St., London WC2E 8LU, United Kingdom
Tel: 44 (0) 1767 604972; Fax: 44 (0) 1767 601640
email: eurospan@turpin-distribution.com

Australia and New Zealand
NewSouth Books
c/o TL Distribution, 15-23 Helles Ave., Moorebank, NSW, Australia 2170
Tel: (02) 8778 9999; Fax: (02) 8778 9944
email: orders@tldistribution.com.au

www.broadviewpress.com

Broadview Press acknowledges the financial support of the Government of Canada through the Canada Book Fund for our publishing activities.

Copy-edited by Martin Boyne

This book is printed on paper containing 100% post-consumer fibre.

Typesetting and assembly: True to Type Inc., Claremont, Canada.

PRINTED IN CANADA

Contents

Acknowledgements

I am grateful to the Social Sciences and Humanities Research Council and to the Trent University Research Office for financial support, allowing me to examine the manuscripts for this edition, to purchase images of their pertinent folios, and to present my findings and ideas at many conferences from 1991 onward.

I wish to thank many colleagues for advice on this project over the years, in particular Dr. Patricia Hollahan of the Medieval Institute Press, Western Michigan University, for her major role in the initial stages of the edition. I am immensely grateful to Professors Rolf H. Bremmer, Joyce Hill, and Roy Liuzza for their detailed commentaries and suggestions on parts of the final draft of the volume. I am also very grateful to Professor Toni Healey at the Dictionary of Old English Project for patience, advice, solutions, and prompt replies. Thanks are also due to Dr. Debby Banham for checking manuscript readings for me from afar, and to Professor Catherine Karkov for advice on the "Mary and the Trinity" image. Without the assistance of so many generous scholars, this book would not have been written. Errors to be found in it will have come from my own desk alone.

I extend my sincerest gratitude to Marjorie Mather, who guided me through the initial stages of the very enjoyable relationship over this book that I have had with Broadview Press, and to Martin Boyne, who has served me so capably and constructively at every step of the volume's preparation. I have been encouraged and supported by Broadview's staff at each turn of the road in a truly and uniquely positive experience that is only too rare for an author, and I am very aware of how lucky I have been with such assistance.

My final thanks are to my husband Richard, who now knows more about Old English liturgical poetry than he ever expected to; his presence at conferences, his tireless role as reader or audience for every section of this book, and his patient support of a frenzied editor for over twenty years have all been deeply appreciated.

Sarah Larratt Keefer, Professor and 3M National Teaching Fellow
Department of English, Trent University
Peterborough, Ontario

List of Figures

Abbreviations

ASE	*Anglo-Saxon England*
ASMMF	*Anglo-Saxon Manuscripts in Microfiche Facsimile,* ed. Phillip Pulsiano, A.N. Doane, et al. (Tempe: ACMRS, 1990-)
ASPR	*Anglo-Saxon Poetic Records: A Collective Edition*, ed. George P. Krapp and Elliott van Kirk Dobbie, 6 vols. (New York: Columbia UP, 1931–53)
BL	British Library
BT(S)	Joseph Bosworth and T. Northcote Toller, *An Anglo-Saxon Dictionary* (Oxford: Clarendon Press, 1898); T.N. Toller, *Supplement* (Oxford: Clarendon Press, 1912)
CCCC	Cambridge, Corpus Christi College
CHM	J.R. Clark Hall and H.D. Meritt, *A Concise Anglo-Saxon Dictionary* (Cambridge: Cambridge University Press, 1969)
CSASE	Cambridge Studies in Anglo-Saxon England
DOE	*Dictionary of Old English: A to G on CD-ROM*, ed. Angus Cameron, Ashley Crandell Amos, and Antonette di Paolo Healey (Toronto: Pontifical Institute of Mediaeval Studies for the Dictionary of Old English Project, 2008)
DOEC	Dictionary of Old English Corpus online (www.umdl.umich.edu/cgi/oec)
EEMF	Early English Manuscripts in Facsimile
EETS	Early English Text Society
HBS	Henry Bradshaw Society
MS	manuscript
OE	Old English
WTH	Worcester Tremulous Hand

Introduction and Background

This book is unusual in a number of ways. It brings together a group of poems that are, with the exception of *Vision of the Rood*, almost unknown and never studied as part of the Old English verse canon. In a 1998 volume of essays on editing Old English poetry, Don Scragg advised that "a new ASPR can and must do something about improving . . . titles."[1] I have accordingly re-titled each piece as needed in this volume, with an explanation set out in its introduction; throughout the book, ASPR (*Anglo-Saxon Poetic Records*) titles are provided in quotation marks, and new titles of the pieces are set in italics. The edition is also unique in bringing these poems together as a dedicated subgenre of verse: inspired by the liturgy, or the public ritual language of the Christian Church, all of these pieces reflect liturgical practice as it was known in Anglo-Saxon England between AD 600 and 1100. Finally, this edition is innovative in presenting the text of each poem as a piece with two faces. On the left-hand page the layout of the poem appears much as it does in the manuscript itself, in the format known as "semi-diplomatic," preserving spatial and scribal information evident in the manuscript witness, but set out in Roman orthography with necessary expansions of scribal abbreviations and regularization of morphology. On the right-hand page is the critical text of each poem, the conventional format for presenting Old English verse, laid out in alliterating half-lines to indicate metrical structure, and with any emenda-

1 D.G. Scragg, "Towards a New Anglo-Saxon Poetic Records," *New Approaches to Editing Old English Verse*, ed. Sarah Larratt Keefer and Katherine O'Brien O'Keeffe (Cambridge: Brewer, 1998), 67–77, 70.

tions of what appear to be scribal errors.[2] Notes accompany the text of each poem, providing background and explanation.

While it has become customary to edit Old English verse by dividing it into its half-lines, with the caesura (or rhythmic pause) that separates them being indicated by a blank space (i.e. as in the critical format), no poem appears in its manuscript as anything other than a block of what is apparently prose. The semi-diplomatic version therefore allows us a readable snapshot—original layout that is nevertheless in familiar orthography—of evidence to be found in the original manuscript. The reader thus has access both to information contained by the layout of poem-texts while in their manuscript form, and to the conventional presentation of Old English poetry, which allows for easy translation and appreciation of metre. It is nevertheless clear that Anglo-Saxon scribes understood that this "prose-block" was poetry, and we will see that one of our pieces (*Ah, Beloved Lord*) is actually laid out in its only complete version in a twelfth-century manuscript in such a way that, despite the "prose" format, words that have semantic relationships to one another are to be found in identical locations (beginning, middle or end) on different lines of that "prose-block."

In the critical texts of these poems, I provide a minimum of modern punctuation, following the scribes' own use of majuscules and *puncti elevati* (evident in the semi-diplomatic texts) to guide my use of new sentences and of periods or semicolons. I insert commas primarily to aid readers in seeing parallel constructions and appositions. Proper names are capitalized and, although they never appear in the manuscript with majuscules, I capitalize "God" (and therefore "Christ") to assist with readers' comprehension of the poetry. Vowel length is added to critical texts (and reflected in the Glossary), as is appropriate for this kind of edition. Wherever possible I preserve the manuscript reading instead of emending, to provide as accurate an impression as possible of each scribe at work. Words underlined in the text are addressed in the notes that follow, where I explain errors or problems that can affect comprehension, and provide grammatical guidelines to allow for accurate translation.

The world has changed so much in the last millennium that we are hard put to remember that education and learning were once wholly the province of the

2 The inspiration for this model lies in the work of Katherine O'Brien O'Keeffe; see her "Texts and Works: Some Historical Questions on the Editing of Old English Verse," *New Historical Literary Study: Essays on Reproducing Texts, Reproducing History*, ed. J.N. Cox and L.J. Reynolds (Princeton: Princeton UP, 1993), 54–68, 64.

Church and, particularly after the Reform of the later tenth century, that they lay in the hands of monasteries and nunneries. Although there were certainly members of the laity who could read and write, the production of manuscripts and the keeping of libraries and records resided to a substantial degree with ecclesiastical and monastic foundations. The language, rhythms, imagery, and culture of the church year were therefore an integral part of the aesthetic that governed the recording, construction, and presentation of Anglo-Saxon learning and thought.

However, writing a poem that focuses on something familiar makes the poet regard the subject with new eyes. So, far from being self-evident, the liturgical poems collected here are fascinating for what they tell us about the ways in which the creative Anglo-Saxon minds responded self-consciously to the culture of Christian ritual with which they lived so closely. In order to write such verse, the Anglo-Saxons who created it had to "step outside the box" to look at what was all around them and to respond in a mindful and deliberate fashion. Such poetry provides an insight into the creation *not* of distanced narratives about heroism (driven either by scriptural account or by Germanic epic legend), *nor* of exercises in wit or preaching or translation of learned Latin material, but of something markedly different. The writing of a poetic meditation based on a prayer that one repeats many times in a single day is an unusual act of self-awareness, since it must examine the supremely obvious for a deeper resonance of belief. As such, these liturgical pieces give us a special insight into the Anglo-Saxon creative aesthetic turned inward to explore the immanent spiritual dimensions of the human soul.

It is nevertheless important to remember that "meditation" does not automatically presume a private rather than a communal act. The poets and scribes who composed and preserved these poems were almost certainly Benedictine monks and nuns, and the reformed Benedictinism of the period during which these poems were most likely produced stressed the communal over all else, such that the concept of ownership was set aside: "no one is to presume to give or receive anything without the Abbot's permission, or to keep anything at all as his own, neither book nor writing-tablet nor pen, nothing whatsoever. . . . Let all share in everything in common, as it is written, and let no one say or suppose that anything is his own."[3] Reading was encouraged for professed Benedictine men and women in times of rest, particularly after the midday

3 Richard Crotty, trans., *Rule of St. Benedict* (Nedlands: U of Western Australia P, 1963), 45–47. See also H. Logeman, ed., *The Rule of St Benet* (London: Trübner, 1888), 63–64, where this chapter appears in Latin with Old English translation above it.

meal, so opportunities for composing poems like these for the benefit of the community would not have been lacking. The observance of Lent in a Benedictine house made provision for additional duties, including "private prayers . . . so everyone will be voluntarily offering to God something above the measure required of him,"[4] and the Benedictine Rule's chapter on craftsmen teaches against anyone who regards such work as "an occasion of pride" such that "[he] be taken away from his craft, and not work at it again."[5] Therefore we may assume that we are catching a glimpse not only of Anglo-Saxon aesthetic sensibilities regarding the ritual language of the Church, but also of the ways in which something that comes from the individual heart at prayer was framed so as to belong to the community as a whole.

Scholarship concerning Old English liturgical poetry is scanty. Since their Latin sources are frequently obvious through being intercalated with the vernacular verse-texts, these poems have been regarded as pedestrian translations and therefore not interesting enough for study. The reason for their creation has been assumed to have been primarily educational, a suggestion probably true in part but certainly limited in its outlook. When examining the larger canon of Latin liturgy glossed by or free-translated to Old English, we encounter circumstances where the translation of a Latin liturgical text into the vernacular can not have been made for educational purposes.[6] Such translations appear devotional in impulse, so explaining away the rendering of well-known prayers or hymns in vernacular poetry as "educational" is shortsighted.

It is my considered opinion that Old English liturgical verse is an articulation of meditation upon prayer that is expressed in the specialized structure of poetry in order to set it apart from the world in which we speak and think without self-conscious structure. In such verse, the interactions between private and public, personal and communal, become spiritual paradoxes that the poets invite their audiences to ponder. So at least for liturgical poetry that

4 Crotty, *Rule of St. Benedict*, 63; see also Logeman, *Rule of St Benet*, 84–85, for the Old English counterpart.

5 Crotty, *Rule of St. Benedict*, 71; Logeman, *Rule of St Benet*, 94.

6 A case in point is the meticulous Old English glossing by Aldred the Provost of virtually all the material in Durham Cathedral Library A. iv. 19. This manuscript contains early tenth-century Latin Office chapters and collects (those readings and prayers prescribed for the individual monastic services of each day), and then later tenth-century miscellaneous Latin liturgical texts, none of which would ever have been recited in Old English, so glossing it would not have been for performative purposes; nor would its contents have been useful within a classroom setting to teach monks Latin, since so many other more appropriate texts were available.

relies upon a single Latin source, and quite possibly for all liturgical verse, we may suggest that

> [i]t locates individual experience within a social and intellectual community as a reinvestigation of the phenomenon of monasticism, or perhaps a revisitation of it, and prefers the cenobitic to the anchoritic impulse. Rather than being a translation exercise for young monks, liturgical poetry based on a single discrete synactic source may have framed a cross-over point where the "words of our mouth" and the "meditation of our hearts" were made public with written text, suggesting a performative reenactment of synactic worship, but within the medium of private thoughts, the vernacular.[7]

"Liturgy" is the most commonly used term for the prayers and ritual constructing the services of the Christian church throughout its particular calendar year and designed for its individual elements of importance. The life of the individual Christian man or woman in Anglo-Saxon England was marked by different rites of passage[8]—baptism, usually as an infant (or, if as an adult, as a result of conversion); the blessing of a marriage (no church service other than a nuptial mass and various blessings was known in pre-Conquest England); pastoral anointing of the sick; and burial of the dead. If a member of the laity chose a vocation in the Church as a priest or member of a professed order, there were rituals that consecrated a man as a deacon, priest, bishop or archbishop, or as a monk, and consecrated a woman as a nun.

During the later centuries of the Anglo-Saxon period, men and women who took up the professed life as monks and nuns lived according to the *Regula Sancti Benedicti* ("Rule of St. Benedict"). This early monastic rule developed in Italy in the sixth century, influencing a number of monastic communities who nevertheless followed various individual practices as well.[9] Monasticism

---

7 Sarah Larratt Keefer, "'Ic' and 'We' in Eleventh-Century Old English Liturgical Verse," *Unlocking the Wordhord: Anglo-Saxon Studies in Memory of Edward B. Irving, Jr.*, ed. Mark C. Amodio and Katherine O'Brien O'Keeffe (Toronto: U of Toronto P, 2003), 123–46, 141. The quoted phrases derive from the Book of Psalms and were used within the monastic Offices before readings. "Cenobitic" refers to communal monastic life, "anchoritic" to professed men and women living as hermits, and "synactic" to the public ritual language or performance of the Church.

8 See Sarah Larratt Keefer, "Manuals," *The Liturgical Books of Anglo-Saxon England*, ed. R.W. Pfaff, Old English Newsletter Subsidia 23 (Kalamazoo, MI: Medieval Institute Press, 1995), 99–110, for a description of these rites.

9 See Dom David Knowles, *The Monastic Order in England*, 2nd ed. (Cambridge: Cambridge UP, 1966), 1–30, for an overview of the complexities of monastic life as it was known in western Europe prior to the tenth century.

as it was practised in Italy was established in the south of England by St Augustine of Canterbury ca. 597,[10] while Irish missionaries brought a more ascetic form of monasticism to the north of England a generation or so later. Yet once again there was no single rule that was followed in any one location; indeed, the Rule of St Benedict was not unknown in the north, but the degree to which it was followed remains unclear. Conflict arose later between Roman and Irish practice: both emphasized education, teaching, and learning, but the Roman way was chosen over the Irish at the Synod of Whitby in 663 or 664, and Roman liturgical practice both in churches and monasteries was established throughout England. Anglo-Saxon missionaries and teachers were sent to the continent during the eighth century; their activities helped to establish new continental foundations and regularize existing monastic life and church liturgical practice in general during that period. By the end of the eighth century, scholars of both sexes trained in English monasteries and nunneries were leaving a substantial cultural and literary footprint for posterity, and men such as Alcuin of York, liturgical consultant to Charlemagne himself, were considered among the greatest intellectual luminaries of their age.

However, the coming of Danish invaders from the north in the last years of the eighth century caused devastation to the English monastic houses and their centres of learning. Raids led to more systematic attacks and then invasion, as the newcomers sought first plunder and then settlement, and many aspects of the Anglo-Saxon social structure suffered substantial collapse during these "viking" raids by Danes during the course of the ninth century. As a result, teaching and education, a professed life of prayer and meditation, and the leisure to pursue the writing and copying of books were interrupted, destroyed or irrevocably changed. Many houses were closed due to attrition or social devastation, and those that remained often became secularized, since few men or women were in a position to follow a vocation when there was so much to recover from in the wake of the Danish invaders. In the late ninth century, Alfred, king of the West Saxons (r. 878–899), successfully met and defeated the last of the now-waning Danish invading forces, constructing peace by negotiated treaty and providing lands for the Danes (thereby incorporating them into Anglo-Saxon society), and ultimately establishing the House of Wessex as the foremost dynasty within England. Alfred was committed to a

---

10 "No precise statement exists to show that the Rule was the code of the Canterbury house, and with our knowledge of Gregory we may assume fairly confidently that it was not so, or, if it was, that it was regarded as a rule to be used within a given framework of life, rather than as a code upon which every detail of that life was to be built" (Knowles, *Monastic Order*, 21).

program of education for all freeborn Anglo-Saxons and to a campaign of translating those texts that he and his advisors considered central to western culture, into a vernacular that could be more widely understood. Yet Alfred was able to found or re-establish only a few monastic centres where learning could flourish. It was left to his great-grandson Edgar (959–975), known as "the Peaceful," to provide royal patronage and direction for the movement known as the Tenth-Century Reform.[11]

Interest in monasticism, higher learning, and intellectual excellence, and rededication to the service of God were all being renewed before Edgar's reign began, and scholarship has successfully sought the roots of the Reform in the late ninth century. However, it was the happy convergence of a king's astute political vision and the talents of three charismatic and highly placed monastic administrators—Dunstan, Æthelwold, and Oswald—that has traditionally been considered the spearhead of this intellectual and political movement. Dunstan and Æthelwold were both born into the aristocratic circles of Wessex and came under the influence of the Mercian court, where cultural aestheticism flourished under King Æthelstan's aunt Æthelflæd. Both men chose monasticism over a secular political life, perhaps through enthusiasm for a higher calling or for a more direct route to power; although a monk, Dunstan held a court position as counsellor under King Edmund, Alfred's grandson. To fulfill an oath in 939 or 940, Edmund re-established Glastonbury as a regular monastic centre of learning and placed Dunstan as its abbot: from the account of Dunstan's life, we know that the newly gathered Glastonbury monks, among them his friend Æthelwold, lived by the Benedictine Rule. In 954, King Edmund's successor Eadred gave Abingdon, a derelict monastery, to Æthelwold for much the same purposes.

Dunstan fell out with the succeeding king Eadwig and was exiled to the continent; there he came under the influence of the Benedictinism whose revitalization had begun with Charlemagne's liturgical reforms a century earlier, a legacy of the continental activities of Anglo-Saxons in the eighth century and now in full flower. In 957, Dunstan was recalled to England by Eadwig's brother Edgar, who as king in Mercia appointed him bishop of Worcester and also of London; when Edgar succeeded Eadwig as king in Wessex in 959, he placed Dunstan to the see of Canterbury, where he was also to serve as the king's main counsellor. Æthelwold moved from Abingdon, now a thriving

11 For a complete discussion of literacy both in Latin and the vernacular, see George H. Brown, *The Dynamics of Literacy in Anglo-Saxon England* (Manchester: Manchester Centre for Anglo-Saxon Studies, 1995), *passim*.

monastery, to become Bishop of Winchester, the capital of Wessex and the city housing the royal palace, the main cathedral of the kingdom, and the Old and New Minsters, formerly great centres of learning but, as with all else, fallen into bad habits. It was Æthelwold's task to restore correct ecclesiastical and liturgical practice within the diocese and to revitalize monasticism, education, learning, and scholarship in the Winchester Minsters and their scriptoria.

The third Reformer was Oswald, likely younger than his two West Saxon colleagues, and the nephew both of Oda, archbishop of Canterbury before Dunstan, and of Oskytel, archbishop of York. These archbishops were of Danish lineage, descendants of the invaders whose incursions had destroyed so much of the fabric of Anglo-Saxon society a century earlier. Like Dunstan, Oswald spent time in one of the reformed Benedictine monasteries of the continent, learning new monastic practice and adopting new ideas and models upon which an English revival might be constructed. Upon Oswald's return to England in 961, Dunstan had King Edgar appoint him bishop of Worcester.

The Reform effected by these three monastic bishops with the guidance and support of their king had all the hallmarks of a new intellectual or ideological movement. The foundation or revitalization of monastic houses progressed in lockstep with the establishment of educational centres, a revival in literacy and learning, the composition, adaptation or translation of sermons to improve the spiritual wellbeing of all Anglo-Saxons, and the rapid production of service-books containing newly developed liturgical rituals and forms. And although each new monastic daughter-house tended to develop the character of its mother-house's individual traditions, an attempt was made, at Easter of what was probably 972, to standardize the monastic way of life that every house in Anglo-Saxon England was to follow, with all foundations under the protection of the king and queen of Wessex. This was a master-stroke of political astuteness, confirming the House of Wessex as the foremost royal line in England by associating it with the rise of intellectual and educational excellence everywhere, and ensuring the obedience and cooperation of men and women who were to pray for the king and queen at the same time that they reaffirmed their dedication to God at every Office.

Benedictine monks and nuns in Anglo-Saxon England lived, as mentioned, according to the Rule of St Benedict, which divided their days into eight periods of prayer (or "Offices"), making up the *Opus Dei* ("work of God"); therefore, approximately every three hours, regardless of the task at hand, each member ceased work and went to the chapel to pray as a community. Some of these Offices were of considerable duration; others, particularly the daytime Offices, were shorter. Such a design deliberately interrupted the tasks of the physical world, whether these were labour in and management of lands or the writing and copying of manuscripts, so as to recall the mind to prayer, diminish the individual sense of self with all its potential for deviant behaviour, and rededicate the soul to God. Communal recitation of the Psalter (or Book of Psalms) once every week lay at the core of these daily Offices, and Benedictine monks and nuns were expected to know all one hundred and fifty psalms *memoriter* ("by memory") or *ex corde* ("by heart").[12] **Mattins** was the Night Office of the monastic life, also called **Nocturns** when grouped together with the dawn office of **Lauds** early on in the Middle Ages: depending on the season, Mattins was generally sung after midnight, and Lauds around 3:00 or 4:00 a.m. **Prime** ("first hour after dawn"), **Terce** ("third hour"), **Sext** ("sixth hour"), and **None** ("ninth hour") were known as the "Little Hours," said around 6:00 a.m., 9:00 a.m, noon, and 3:00 p.m. respectively, and because they interrupted daily tasks, were considerably more brief than the two Offices before them and the two following them. **Vespers** was the evening Office, sung around sunset, and **Compline**, the final Office of the day, was said just before bedtime around 9:00 p.m.

But week by week, each Christian soul, lay or professed, was expected to attend Mass, the centre of which was the celebration of the Holy Eucharist. This fundamental Christian ritual was a reaffirmation of faith in Jesus Christ's redemption of humanity by crucifixion on Good Friday, which began with his breaking bread and pouring wine out for his disciples at the Passover feast the day before, and identifying his body and blood with these gifts he offered them. To prepare to receive the Holy Eucharist, or even to be present at its sharing, a Christian was expected to cleanse the soul through confession. To approach God who had freed humanity from sin was to praise him and acknowledge the deepest gratitude. Over the centuries from the time the Church developed, the Old and New Testaments were explored for appropriate texts of contrition and praise, while new prayers and hymns were written

12 Two versions of the Latin Book of Psalms—the *Romanum* and *Gallicanum* (found in the Vulgate Bible)—based respectively on St Jerome's first and second translations from the Greek, were used actively during the Anglo-Saxon period; Jerome's third translation, known as the *Hebraicum*, was certainly known in Anglo-Saxon England but never used liturgically. The *Gallicanum* was known early on through Irish influence but was then superseded by the *Romanum*, which is the text used by the *Kentish Great Miserere* poet; as a result of the Tenth-Century Reform, the *Gallicanum* version was re-introduced into England from continental houses, and it informs Latin psalter texts from the late tenth century on.

and became part of ritual Eucharistic practice that embodied these right attitudes.

By the tenth century, Ælfric and Wulfstan, names best known to us today as exemplary teachers and the most prolific writers of spiritual guidance of their generation, had both set down those liturgical forms they believed *ælc cristene mann* ("every Christian person") should know. In his homily *To Eallum Folke* ("To All People"), Wulfstan identifies three prayers that should be known, if not in Latin then in English; Ælfric lists only the first two. These are the Lord's Prayer (also known as the *Pater Noster* from its first two words, "Our Father," in Latin) and the statement of spiritual belief or Creed, recited at baptism and known as the Apostles' or baptismal Creed. To the Lord's Prayer Wulfstan adds the Doxology, or *Gloria Patri*, a short ascription of praise to the Holy Trinity (God the Father, God the Son, and God the Holy Spirit) frequently used at the end of other prayers.[13] These three liturgical elements form the core of six of our poems in this edition: the *Pater Noster* is the source for the *Exeter Lord's Prayer*, *Corpus Lord's Prayer*, and *Junius Lord's Prayer*; the Creed stands behind the *Baptismal Creed* in Oxford, Bodleian Junius 121 (and is quoted in *Vision of the Rood*); and the *Gloria Patri* is the source for the *Old English Doxology* and the *Titus Alphabet Doxology*.

The **LORD'S PRAYER**
(*Exeter Lord's Prayer*, *Corpus Lord's Prayer*, and *Junius Lord's Prayer*)

The Lord's Prayer derives directly from two gospel versions (Matthew 6:7–14, and a shorter version in Luke 11:2–4) of the same episode in Jesus Christ's life: when his disciples ask that he teach them how to pray, he gives them a model, and this passage in the Bible, known as *oratio dominici,* "prayer of the Lord," was incorporated into the liturgy of the young Church from its earliest days. It is the "summary of all prayer, containing in its seven petitions the substance of all that man can ask of God,"[14] and was used daily within the celebration of Mass. It is included in most private prayer-books from both continental and Anglo-Saxon sources in the early medieval period and is also

13 *To Eallum Folke*, in Dorothy Bethurum, ed., *The Homilies of Wulfstan* (Oxford: Clarendon Press, 1957), 166–68; see also Benjamin Thorpe, ed. and trans., *The Homilies of the Anglo-Saxon Church: The First Part, Containing the Sermones Catholici or Homilies of Ælfric* (New York: Johnson Reprint Corporation, 1971; orig. publ. London, 1846, 2 vols.), II, 596–98.

14 F. Cabrol, *Le livre de la prière antique* (Paris: H. Oudin, 1900); trans. anon. by a Benedictine of Stanbrook as *Liturgical Prayer* (Westminster, MD: The Newman Press, 1950), 88.

singled out in ecclesiastical council canons as a central teaching to be used both with candidates for baptism ("catechumens") and in homilies further expounding the Christian faith.[15] Within a monastic community it was recited by the Prior on behalf of the community, at the end of both Lauds, the major early-morning Office, and Vespers, the major evening Office of the Benedictine Rule. As I have noted elsewhere, "It was the prayer of the faithful, performed publicly only by baptized Christians. St Ambrose, St John Chrysostom, St Augustine, and many others, exhort the faithful to say it often in their private devotions."[16]

From Anglo-Saxon England itself, we find evidence of the use of the Lord's Prayer throughout the monastic life, both in the *Regularis Concordia* from ca. 972, the synod document that records agreed-upon monastic practice in England during the reign of Edgar the Peaceful (960–975), and in Ælfric's Letter to the Monks at Eynsham, written ca. 1005. English monks and nuns would have recited the Lord's Prayer many times during the course of each day throughout the church year as private devotion, as part of the Office hours, and with specific intent: "For the king and benefactors two psalms are to be sung, together with the Lord's Prayer, *preces* [petitionary prayers] and a collect, at every one of the hours."[17] It is also prescribed for some of the major temporal festival offices of the Church.[18]

Following is the Latin version of the Lord's Prayer from St Jerome's second bible translation called the Vulgate, known to all of western Christendom. The Latin of this prayer appears in two of the three Old English Lord's Prayer poems, intercalated with their vernacular translations, and stands as the single source behind the third. A literal translation appears after each petition of the Latin text, and I have identified the traditional "seven petitions":

---

15 Canon X of the Council of Clovesho (747) requires that a priest be able "to explain in the native tongue the services and the Creed and *Pater noster*," and councils convened at Mainz, Chalon, and Arles in 813 confirm provision made for the Lord's Prayer as catechetical teaching; see Milton McC. Gatch, *Preaching and Theology in Anglo-Saxon England* (Toronto: U of Toronto P, 1977), 33–35, 51–52.

16 Keefer, "'Ic' and 'We,'" 135.

17 Dom Thomas Symons, ed., *Regularis Concordia: The Monastic Agreement of the Monks and Nuns of the English Nation* (London: Nelson, 1953), 12, 15, 21, 23, 24, 32, 34, 38, 45, 51; Christopher A. Jones, ed., *Ælfric's Letter to the Monks at Eynsham*, CSASE 24 (Cambridge: Cambridge UP, 1998), 113.

18 Feast days celebrating events in the life of Jesus Christ, such as the Purification of the Virgin (Jones, *Ælfric's Letter*, 119), or Ash Wednesday and then all subsequent Wednesdays and Fridays until Holy Week (123).

Pater noster, qui es in cęlis ("our Father, who is in heaven")
(i) *sanctificetur nomen tuum* ("may thy name be hallowed")
(ii) *Adueniat regnum tuum* ("may thy kingdom come")
(iii) *fiat uoluntas tua* ("may thy will be done") *sicut in cælo et in terra* ("as [it is] in heaven, so [may it be done] on earth")
(iv) *Panem nostrum cotidianum da nobis hodię* ("our daily food give to us today")
(v) *Et dimitte nobis debita nostra* ("and dismiss from us our debts") *sicut et nos dimittimus debitoribus nostris* ("just as we forgive [sins] from our debtors")
(vi) *Et ne nos inducas in temptationem* ("and do not lead us into temptation")
(vii) *Sed libera nos a malo. Amen.* ("but free us from evil. amen").[19]

Wulfstan translates the Lord's Prayer into Old English for those of his congregation unable to read or understand Latin: *Eala ure fæder þe on heofonum eart, a sy ðin nama ecelice gebletsod; and ðin ricedom ofer us rixie symble, and ðin willa gewyrðe swa swa on heofonum eac swa on eorðan. Geunn us to þissum dæge dæghwamlices fostres. And us gemilda swa swa we miltsiað þam ðe wið us agyltaþ; and ne læt ðu us costnian ealles to swyðe, ac alys us fram yfele, amen*[20] (lit., "Oh, our father that in heaven art, ever be thy name eternally blessed; and [may] thy kingdom over us rule always, and [may] thy will be accomplished, just as in heaven so also on earth. Grant to us for this day daily nourishment. And to us show mercy just as we show mercy to those that against us offend; and let not thou us test entirely too greatly, but redeem us from evil, amen").

In his homily on the Lord's Prayer, Ælfric sets it out this way: *Pater noster, þæt is on Englisc, Þu, ure Fæder, þe eart on heofonum, Sy þin nama gehalgod. Cume ðin rice. Sy ðin wylla on eorðan swa swa on heofonum. Syle us todæg urne dæghwamlican hlaf. And forgyf us ure gyltas, swa swa we forgyfąð ðam þe wið us agyltað. And ne læd ðu na us on costnunge. Ac alys us fram yfele. Sy hit swa*[21] (lit., "*Pater noster*, that is in English, Thou, our Father, that art in heaven, Be thy name hallowed. [May] come thy kingdom. Be thy will [done] on earth just as in heaven. Give us today our daily loaf. And forgive us

19 The Latin prayer text is taken from Salisbury Cathedral 150, a psalter whose Latin dates to ca. 975, contemporary with the Reform period (Celia Sisam and Kenneth Sisam, eds., *The Salisbury Psalter*, EETS 242 [London: Oxford UP, 1959], 304).

20 Bethurum, *Homilies*, 166; translation mine.

21 Thorpe, *Homilies*, I, 258–74, 258–59; translation mine.

our sins, just as we forgive those that against us offend. And lead not thou us never into testing. But redeem us from evil. Be it thus [amen].") In this homily, Ælfric explores the different clauses of the Lord's Prayer, noting the traditional divisions (*Seofon gebedu sint on þam Pater noster* ["In the *Pater Noster* are seven prayers"]) and working his way through the relevance of each one to his congregation: *Þa ðreo forman gebedu beoð us ongunnene on ðysre worulde, ac hi beoð a ungeendode on þære toweardan worulde* ("the first three prayers are begun by us in this world, but they will ever be unended in the world to come") . . . *Se ðe þe inundað swa swa fæder, he bið swylce he ðin heafod sy. Ealswa wel behofað þæt heafod þæra oðera lima, swa swa ða lima behofiað þæs heafdes* ("He who protecteth thee as father is, as it were, thy head. As the head requireth the other members, so these members require the head").[22]

Consequently, there is no standardized Old English version for the Lord's Prayer as we might have expected; instead, for the Anglo-Saxons it was a dynamic and living act of commitment, praise, and humble request, whose various translations allowed its spiritual immediacy to be accessible both to well-read monastic scholars and to illiterate members of the parish. Regarding it in this way—energetic, applicable to the lives of men and women in all walks of Anglo-Saxon life, the single most important articulation of humanity's dependence on God because its authority came from Jesus Christ himself—allows us to understand how the three poems based on the *Pater Noster* prayer had their genesis.

The **BAPTISMAL CREED**

(*Baptismal Creed, Vision of the Rood*)

It is important to realize that catechesis—the teaching and examining of candidates for baptism—gave rise to the formulation of those statements of faith called "creeds" (from the Latin *credo*, "I believe"), rather than the other way around. Baptism, worship, preaching, catechetical instruction, anti-heretical and anti-pagan polemics, and exorcism all provided occasions for giving concrete expression, along lines determined by the needs of the moment, to the cardinal articles of Christian belief.[23] Oft-repeated legend had it that the twelve apostles gathered together after Pentecost[24] to establish a common

22 Thorpe, *Homilies*, I, 262–63, 270–71, 274–75.

23 J.N.D. Kelly, *Early Christian Creeds* (Harlow: Longman, 1950; 3rd ed., 1972), 30.

24 Acts 2:1–47.

basis for their preaching, and that each contributed to a general statement of faith.[25] So from the very earliest period of the development of organized Christianity, statements of belief were known and used to help the Church grow.

The credal form that eventually developed into what is now known as the Apostles' Creed and was used at baptism throughout the Western Christian church is known technically as the Old Roman Creed, described at the beginning of the fifth century in detail by Rufinus, who was responsible for promulgating the legend of its apostolic composition, mentioned above.[26] It lacks some of the statements to be found in the baptismal Creed that the Anglo-Saxons knew but was its immediate ancestor. For some time, this Creed and the Lord's Prayer were guarded as "holy secrets," not to be set down as text ill-advisedly, lest the uninitiated gain access to them; as such, tracking the history of credal development can be sketchy for the liturgical historian.[27] But we know how the baptismal Creed used in Anglo-Saxon England was fleshed out along the road of its development, since it served not only for preaching, catechesis, and baptism, but also within the liturgical context of the Offices of Benedictinism as early as the ninth century on the continent. In Anglo-Saxon monastic use, we find it prescribed for Compline of Easter Sunday and the six remaining days of Easter Week.[28]

The text in Latin, with its translation, follows:

(i) *Credo in deum patrem omnipotentem creatorem cæli et terrę* ("I believe in God the Father Almighty, creator of heaven and earth");

(ii) *Et in Iesum Christum filium eius unicum dominum nostrum qui conceptus est de spiritu sancto Natus ex Maria uirgine, Passus sub Pontio Pilato Crucifixus, mortuus et sepultus, Descendit ad inferna tertia die resurrexit a mortui, Ascendit ad cælos sedet ad dexteram dei patris omnipotentis Inde uenturus (est) iudicare uiuos et mortuos* ("And in Jesus Christ, His only Son, our Lord, Who was conceived by the Holy Spirit, born from the Virgin Mary, suffered under Pontius Pilate, was crucified, dead and buried, descended into hell, on the third day rose again from the dead, ascended to heaven, sits on the right hand of God the Father almighty; thence He will come to judge the living and the dead");

---

25 J.N.D. Kelly, ed. and trans., *Rufinus: A Commentary on the Apostles' Creed* (London: Longman, 1955), 29–30; see also Kelly, *Early Christian Creeds*, 1–6.

26 Kelly, *Rufinus*, *passim*.

27 Kelly, *Early Christian Creeds*, 168–71.

28 Jones, *Ælfric's Letter*, 137.

(iii) *Credo in spiritum (sanctum), sanctam ęcclesiam catholicam sanctorum communionem Remissionem peccatorum Carnis resurrectionem, uitam æternam. Amen* ("I believe in the (Holy) Spirit, the holy catholic Church, the communion of saints, the remission of sins, the resurrection of the flesh, and eternal life. Amen").[29]

Wulfstan and Ælfric both wrote sermons on the baptismal Creed as essential to the salvation of the soul, providing translations of it as they did so.[30] Ælfric includes a text with the heading *Her is geleafa, and gebed, and bletsung, læwedum mannum ðe ðæt leden ne cunnon* ("Here is belief, and prayer, and blessing, for laymen who know not Latin"), in which he presents the Lord's Prayer, the baptismal Creed, and the Niceno-Constantinopolitan Creed (here called the *Mæsse Creda* ["the Mass Creed"] and for which, see below) in Old English.[31] His homily for the penitential season of Lent once again makes plain the need for each man or woman to know certain prayers for the salvation of their souls: *Ælc cristen man sceal cunnan his Pater noster and his Credan. Mid þam Pater nostre he sceal hine gebiddan, and mid þam Credan he sceal his geleafan getrymman. Se lareow sceal secgan ðam læwedum mannum þæt andgit to ðam Pater nostre and to þam Credan, þæt hi witon hwæs hi biddon æt Gode, and hu hi sceolon on God gelyfan* ("Every Christian man shall know his *Pater noster* and his Creed. With the *Pater noster* he shall pray, and with the Creed he shall confirm his belief. The teacher shall explain to the laymen the sense of the *Pater noster* and of the Creed, that they may know what they pray for to God, and how they shall believe in God").[32]

The baptismal Creed is to be distinguished from the later and formulaically more complex Niceno-Constantinopolitan Creed (Ælfric's *Mæsse Creda*) of the fourth century, whose initial role was to make reply to the heresy of Arianism.[33] Its use in the West was confined primarily to the Mass. The baptismal Creed must also be distinguished from the so-called "Athanasian Creed," more a doctrinal exposition than a creed *per se*, and before the

29 Sisam and Sisam, *Salisbury Psalter*, 304–5, translation mine; see also Kelly, *Early Christian Creeds*, 369.

30 Thorpe, *Homilies*, I, 275–93, and Bethurum, *Homilies*, 157–65, in a sermon to which *To Eallum Folke* is related.

31 Thorpe, *Homilies*, II, 597–99.

32 Thorpe, *Homilies*, II, 605.

33 The main heresy espoused by Arius questioned the co-equality of the Son with the Father: "The Nicene Creed was a theological statement of the church's faith for Christians, not a test for converts from paganism" (Dom Gregory Dix, *The Shape of the Liturgy* [London: Dacre Press, 1945], 486). See also Kelly, *Early Christian Creeds*, 205–367.

eleventh century called only "the Catholic faith" (being a lengthy summation of orthodox Christian belief) or by its opening Latin words, *Quicumque vult* ("Whosoever desires"). Because these two other creeds were known in pre-Conquest England, I have chosen to rename the poem in Oxford, Bodleian Junius 121, as *Baptismal Creed*, to distinguish it clearly from the other two.

The **GLORIA PATRI**

(*Titus Alphabet Doxology, Old English Doxology*)

This short formula began as a free-standing glorification of God, known as a "doxology" ("words of praise"): *Gloria Patri et Filio et Spiritui Sancto; sicut erat in principio et nunc et semper et in saecula saeculorum. Amen* ("Glory to the Father and to the Son and to the Holy Spirit; as [it was] in the beginning, [is] now and ever [shall be], throughout all ages. Amen"). Like the Niceno-Constantinopolitan Creed, it was perfected at the time (and as a result) of the Arian heresy, and came to be used at the end of other prayers, hymns or psalms to reconfirm the orthodox Trinitarian belief. Its second sentence (*sicut erat . . .*) derived from this Arian controversy in the West, "since the co-equality and co-eternity of the Son was one of the tenets of faith rejected by Arius, and its final phrase, 'per saecula saeculorum,' reaches back once again through the apostolic tradition to Judaic use in the synagogue."[34]

Because of its use as a closure formula, the *Gloria Patri* is to be found throughout the public and private prayer of the Anglo-Saxon Church: within the Old English translation of the Rule of St Benedict, it was considered so self-evident that it was either left unglossed altogether or rendered as *gloria* only.[35] However, Wulfstan adds it at the end of the Lord's Prayer and before the baptismal Creed, as a third element which all Christians, lay, ordained, and professed alike, must know in order to achieve salvation. He provides only the first sentence of the Latin but the entire prayer in Old English: *Gloria patri et filio et spiritui sancto. A sy lof and wuldor fæder and suna and halgum gaste, swa swa on fruman wæs and gyt is and symble bið in ealra worulda woruld, amen* ("Ever be praise and glory to the Father and Son and Holy Ghost, just as it was in the beginning and yet is and ever shall be throughout all worlds, amen").[36]

Ælfric does not include it in his section of prayers in English, nor do we

34 Sarah Larratt Keefer, "In Closing: Amen and Doxology in Anglo-Saxon England," *Anglia* 21 (2003): 210–37, 221–22.

35 See Logeman, *Rule of St Benet*, 38.

36 Bethurum, *Homilies*, 166; translation mine.

generally find it among the canticles and hymns that follow the psalms in the English psalter-books, but this seems most probably the result of its ubiquity. The *Regularis Concordia* refers to it as in the Old English *Regula Sancti Benedicti* only as *gloria*,[37] and makes mention of when it should be used and when omitted, provisions that are generally confirmed by Ælfric's Letter to the Monks at Eynsham.[38]

The **GLORIA IN EXCELSIS** and the **TE DEUM** (*Kentish Hymn of Praise*)

Known as the Greater Doxology or the Angels' Hymn, the *Gloria in Excelsis* takes its origin from Luke 2:14 and was composed early on as a *psalmus idioticus* (privately written hymn)[39] for use in the Eastern Christian church. The presence of Eastern variants makes its composition date perhaps as early as the third or even second century, where it was sung at dawn; coming west, it was used at the Mass but only for specific festivals.[40] The *Te Deum* is another private Latin hymn of praise, thought to have been written by Nicetas of Remisiana and, as such, probably the work of the fourth century. It was used in the early Church strictly during the Offices and thus would have been known only to monks or nuns.

We therefore see that these two hymns of praise were intended for quite different purposes.[41] The *Gloria in Excelsis* was used at the Mass, particularly on major feast days of Christmas, Eastertide or Pentecost, while the *Te Deum* was a canticle generally reserved for the Office of Nocturns, once again used for the major feasts of the Christian year. Neither was sung during the penitential season of Advent or on days of fasting, so their association with Christian celebration and praise belongs to the very earliest days of their inclusion

37 Symons, *Regularis Concordia*, 11, 21, 30, 32, 33, 49.

38 Jones, *Ælfric's Letter*, 123, 125, 127, 135; Jones discusses the omission of the *Gloria Patri* during the week before Palm Sunday (181–82) and its use during the last three days of Holy Week (185–86).

39 Pierre Batiffol, *History of the Roman Breviary*, trans. A.M.Y. Baylay (London: Longman, 1898), 109.

40 See Dix, *Shape of the Liturgy*, 456–57, and L. Duchesne, *Origines du culte chrétien* (Paris: Thorin et Fils, 1898), 158.

41 For an interesting discussion of these two hymns, see Samuel W. Duffield, *The Latin Hymn-writers and their Hymns* (New York: Funk and Wagnall, 1889), 348–50.

in the liturgy.[42] The *Gloria in Excelsis* would almost certainly have been a better-known hymn than the *Te Deum*, because it was more widely used (at the celebration of Mass in parishes, that is, every Sunday and on feast days) and by a greater number of people (both the laity and secular clergy, as well as monastic men and women who heard Mass more frequently).

The *Gloria in Excelsis* is found in many service-books from the Anglo-Saxon period, but in particular it is included in the group of canticles and hymns following the psalms, under the heading *Oratio pura cum laudatione* ("a pure prayer with praising") in many of the Latin psalters from the Anglo-Saxon period:

(i) *Gloria in excelsis deo Et in terra pax hominibus bone uoluntatis* ("Glory in the highest to God and on earth peace to men of good will");

(ii) *Laudamus te. Benedicimus te. Adoramus te. Glorificamus te. Gratias agimus tibi propter magnam gloriam tuam* ("We praise thee. We bless thee. We worship thee. We glorify thee. We give thee thanks for thy great glory");

(iii) *Domine deus rex caelestis. Deus pater omnipotens. Domine fili unigenite Iesu Christe. Domine deus. Agnus dei. Filius patris. Qui tollis peccata mundi miserere nobis* ("Lord God, king of heaven. God the almighty father. Lord the only-begotten son Jesus Christ. Lord God, Lamb of God, Son of the Father. Who takes away the sins of the world, have mercy on us");

(iv) *Qui tollis pæccata mundi. Suscipe deprȩcationem nostram. Qui sedes ad dexteram patris miserere nobis* ("Who takes away the sins of the world, receive our prayer. Who sits at the right of the Father, have mercy on us");

(v) *Quoniam tu solus sanctus. Tu solus dominus. Tu solus altissimus. Iesu Christe cum sancto spiritu. In gloria dei patris. AMEN* ("Because thou alone art holy, thou alone art the Lord, thou alone art most high, Jesus Christ, with the Holy Spirit, in the glory of God the Father. Amen").[43]

The *Te Deum* is found almost exclusively in Latin psalters remaining to us from Anglo-Saxon England, where it is customarily headed *Ymnus ad matutinum diebus dominici* ("Hymn for Sunday Mattins"):

(i) *Te deum laudamus; te deum confitemur. Te (e)ternum patrem omnis terra ueneratur* ("We praise thee, God; we confess thee [to be] God; all the earth worships thee as the eternal Father");

(ii) *Tibi omnes angeli; tibi cȩli et uniuerse potestates; Tibi Cherubin et*

42 For further study on their roles in the liturgy of the Anglo-Saxon church, particularly of monastic communities, see Symons, *Regularis Concordia*, 28–29, 30, 48, 50, 57–58, and Jones, *Ælfric's Letter*, 117, 119, 134–35, 139, 164–67, 173–74, 185, 206, which reflects more specific evidence of *Regularis Concordia* usage.

43 Sisam and Sisam, *Salisbury Psalter*, 303; translation mine.

Seraphim incessabili uoce proclamant. SANCTUS SANCTUS SANCTUS dominus deus Sabaoth. Pleni sunt cæli et terra maiestatis gloriæ tuæ ("to thee all angels [proclaim], to thee the heavens and universal powers [proclaim]; to thee Cherubim and Seraphim proclaim with unceasing voices 'Holy Holy Holy Lord God Sabaoth. Full are the heavens and the earth of the majesty of thy glory'");

(iii) *Te gloriosus apostolorum chorus; Te prophetarum laudabilis numerus; Te martyrum candidatus laudat exercitus* ("The glorious choir of apostles [praise] thee; the praiseworthy company of prophets [praise] thee; the white-shining army of martyrs praise thee");

(iv) *Te per orbem terrarum sancta confitetur ęcclesia Patrem inmense maiestatis* ("the holy church throughout the globe acknowledges thee the Father of immeasurable majesty");

(v) *Uenerandum tuum uerum et unicum filium Sanctum quoque paraclitum spiritum* ("Thy praise-worthy, true and only Son, also the Holy Spirit, the Comforter");

(vi) *Tu rex gloriæ Criste. Tu patris sempiternus es filius. Tu ad liberandum suscepisturus hominem non horruisti uirginis uterum* ("Thou art the king of glory, Christ; thou art the eternal Son of the Father; thou having taken it upon thyself to liberate humanity did not disdain a virgin's womb");

(vii) *Tu deuicto mortis aculeo aperuisti credentibus regna cælorum. Tu ad dexteram dei sedes in gloria patris* ("Thou, having overcome the pain of death, opened the kingdom of heaven to believers; Thou sittest at the right hand of God in the glory of the Father");

(viii) *Iudex crederis esse uenturus. Te ergo quesumus tuis famulis subueni quos pretioso sanguine redemisti* ("Thou art believed to be coming as our judge; we therefore ask thee to help thy servants whom thou hast redeemed with thy precious blood");

(ix) *Æterna fac cum sanctis tuis gloria munerari [numerari]. Saluum fac populum tuum domine et benedic hereditati tuæ. Et rege eos et extolle illos usque in ęternum* ("Make them to be rewarded [numbered] with thy saints in eternal glory; Save thy people, Lord, and bless thine inheritance, and rule them and raise them up for ever");

(x) *Per singulos dies benedicimus te. Et laudamus nomen tuum in sæculum et in sæculum sæculi* ("Through every day we bless thee and praise thy name forever, forever and ever");

(xi) *Dignare domine die isto sine peccato nos custodire. Miserere nostri domine, miserere nostri* ("Grant, Lord, to keep us safe this day without sin; Have mercy on us, Lord, have mercy on us");

(xii) *Fiat misericordia tua domine super nos quemadmodum sperauimus in te. In te domine speraui non confundar in eternum.* ("Let thy mercy, Lord, be upon us just as we have hoped in thee. In thee, Lord, I have hoped; may I never be confounded").[44]

The **GREAT MISERERE**: **PSALM 50**
(*Kentish Great Miserere*)

The weekly recitation of the 150 psalms comprising the Psalter formed the backbone of the Benedictine *Opus Dei* within each community. However, certain psalms were said daily, and some of them more than once. Psalm 50,[45] known as the *Miserere* or "Great *Miserere*" from its initial word in Latin, belongs to the seven penitential psalms (the others being Psalms 6, 31, 37, 101, 129, and 142) that were sung as a group three times daily to remind each professed man or woman of the soul's innate sinfulness. Psalm 50 was also said with other prayers (including the Lord's Prayer) during the day, with intention "for the King, Queen and benefactors" and "against fleshly temptation."[46] It was prescribed for additional recitation during certain seasons and important services during the ecclesiastical year,[47] including Good Friday's Veneration of the Cross[48] and the public reconciliation of penitents held on Maundy Thursday during Holy Week.[49]

By a tradition well-known to the Anglo-Saxons, Psalm 50 was regarded as the hymn of contrition written by King David after he seduced Bathsheba, the beautiful wife of his general Uriah. On discovering that Bathsheba was pregnant with his child, David attempted to cover his tracks, but Uriah's loyalty in not sleeping with his wife during wartime led David to send Uriah to certain death in the front lines of battle. Once Uriah had been killed, David took Bathsheba as his wife, but the prophet Nathan, inspired by God to know what had happened, reproached David severely, bringing about the act of confes-

---

44 Sisam and Sisam, *Salisbury Psalter*, 301–2; translation mine.

45 By the psalm numbering in the Vulgate Bible; modern psalter versions that follow traditional Hebrew numbering identify this psalm as 51, another reason for my re-titling of the Old English poem based upon it.

46 See Symons, *Regularis Concordia*, 12, 14–15, 22, 23.

47 Symons, *Regularis Concordia*, 26, 34, 43.

48 See Sarah Larratt Keefer, "The Veneration of the Cross in Anglo-Saxon England," *Liturgy of the Late Anglo-Saxon Church*, ed. H. Gittos and M. Bradford Bedingfield, HBS Subsidia 5 (Woodbridge: Boydell, 2005), 141–82.

49 See Sarah Hamilton, "Rites for Public Penance in Late Anglo-Saxon England," *Liturgy of the Late Anglo-Saxon Church*, ed. H. Gittos and M. Bradford Bedingfield, HBS Subsidia 5 (Woodbridge: Boydell, 2005), 63–103, 80.

sion and penance that this psalm apparently represents.[50] Psalm 50 is considered the foremost of the penitential psalms, hence its customary title "Great *Miserere*," which serves to explain the editorial title—the *Kentish Great Miserere*—of the poem in this edition.

The psalm itself also appears in Old English prose in a number of interlinear glossed psalters from the later Anglo-Saxon period, and in Bibliothèque Nationale de France Fonds Latin 8824,[51] where its inclusion at the end of the first 50 psalms in prose may be the product of King Alfred's circle of learning at the end of the ninth century.[52] The Latin Vulgate (*Gallicanum*) text with indications of *Romanum* variants, and a modern English translation follow:

Miserere mei Deus secundum magnam misericordiam tuam ("Have mercy on me, O God, according to thy great mercy");

Et secundum multitudinem miserationum tuarum dele iniquitatem meam ("And according to the multitude of thy tender mercies blot out my iniquity");

Amplius lava me ab iniquitate (Ro. *iniustitia*)[53] *mea et a peccato* (Ro. *delicta*) *meo munda me* ("Wash me yet more from my iniquity, and cleanse me from my sin");

Quoniam iniquitatem meam cognosco (Ro. *agnosco*) *et peccatum* (Ro. *delictum*) *meum contra* (Ro. *coram*) *me est semper* ("For I know my iniquity and my sin is always before me");

Tibi soli peccavi et malum coram te feci; ut iustificeris in sermonibus tuis et vincas cum (Ro. *dum*) *iudicaris* ("To thee only have I sinned, and have done evil before thee; that thou mayst be justified in thy words, and mayst overcome when thou art judged");

Ecce enim in iniquitatibus conceptus sum et in peccatis concepit me mater mea ("For behold! I was conceived in iniquities; and in sins did my mother conceive me");

Ecce enim veritatem dilexisti incerta et occulta sapientiae tuae manifestasti mihi ("For behold! thou has loved truth; the uncertain and hidden things of thy wisdom thou hast made manifest to me");

---

50 See 2 Samuel 12–13.

51 See Sarah Larratt Keefer, *The Old English Metrical Psalter: An Annotated Set of Collation Lists with the Psalter-Glosses*, Garland Reference Library of the Humanities 189 (New York: Garland, 1979), xii and *passim*.

52 Janet Bately, "Lexical Evidence for the Authorship of the Prose Psalms in the Paris Psalter," *ASE* 10 (1982): 69–95, 95.

53 This translation is from Douay-Rheims, which follows the *Gallicanum* rather than the *Romanum* text used by the *Kentish Great Miserere* poet. However, the differences are not major and the sense is apt. Notable differences in the *Romanum* text are noted.

Asparges (Ro. *asperies*) *me hysopo et mundabor; lavabis me et super nivem dealbabor* ("Thou shalt sprinkle me with hyssop and I shall be cleansed; thou shalt wash me and I shall be made whiter than snow");

Auditui meo dabis gaudium et laetitiam exultabunt ossa humiliata ("To my hearing thou shalt give joy and gladness: and the bones that have been humbled shall rejoice");

Averte faciem tuam a peccatis meis et omnes iniquitates meas dele ("Turn away thy face from my sins, and blot out all my iniquities");

Cor mundum crea in me Deus et spiritum rectum innova in visceribus meis ("Create a clean heart in me, O God; and renew a right spirit within my bowels");

Ne proicias me a facie tua et spiritum sanctum tuum ne auferas a me ("Cast me not away from thy face; and take not thy holy spirit from me");

Redde mihi laetitiam salutaris tui et spiritu principali confirma me ("Restore unto me the joy of thy salvation, and strengthen me with a perfect spirit");

Docebo (Ro. *doceam*) *iniquos vias tuas et impii ad te convertentur* ("I will teach the unjust thy ways; and the wicked shall be converted to thee");

Libera me de sanguinibus Deus Deus salutis meae; exultabit lingua mea iustitiam tuam ("Deliver me from blood, O God, thou God of my salvation; and my tongue shall extol thy justice");

Domine labia mea aperies et os meum adnuntiabit laudem tuam ("O Lord, thou wilt open my lips; and my mouth shall declare your praise");

Quoniam si voluisses sacrificium dedissem; utique holocaustis non delectaberis ("For if thou hadst desired sacrifice, I would indeed have given it; with burnt offerings thou wilt not be delighted");

Sacrificium Deo spiritus contribulatus; cor contritum et humiliatum Deus non spernit ("A sacrifice to God is an afflicted spirit; a contrite and humbled heart, O God, thou wilt not despise");

Benigne fac Domine in bona voluntate tua Sion et aedificentur muri Hierusalem ("Deal favourably, O Lord, in thy good will with Sion; that the walls of Jerusalem may be built up");

Tunc acceptabis sacrificium iustitiae oblationes et holocausta; tunc inponent super altare tuum vitulos ("Then shalt thou accept the sacrifice of justice, oblations and whole burnt offerings; then shall they lay calves upon thy altar").[54]

54 Robert Weber, ed., *Biblia Sacra iuxta Vulgatam Versionem*, 2 vols. (Stuttgart: Deutsche Bibelgesellschaft, 1969), I, 830–32.

CONFESSIONAL PRAYERS

(Ah, Beloved Lord)

Penitent: *Confiteor deo et omnibus sanctis eius et tibi frater quia peccaui in cogitatione, in locutione et opere, propterea precor te ora pro me* ("I confess to God and to all his saints and to you, brother, that I have sinned in thought, in speech and in deed, and therefore I ask that you pray for me").
Confessor: *Misereatur tui omnipotens deus et dimittat tibi omnia peccata tua; liberet te ab omni malo, conseruat et confirmat in omni opere bono, et perducat te ad uitam eternam* ("May almighty God have mercy on you and dismiss from you all your sins; may he free you from all evil, conserve and confirm you in all good work, and bring you to life eternal").[55]

Although most modern church liturgies make provision for a confession during Mass to be said by both priest and congregation, in the early Church this was an individual rather than communal act, and *Confiteor* ("I confess") forms were found primarily in private prayer-books rather than in psalters, sacramentaries or pontificals. W. de Grey Birch notes its presence in his edition of ninth-century London, British Library Harley 2965, one of the earliest of the English prayer-books remaining to us today.[56] Muir's edition of early eleventh-century prayer-book texts is quoted above for its Latin version of the *Confiteor*, but although this seems safely formulaic, we must remember that for the Anglo-Saxons, prayer was a living and dynamic force to be used by individuals intent on salvation. The prayer-book that Muir has edited also preserves an Old English confessional prayer that is found nowhere else, partly deriving from traditional liturgical Latin language, partly the result of Old English's Germanic resonances of metre and sound, and partly influenced by the Irish Church's *lorica* tradition.[57] Prayers of this kind therefore resisted orthodox formulism and remained the spontaneous result of the individual voice with individual sins and petitions, directly addressing God in whom each convert or Christian child had been taught unequivocally to believe.

---

55 Bernard James Muir, ed., *A Pre-Conquest English Prayer-Book*, HBS 103 (Woodbridge: Boydell, 1988), 154; translation mine.

56 W. de Grey Birch, ed., *An Ancient Manuscript of the 8th or 9th Century* (London: Simpkin and Marshall, 1889), 97.

57 See Muir, *Pre-Conquest English Prayer-Book*, 136–37. A *lorica* is a breastplate, and prayers of this nature invoked the power of God for protection, much as a warding spell might do. Since the Anglo-Saxons thought nothing of including charms in liturgical texts, or prayers in manuscripts containing remedies and charms, overlaps between the two occurred frequently.

Within Benedictine life for Anglo-Saxon monks and nuns, the *Regularis Concordia* encourages personal confession every week, although no individual prayer is prescribed for its practice.[58] The *Confiteor* may have been reserved for the public confession to be made at Chapter each day after Prime, where each monk "shall . . . with lowly devotion, beg pardon of the abbot, who takes the place of Christ, and ask[s] forgiveness of [his] many failings, saying the *Confiteor*."[59]

* * *

A new convention in editing considers individual pieces in light of the manuscript context where they are to be found, exploring both the contents of that manuscript in which they travel, and the specific form that the codex itself takes.[60] For example, it is noteworthy that three of the manuscript witnesses for poems in this edition (London, B.L. Cotton Vespasian D. vi, Cotton Titus D. xxvii and xxvi, and Cotton Julius A. ii) contain chronological/prognostic entries concerned with measurement, age, numbers or alphabets. It is also significant that many of these poems are found in manuscripts of disparate natures (i.e. a very diversified anthology of poetry, a collection of religious verse and sermons, a personal prayer-book, a miscellany made up in part of regional texts, a glossed psalter, and two large but differing compendia which include homilies, laws, and singular collections). This suggests that the subgenre of liturgical poetry had no natural home in any single type of collection and may not have been large when at its most complete. On the other hand, because two of the ten liturgical poems remain in more than one full or fragmentary copy, we may assume that, while there may not have been many of these liturgical poems, they seem to have been popular. If the canon were indeed not large, a suitable explanation might be that the desire to write this kind of verse was limited to a relatively short period, a time when so many other texts were being generated that such an impulse might have had to compete for composition or compilation time on the part of their poets and scribes. Arguably, these poems were sparked by the Tenth-Century Reform enthusiasm for a reaffirmation of faith in the Church, monasticism, and edu-

58 Symons, *Regularis Concordia*, xxxix, 18 (n. 6).

59 Symons, *Regularis Concordia*, 29.

60 I list all critical editions of these manuscripts along with valuable works like that of Neil R. Ker, *Catalogue of Manuscripts Containing Anglo-Saxon* (Oxford: Clarendon Press, 1957; repr. 1990), to encourage readers to explore manuscript history and context on their own.

cation. Resulting from this Reform, we find a translation of the first six books of the Old Testament,[61] the copying into multiple manuscripts of a West Saxon version of the Gospels,[62] the writing of impressive bodies of homiletic or sermon material in the language of the Anglo-Saxon people, and a remarkable number of vernacular prose texts included in Latin liturgical service-books of the late tenth and eleventh centuries: all of these point to a cultural milieu wherein the writing of metrical English meditations on central texts of the liturgy would be most likely to occur.

This edition presents its ten liturgical poems systematically by source rather than chronologically by manuscript age, so as to to make the collection most accessible to the reader. While books are to some degree dateable on a timeline, dating the material within them is quite a different matter. Only if chronologically specific information (historical events, the names of people of whom we know something from other sources) appears in a poem can we begin to guess its date of composition. Linguistic evidence plays a role here to some degree, but it can be misleading: it is quite possible, for example, to find a poem originally composed in Northumbria in the eighth century which has nevertheless been preserved in the West Saxon dialect in a book that is conventionally dated to the tenth century: a West Saxon–speaking scribe of the tenth century has copied the piece into his own dialect.

For these reasons scholars are careful when trying to date Old English poetry. However, the canon of liturgical verse seems most likely the result of the Benedictine Reform of the mid-tenth century; most, if not all, of our poems were probably composed no earlier than 950. In cases like the *Exeter Lord's Prayer*, the *Kentish Great Miserere* or *Hymn of Praise*, or the *Vision of the Rood*, whose manuscripts all fall before or just at the turn of the eleventh century (i.e. the beginning of the 1000s), we might therefore suppose a composition date for the form in which they are presented in their witnesses as being no more than 25 or 30 years earlier than the date of each compilation.[63]

---

61 S.J. Crawford, ed., *The Old English Version of the Heptateuch*, EETS 160 (London, 1922; repr. 1969); for a recent collection of studies on this translation, see also B.C. Withers and R. Barnhouse, eds., *The Old English Hexateuch: Aspects and Approaches* (Kalamazoo, MI: Richard Rawlinson Center in association with Medieval Institute Publications, 2000).

62 See Roy Michael Liuzza, ed., *The Old English Version of the Gospels*, 2 vols., Early English Text Society 304 and 314 (Oxford: Oxford UP, 1994–2000).

63 But see Éamonn Ó Carragáin, "Sources or Analogues? Using Liturgical Evidence to Date 'The Dream of the Rood,'" *Cross and Cruciform in the Anglo-Saxon World*, ed. Sarah Larratt Keefer, Karen L. Jolly, and Catherine E. Karkov (Morgantown: West Virginia UP, 2010), 135–65; and also his *Ritual and the Rood: Liturgical Images and the Old English Poems of the* Dream of the Rood *Tradition* (London: British Library Publications; Toronto: U of Toronto P, 2005), 189–95, 228–36. Ó Carragáin argues for an early

For liturgical verse in manuscripts of the eleventh century, we have no way of knowing whether their composition was coeval with that of poems in later tenth-century books, or whether they derive from a period more contemporary with the manuscripts in which they are to be found. Although *Ah, Beloved Lord* exists in full only in a witness of ca. 1150, the presence of its first fifteen lines copied into London, Lambeth Palace 427, around 1050 indicates that, for it to have been appreciated and excerpted from in this fashion, it was almost certainly a complete piece by the first half of the eleventh century.

Some liturgical poems in manuscripts that date earlier or later than one another may share lexical features such as identical vocabulary or even half-lines, or structural similarities like the intercalated Latin of the source-text within each poem proper. This could point to a relatively early date of composition for most of the canon which drew from a common lexical register that was fashionable at a specific period, but it could just as easily be argued that a group of later liturgical compositions might have been emulating the lexicon and style of an earlier group. Therefore I am not going to attempt to locate the majority of these pieces in any kind of common historical context, although specific observations in the introductions to individual poems may present evidence that is ultimately significant in better understanding these pieces.

Four of these poems were edited by James Ure in 1957 as part of the "Old English Benedictine Office." This is a misleading term, since at no time would the Benedictine monastic Offices have been recited in anything but Latin. The "text" that Ure edits is a curiosity: preserved in Cambridge, Corpus Christi College (CCCC) 201, and Oxford, Bodleian Junius 121 (written roughly a quarter century apart), the versions are not identical, and if purporting to cover the Offices in a day, the "text" is incomplete. The presence of hymn, psalm, and collect incipits ("opening words") and of psalter verses first in Latin and then in Old English creates a peculiar effect whose intended purpose has evaded scholars. Finally, the inclusion, in this bilingual and largely shorthand compilation, of substantial vernacular poems based on the liturgy is unprecedented: in CCCC 201 we find one vernacular Lord's Prayer poem, in Junius 121 we find a wholly different Lord's Prayer poem as well as a verse baptismal Creed piece, and in both manuscripts we find recensions of the metrical *Old English Doxology* poem. Ure has no clear conclusions to make about this "text," nor can he explain the presence of the poems

---

date for *Vision of the Rood* even as it appears in the Vercelli Book, such that it might have influenced tenth-century English liturgical practice rather than being influenced by it.

within it. He concludes only that "the four metrical paraphrases [in the "Old English Benedictine Office"] . . . afford evidence of the persistence of the Cædmonian tradition of Anglo-Saxon religious writing," evidently focusing here on *Cædmon's Hymn* only, rather than on the scriptural verse narratives ascribed to Cædmon by Bede.[64] However, *Cædmon's Hymn* is not a liturgical poem: it consists primarily of names for God and praise for those names, it quotes no liturgical source, it contains no intercalated Latin pointing to a source, and as such, it is in no way comparable to the liturgical poetry contained in the "Old English Benedictine Office," and with which this edition is concerned.

Figure 1 presents a time-line that indicates our best assumptions concerning manuscript compilation: the codices that contain the extant examples of liturgical vernacular poetry range in date from ca. 965 to the mid-twelfth century. At one end of the time-line, three books (Exeter Cathedral 3501, London, BL Cotton Vespasian D. vi, and Vercelli, Biblioteca Capitolare CXVII) can be safely assigned to the late tenth or turn of the eleventh century; two of them contain a significant percentage of the canon of extant Old English poetry, and the third is a miscellany of the sort so commonly found in later Anglo-Saxon England. At the other end, the only complete copy of one of our pieces (*Ah, Beloved Lord*) was copied into a short manuscript in a scribal hand of ca. 1150. We can therefore propose some relatively safe theories about the poems that these contain—namely, that *Exeter Lord's Prayer* and the two Kentish poems were probably composed between 950 and 975, and *Vision of the Rood* as it stands in the Vercelli Book, in the 30 years between 960 and the 990s.[65] We may also suggest that at least one poem in this edition—*Ah, Beloved Lord*—was still interesting enough to have been included a century after the Norman Conquest by an Anglo-Norman scribe in a collection of Old English texts loosely identifiable as wisdom and colloquy material.

---

64 James Ure, ed., *The Benedictine Office: An Edition of the Old-English Text* (Edinburgh: Edinburgh UP, 1957), 56. See Bertram Colgrave and R.A.B. Mynors, eds. and trans., *Bede's Ecclesiastical History of the English People* (Oxford: Oxford UP, 1969), IV.24, for an account of Cædmon's life.

65 See my study of the Good Friday Veneration of the Cross ritual comparison with *Vision of the Rood* ("Revisiting Good Friday, Nones: The Veneration of the Cross and *The Dream of the Rood*," *Poetry, Place and Gender: Studies in Medieval Culture in Honor of Helen Damico*, ed. Catherine Karkov [Kalamazoo, MI: Medieval Institute Press, 2009], 38–59), which suggests a composition date for the poem coeval with or later than that of the Regularis Concordia synod of the 970s.

FIG. 1 Timeline of the manuscripts contained in this edition

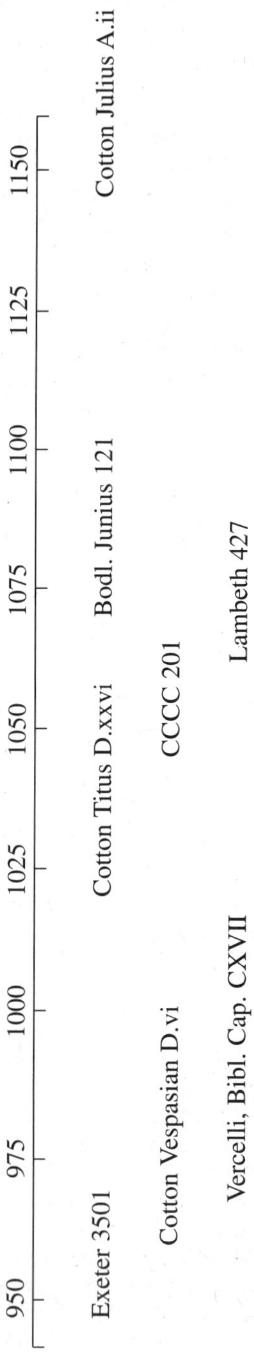

The manuscript witnesses can be laid out more or less chronologically as follows, with the poems of each identified with their traditional ASPR titles in brackets:

1. Exeter Cathedral 3501: second half of 10c: *Exeter Lord's Prayer* ("Lord's Prayer I");
2. London, British Library Cotton Vespasian D. vi: second half of 10c: *Kentish Hymn of Praise* ("The Kentish Hymn") and *Kentish Great Miserere* ("Psalm 50");
3. Vercelli, Biblioteca Capitolare CXVII: late 10c: *Vision of the Rood* ("Dream of the Rood");
4. London, British Library Cotton Titus D. xxvii: early-mid 11c: *Titus Alphabet Doxology* ("Gloria II");
5. Cambridge, Corpus Christi College 201: early-mid 11c: *Old English Doxology* ("Gloria I") and *Corpus Lord's Prayer* ("Lord's Prayer II");
6. London, Lambeth Palace 427, fol. 183v: early 11c but poem fragment added later 11c: *Ah, Beloved Lord* ("A Prayer"), 1–15;
7. Oxford, Bodleian Junius 121: third quarter of 11c: *Old English Doxology* ("Gloria I"), *Baptismal Creed* ("The Creed"), and *Junius Lord's Prayer* ("Lord's Prayer III");
8. London, British Library Cotton Julius A. ii: mid 12c: *Ah, Beloved Lord* ("A Prayer"), complete.

Lord's Prayers

(a) *Exeter Lord's Prayer*

The *Exeter Lord's Prayer* (edited as "Lord's Prayer I" by Krapp and Dobbie in ASPR) is the shortest of the three poems based on the *Pater Noster*, and likely the earliest. Included in the mid-tenth-century Exeter Book, which was compiled perhaps between 970 and 990, it shows none of the sophistication of the longer *Pater Noster* poems which may have been composed under different circumstances. It has no intercalated Latin text of its liturgical (and scriptural) original as we find elsewhere, and despite its clear dependence on the liturgical prayer *Pater Noster*, the *Exeter Lord's Prayer* does not end with *amen* like most of its later counterparts, and it is incomplete as a paraphrase. This lack of the customary liturgical closure marker *amen* for a poem that is modelled on the best-known prayer of Christendom is indeed odd and difficult to account for, but the *Exeter Lord's Prayer* is not merely a paraphrase: the poem as we have it omits entirely the Lord's Prayer's fifth petition *Et dimitte nobis debita nostra sicut et nos dimittimus debitoribus nostris* ("and forgive us our debts as we forgive our debtors"); this seems part of its original construction and not an error by poet or scribe.

The *Exeter Lord's Prayer* is described by Krapp and Dobbie as "a versified text of the Lord's Prayer . . . which follows the Latin original very closely, with no additions to the sense."[1] It is to be found in their section 19,[2]

1 George P. Krapp and Elliott van Kirk Dobbie, eds., *Anglo-Saxon Poetic Records: A Collective Edition* (ASPR) III (New York: Columbia UP, 1931–53), xiii.

2 Krapp and Dobbie, ASPR III, lxiii.

which they call "the shorter religious poems," but in fact it is the only one of the group with any evident reliance on a liturgical source. Of the others, "Almsgiving" (folio 121v–122r) contains more in the way of moral or spiritual teaching, and it is followed by "Pharaoh" (folio 122r), which deals with the number of men in Pharaoh's army. Like the "Age of the World" chronology that separates the Kentish liturgical poems in London, BL Cotton Vespasian D. vi, and the "Age of the Virgin" that accompanies the Cotton Titus D. xxviii Alphabet and its metrical Doxology, "Pharaoh," which immediately precedes the *Exeter Lord's Prayer*, is a numerological curiosity. It resembles the groups of Exeter Book riddles that surround it (folios 101r–115r, 122v–123r, and 124v to the end of the extant manuscript) in its opening words *saga me hwæt* ("tell me what"); for this reason "Pharaoh" may once have been cast as a riddle itself, or be part of a question-and-answer dialogue that emulates the process of catechesis (training within faith whereby each answer, elicited by a question from an examiner, forms part of a doctrine of belief). Such a catechetic form also appears in the Old English prose dialogue called "Adrian and Ritheus," found in the same twelfth-century manuscript (London, BL Cotton Julius A. ii) as the liturgical poem edited here under the title *Ah, Beloved Lord*.[3] A twenty-line piece editorially titled "Homiletic Fragment II" (folio 122rv) follows the *Exeter Lord's Prayer*, but despite this title it may or may not be a complete unit. Like "Almsgiving," it is didactic in its impulse, and Krapp and Dobbie argue that a summary section within it ("Faith is one, one living unity, baptism is one, the eternal Father is one, one is the Lord of men," lines 8–10) marks it as "late homiletic style," distinct from its three predecessors, and contemporary with the manuscript.[4] However, they do not explain what elements about "Almsgiving," "Pharaoh," and the *Exeter Lord's Prayer* might make them necessarily earlier.

Despite such a grouping, no thematic design appears evident in the layout of this part of the Exeter Book. It belongs to the section of the manuscript that suffered from severe scorching: the end of the "Pharaoh" poem and the beginning of the *Exeter Lord's Prayer* are affected on folio 122r. Each piece on this page begins with a simple large capital drawn in the inside gutter to

3 Editorially titled as "A Prayer" by Dobbie in ASPR VI, lxxxv–lxxxviii and 94–96.

4 Krapp and Dobbie, ASPR III, lxiv.

the left of the writing block, and each poem ends with the singular terminal punctuation found marking off section or unit endings throughout the Exeter Book (:,). Where a few words are left at the close of a text, they are placed on the end of the next line rather than at its beginning, to keep as pristine and solid as possible the vertical line of text standing in from the capitals on the left and forming the inside margin of the writing block. Thus we find with "Pharaoh" that its final words *in woruldrice* are split across the ends of manuscript lines 11 and 12; line 11 closes with *in wo*, and line 12 is blank until its final 2.5 centimetres, where we find *ruldrice* completing the poem and marking its termination. The initial capital of the *Exeter Lord's Prayer* is damaged beyond recognition by the scorch-mark; it has a tall ascender rising from the edge of the scorch which may once have been a majuscule thorn to begin the word *Þu*.

The *Exeter Lord's Prayer* does not readily follow the conventional design of two alliterators[5] on strong beats in the a-line, with the first strong beat of the b-line alliterating with them. Looking at a reconstruction of the damaged first line, it is possible to suggest that the barely discernible "g," evident as the poem's first visible letter at the end of a word, may be part of *halig*,[6] to modify *fæder* and alliterate with *heofonum* in the first b-line. A conjectured reconstruction of *Þu halig fæder* would scan out as "x / x / x," which would create an acceptable example of anacrusis in the A-Type half-line, but for the fact that, even allowing for *halig* and with *Þu* presumed at the start of the line, there are still nearly 2 centimetres of room for another word between them. Given the opening words of its liturgical source (*Pater noster*, "our Father"), I suggest the emendation *Þu ure halig fæder*, since *ure* in this size of scribal hand would fill out the line correctly. If we assume that the terminal "e" of *ure* is not sounded (or is elided with the aspirant [h] which begins *halig*), this suggestion still allows for anacrusis, providing us with "x x / x / x," recognizable once again as an A-Type half-line.

The structure of the b-line presents more difficulties: *þu þe on heofonum eardast* can be read metrically as "x x x / x x / x," with the alliteration on the

5 For further information on this and other metrical terms, see Appendix A, pp. 205–10 below.

6 Evidently without inflectional ending: although a weak nominative singular adjective would more correctly be *halga* or *haliga,* a reading of *halig* in this construction is not impossible.

first lift of the half-line, but if so, it cannot be another A-Type line, since we understand anacrusis to work for the first half-line of a pair but not the second. It could be taken as a hypermetric line with three lifts, one each on *þu*, *heo-* and *ear-*, but there is no indication of hypermetrics within the poem's context. Finally, we might assume that the alliteration pattern is faulty (alliteration would lie on the second and not the first stressed syllable of the b-line) and the two lifts lie on *þu* and *heo* (where the pronoun *þu* refers to God, it could well have been considered more important than the root syllable of the verb *eardast*), creating a second A-Type line which scans / x x / x x x x. This b-line presents the nominative form of the second-person singular (*þu*) so as to introduce a relative clause (*þe on heofenum eardest*) before the main clause *geweorðad wuldres dreame* in the next line. The first sentence of the poem thus becomes *Þu ure halig fæder þu þe on heofonum eardast/ geweorðad wuldres dreame*, meaning "Thou, our holy Father, thou who dwellest in heaven, honoured with the joy of glory."

We must remember that, simple as it is, this is not a verbatim text-to-text translation as we find in the canticle section of an interlinear glossed psalter. I have already noted that it omits the petition for the forgiveness of sins; since the omission seems part of the poem's original design, it would reinforce the theme of humanity's response to the divine alone and not humanity's treatment of fellow men. The rest of the poem is understated in its elaboration in the same fashion but continues to expand delicately on the original: we find *cyme þin rice wide* (line 4a), "may thy kingdom come far and wide" for *adveniat regnum tuum*, rather than an Anglo-Saxon version of "may thy kingdom happen"; and *ac þu us freodon gief . . . fram yfla gehwam* (lines 10 a,11a), "but thou, give to us freedom . . . from every evil" for *sed libera nos a malo*, "deliver us from evil." Whitbread assumes that it is a monastic exercise, calling it "a straightforward workmanlike version, unadorned except by the addition of several titles for God reminiscent of those in *Cædmon's Hymn*."[7] Why this poem was included in Exeter Cathedral 3501 is perhaps an important question to consider. The compiler of the Exeter Book evidently deemed it of value, and it seems to have been included among the miscellaneous texts near the end, for want of a better place to put it but so as not to leave it out.

---

7 Leslie Whitbread, "The Old English Poems of the *Benedictine Office* and Some Related Questions," *Anglia* 80 (1967): 37–49, 42.

SEMI-DIPLOMATIC TEXT
(folio 122r, lines 12–20)

[ ]g fæder þu þe on heofonum eardast ge

[ ]ordad wuldres dreame sy þinu<m> weorcu<m> halgad noma

niþþa bearnum þu eart nergend wera cyme þin rice wide

⁊ þin rædfæst willa aræred under rodores hrofe eac

þon on rumre foldan syle us to dæge domfæstne blæd

hlaf userne helpend wera þone singalan soðfæst meo

tod ne læt usic costunga cnyssan to swiðe ac þu us

freodon gief folca waldend from yfla gehwam a to

widan feore :,

CRITICAL TEXT

[Þū ūre hāli]g fæder,   þū þe on heofonum eardast
geweorðad wuldres dreame; sy þinum weorcum hālgad
noma niþþa bearnum;   þū eart nergend wera;
cyme þīn rīce wīde   ond þin rædfæst willa
ārǣred under rodores hrōfe, ēac þon on rūmre foldan;
syle us tō dæge   dōmfæstne blǣd,
hlāf ūserne,   helpend wera,
þone singālan,   sōðfæst meotod;
ne lǣt ūsic costunga   cnyssan tō swīðe
ac þū ūs frēodon gief,   folca waldend,
from yfla gehwām   ā tō wīdan feore.

NOTES

2: MS ge[ ]ordad: *This participle needs to be emended to read* geweorðad.
10: MS freodon: *This is a levelled form* (-om > -on), *most commonly found with inflectional endings like the dative plural, which appeared from the tenth century on.*

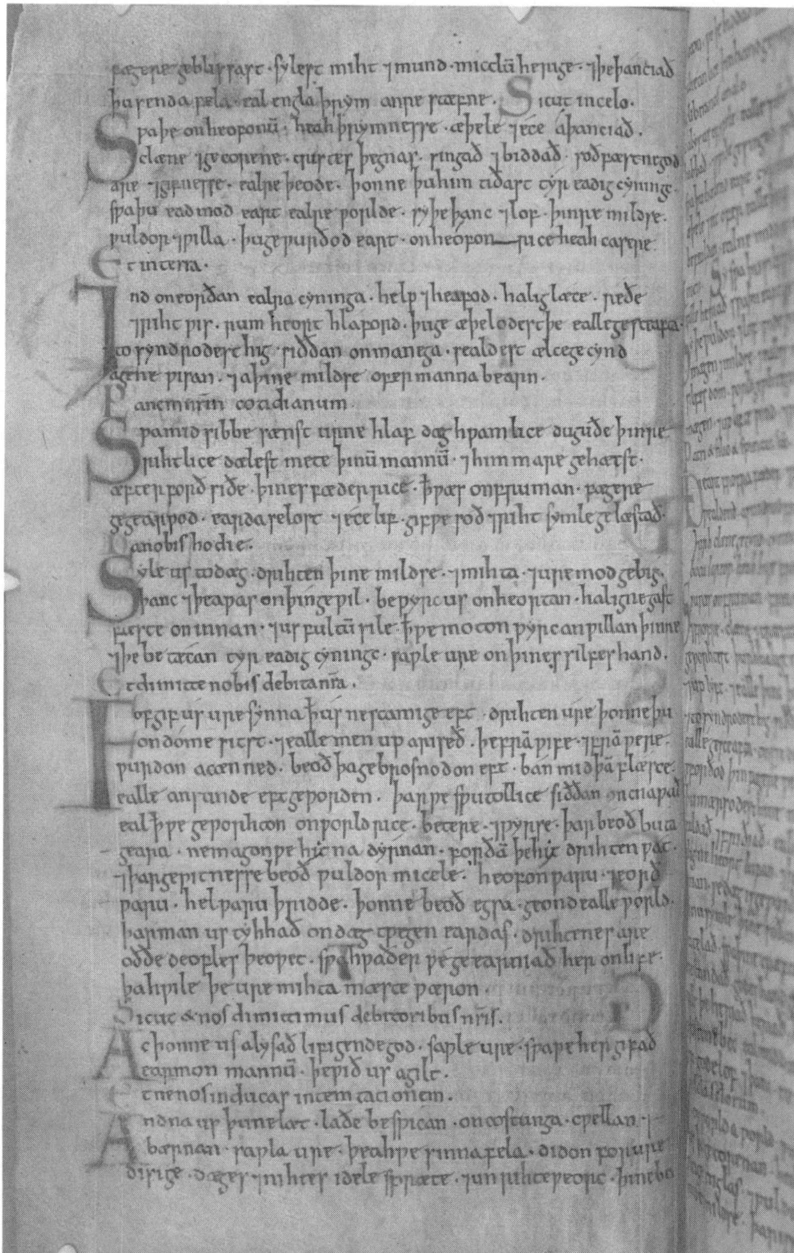

FIG. 2 Cambridge, Corpus Christi College MS 201, page 168, by kind permission of the Master and Fellows of Corpus Christi College, Cambridge

(b) *Corpus Lord's Prayer*

The *Corpus Lord's Prayer* is the most complex and sophisticated of the three *Pater Noster* poems and was taken by Ure as the "alternate" version within the "Old English Benedictine Office," rather than the original one.[8] It shares ideological and lexical similarities with a number of the vernacular liturgical poems in this edition, in particular the *Kentish Hymn of Praise*, *Baptismal Creed*, and *Ah, Beloved Lord*, suggesting a common stock of imagery or lexicon. Together with the *Old English Doxology* (immediately following it in its manuscript), it demonstrates a structural reliance on pairs of nouns, adjectives or verbs within the long line—*hiht and frofor* (line 11), *fæger and wurðlic* (line 45), or *singað and biddað* (line 60)—for a total of thirty such pairs. Its intriguing use of *casere* ("ruler," derived from Caesar's name) in line 66 also appears in the opening narrative of the *Kentish Great Miserere* (*Dauid æt wige/ soð sigecempa, searocyne man/ casere creaftig*, lines 9b–11a). The *Corpus Lord's Prayer* seems "the product of a sophisticated mind. . . . [H]ere we have the individual immanent within the semblance of the communal, just as each soul, reciting within synactic performance, is still reciting for herself and from her own space within creation."[9]

It is worthwhile examining the way that the *Corpus Lord's Prayer* poet sets out his Latin original in the manuscript. Capitals for Latin rubrics and Old English meditations vary between red and green in colour. Of the traditional seven petitions of the *Pater Noster* (see Introduction, p. 24), the first is divided on the page into address (*Pater noster*), relative clause of description (*qui es in celis*), and prayer proper (*sanctificetur nomen tuum*), with an Old English verse meditation separating each section from the other two. The third petition is also divided by accompanying Old English meditations into the core of its prayer (*fiat voluntas tua*) and two prepositional phrases modifying that core (*sicut in celo* and *et in terra*). The poet uses vernacular verse reflections to divide the fourth petition into that which is asked for (*panem nostrum cotidianem*) and the request that it be given (*da nobis hodie*), and the fifth petition is separated by its Old English into the prayer for forgiveness (*et dimitte nobis debita nostra*) and the following consequent clause which promises forgiveness of others (*sicut et nos dimittimus debitoribus nostris*). Each of these internal divisions carries a small coloured capital, suggesting that it

8 Ure, *Benedictine Office*, 51–55. But see Whitbread, "Old English Poems," 41–89, for disagreement.

9 Keefer, "'Ic' and 'We,'" 141.

be treated as a discrete unit on which to concentrate attention, and each has its own Old English following. *Amen* stands independent of the preceding petitions and has its own three-line vernacular reflection, once again presented as a discrete subject for contemplation.

Corpus Lord's Prayer also departs more frequently from its liturgical model than do the other two Lord's Prayer poems, by incorporating material from different prayers or hymns, or from texts at a substantial remove from the ritual language of Mass or Office. In lines 12b–18, we find what initially appears to be an echo from the *Te Deum*; in fact the original text for both comes from Isaiah 6:1–3, wherein the prophet's vision of God includes angels crying aloud to one another "Holy, holy, holy is the Lord God of hosts; heaven and earth are filled with his glory." The poet may therefore have been quoting the Old Testament or the canticle that in part derived its inspiration from it: both are a substantial departure from the *Pater Noster* prayer.

Dobbie addresses the reference in line 23 (his line 20) to "seventy-two" (*manegum gereordum/ twa and hundseofontig, þæs þe secgað bec,* "with many voices, two-and-seventy, of whom the books tell us") by noting that it refers to a non-scriptural tradition of the "number of nations and languages resulting from the confusion of tongues . . . but attested by rabbinical and patristic sources."[10] A simpler explanation lies in the text of Luke 10:1, where St Jerome's Latin Vulgate, widely used throughout the Anglo-Saxon period, reads *designavit Dominus et alios septuaginta duos*, "the Lord chose another seventy-two."[11] The West Saxon text of the Gospels also follows the Vulgate for these verses: *Æfter þam sæ hælend gemearcude oðre twa and hundseofantig and sende hig twam beforan his ansyne on ælce ceastre and stowe þe he to cumenne wæs*, "after that, the Lord designated another seventy-two and sent them out in pairs ahead of him into every city and place which he intended to visit." This association of "seventy-two" with Luke's Gospel makes far more sense, considering that the request, *Drihten, lær us us gebiddan swa iohannes his leorningcnihtas lærde* ("Lord, teach us to pray for ourselves as John taught his disciples"), which produces the Lucan version of the Lord's Prayer, lies only a chapter later in Luke 11:1–4.[12] *Boc* or *bec* (line 23) most commonly refers to a gospel-book, so the *Corpus Lord's Prayer* poet was probably making reference to Luke 10:1 and not to considerably less accessible "rabbinical and patristic sources" in Bede or elsewhere; in either

10 Dobbie, ASPR VI, 185.

11 Weber II, 1627; translation mine.

12 Liuzza, *Old English Version of the Gospels*, I, 122, 125.

case, we evidently have a more educated mind at work than those that composed the other two *Pater Noster* poems.

Some grammatical anomalies appear in the poem (see critical notes to lines 17, 34, 73, 106, and 112–13), but earlier editors have made changes that may not always have been necessary. In verse line 34, Dobbie emends the MS reading *sib and lufu* to read as accusatives, *sibbe and lufe*, the direct objects of *gemetað,* while Ure adjusts the MS reading of *wē* to read *þe*, thus leaving *sib and lufu* as the nominative compound subject of the verb. There is no question about the wyn (ƿ) that begins *we* in the manuscript, and I follow Dobbie's reading with the following justification: the line *þar we sibbe and lufe samod gemetað* is reminiscent of Ps. 84:10, *misericordia et veritas obviaverunt sibi: iustitia et pax osculatae sunt* ("Mercy and truth have met together; justice and peace have kissed one another") since a verb meaning "met" (in the poem, *gemetað*, and in the psalm-verse, *obviaverunt*) appears together with a noun meaning "peace" (in the poem, *sib[be]*, and in the psalm-verse, *pax*), which stands as one of a pair in the subject position. Perhaps the copyist was reminded of this psalm verse and miscopied the nouns' endings as nominative rather than accusative, despite already having correctly set down *wē* as the true subject of *gemetað*. If so, this might be evidence that the copyist knew his or her psalms by heart and was a monk or nun;[13] we might also wonder if the composer of our poem were quoting this psalm-verse indirectly in describing the kingdom of heaven.

Dobbie and Ure both emend the MS reading *þinre . . . hand* ("thine . . . hand") in verse line 47 to *sinre* ("his"), assuming that the Son of God, addressed in these lines, cannot sit on his own right side. However, lines 47b–48a state *þu eart sunu and fæder/ ana ægþer* ("thou art son and father, both one"), a close identification of the first two persons of God that is also found in the *Baptismal Creed* (see p. 91, lines 16b–18), so what seems to be an anomaly may have been intentional. The words ⁊ (= "and") *fæder* appear at the end of the fourth manuscript line from the bottom on page 167, written unusually far into the outer margin and outside the writing boundary; although they appear to be in the same hand as the rest of the text, they are very faint. The word *fyrde* (part of half-line 52a), the last line of the manuscript page, is in the same hand, evidently written at much the same time, and is similarly faint. There is no reason to erase *fyrde*, although I have conjec-

13 The *Regula Sancti Benedicti* required that monks and nuns know much of their Office recitation from memory (Lat. *ex corde,* OE *butan bec*; or Lat. *memoriter*, OE *gemyndlice*). See Logeman, *Rule of St Benet*, 39.

FIG. 3 Drawing (detail), after London, British Library MS Cotton Titus D.xxvii, folio 75v: God the Father and God the Son

tured elsewhere that the very close identification of the Father and the Son in these two poems might constitute a departure from the tenets of orthodoxy,[14] which would explain an attempt at erasing *⁊ fæder*. I can therefore only suggest reasons for the faintness of these words: a) that they have been rubbed by wear, perhaps unlikely since the lines before and after show no such patterns; b) that an attempt was made to erase them, a possibility although no reason occurs, as we have just seen, for erasing *fyrde*; or c) that they were accidentally omitted and added quickly and in paler ink by the scribe when he or she noticed the omission. This latter is the most likely: although *fyrde* falls within the writing area, *⁊ fæder* clearly does not. So if these words were added

14 Keefer, "'Ic' and 'We,'" 136–37 and 146, n. 57. See also below, pp. 61, 70.

as afterthoughts, they were intended to be there, and we must take seriously the import of *þu eart sunu and fæder/ ana ægþer* before making emendations to suit modern thinking.

For this reason I leave the reading *þinre . . . hand* in line 47 unemended, odd as it will be to translate. In support of this decision, Figure 3 presents part of the image of The Trinity and Mary, found on folio 75v of Ælfwine's prayer-book in which the *Titus Alphabet Doxology* is also to be found. In this miniature we see identical figures holding books: these have been identified as "Christ incarnate and God the Father,"[15] and the design of the drawing, presenting a common early medieval aesthetic whereby the Father and the Son are mirror images of each other, offers some rationale for allowing the MS reading *þinre . . . hand* to remain unaltered in the *Corpus Lord's Prayer*.

We can make some educated guesses about how many earlier versions of a piece of text may have existed prior to the one that remains to us for posterity. This poem appears to be missing perhaps two half-lines;[16] we must assume that the missing sections were once part of the original composition, and that the erroneous copy in hand is either the fault of the CCCC 201 copyist (one remove from a first version), or the fault of an earlier scribe whose copy represented or stood behind the exemplar that the CCCC 201 scribe used (more than one remove from the original composition). In like manner, a curiosity occurs at the start of the ninth line of manuscript page 168 (see Figure 2), where the Old English text (copied before the coloured capitals were added) reads "–nd" for OE *And*, awaiting its rubricated majuscule "A." The rubricator instead adds a large tironian nota ("⁊"), the insular scribal abbreviation for *and* that is the Old English equivalent of ampersand ("&"), standing for Latin *et* ("and"). This is less likely an error on the part of the text-scribe, who was almost certainly following his or her exemplar faithfully,[17] than a slip by the rubricator, who also omits the coloured capital from the word *Gloria* (see p. 102, below) that begins the *Old English Doxology* on manuscript page 169. From this it is clear that at least one, and perhaps more than one, recension of the *Corpus Lord's Prayer* existed before the version in CCCC 201.

---

15 Catherine E. Karkov, "Abbot Ælfwine and the Sign of the Cross," *Cross and Cruciform in the Anglo-Saxon World*, ed. Sarah Larratt Keefer, Karen L. Jolly and Catherine E. Karkov (Morgantown: West Virginia UP, 2010), 105–32, 106.

16 See critical notes to lines 7 and 78.

17 Farther down the same page 168, we find *And* written out at the beginning of a section in full, with the correct majuscule "A" preceding it, so we must assume that the scribal abbreviation was not customarily used in this manuscript at the beginning of a sentence.

SEMI-DIPLOMATIC TEXT

(page 167, line 11 – page 169, line 10)
Capitals alternate red and green.

Pater n<oste>r · Þu eart ure fæder ealles wealdend ·

cẏninc on wuldre · forðam we clẏpiað to þe · are biddað

nu þu ẏþost miht · sawle alẏsan þu hig sændest ær · þurh

þine æþelan hand · in to þa<m> flæsce · ac hwar cẏmð heo nu ·

buton þu engla god eft hig alẏse · sawle of sẏnnu<m> þurh

þine soðan miht · Qui es in celis ·

Ðu eart in heofenu<m> · hiht ⁊ frofor · blissa beorhtost ·

ealle abugað to þe · þinra gasta þrẏm · anre stæfne ·

clẏpiað to criste cweþað ealle þus · halig eart þu halig · heofon

engla cẏningc · drihten ure · ⁊ þine domas sẏnd rihte ⁊ rume ·

ræcð efne gehwam · æghwilcu<m> men agen gewẏrhta · wel bið ða<m>

CRITICAL TEXT

Pater noster.

Þū eart ūre fæder, ealles wealdend,

cyninc on wuldre; forðam wē clypiað to þē,

āre biddað, nū þū ȳþost miht

sāwle ālȳsan; þū hīg sændest ǣr,

þurh þīne æþelan hand in tō þām flǣsce

ac hwār cymð hēo nū,

būton þū, engla God, eft hīg ālȳse,

sāwle of synnum þurh þīne sōðan miht.

Qui es in celis.

Ðū eart in heofenum hiht and frōfor,

blissa beorhtost; ealle ābūgað tō þē,

þīnra gāsta þrym, ānre stæfne

clypiað tō Criste, cweþað ealle þus:

"Hālig eart þū, hālig, heofonengla cyningc,

drihten ūre; and þīne dōmas synd

rihte and rūme, rǣcað efne gehwām,

ǣghwilcum men āgen gewyrhta;

þe wyrcð willan þinne · S<an>c<t>ificetur nomen tuum ·
Swa is gehalgod þin heah nama · swiðe mærlice · manegum
gereordu<m> · twa ⁊ hund seofontig · þæs þe secgað bec · þ<æt> þu
engla god · ealle gesettest · ælcere þeode · þeaw ⁊ wisan · þa wur
þiað þin weorc · wordu<m> ⁊ dædu<m> · þurh gecẏnd clẏpiað > ⁊ crist
heriað · ⁊ þin lof lædað lifigenda god · swa þu eart geæþelod
geond ealle world. Adueniat regnum tuum ·
Cum nu ⁊ mildsa · mihta waldend · ⁊ us þin rice alẏf ·
rihtwis dema earda selost · ⁊ ece lif · þar we sib ⁊ lufu
samod gemetað · eagena beorhtnẏs · ⁊ ealle mirhðe · þar bið
gehẏred þin halige lof · ⁊ þin micele miht mannu<m> to frofre ·
swa þu engla god eallu<m> blissast. Fiat uoluntas tua ·

wel bið ðām þe wyrcð willan þīnne."
Sanctificetur nomen tuum.
Swā is gehālgod þīn hēah nama
swīðe mǣrlice manegum gereordum,
twā and hundseofontig þǣs þe secgað bēc
þæt þū, engla God, ealle gesettest
ǣlcere þēode, þēaw and wīsan;
þā wurþiað þīn weorc wordum and dǣdum,
þurh gecynd clypiað and Crīst heriað,
and þīn lof lǣdað, lifigenda God,
swā þū eart geæþelod geond ealle world.
Adueniat regnum tuum.
Cum nū and mildsa, mihta waldend,
and ūs þīn rīce ālȳf, rihtwīs dēma,
earda sēlost and ēce līf
þār wē sibbe and lufe samod gemētað,
ēagena beorhtnysse and ealle mirhðe;
þār bið gehȳred þīn halige lof
and þīn micele miht mannum tō frōfre
swā þū, engla God, eallum blissast.
Fiat uoluntas tua.

Gewurðe þin willa · swa þu waldend eart · ece geopenod ·

geond ealle world · ⁊ þu þe silf eart soðfæst dema · rice

rædbora · geond rumne grund · swa þin heahsetl is · heah

⁊ mære · fæger ⁊ wurðlic · swa þin fæder worhte · æþele ⁊ ece ·

þar ðu onsittest · on þinre swiþran healf · þu eart sunu ⁊ fæder

ana ægþer · swa is þin æþela gecẏnd · micclu<m> gemærsod ·

⁊ þu monegu<m> helpst · ealra cẏninga þrẏm · clẏpast ofer ealle ·

bið þin wuldorword · wide gehẏred · þonne þu þine fyrde

[page 168]

fægere geblissast · sẏlest miht mund · micclu<m> herige · ⁊ þe þanciað

þusenda fela · eal engla þrẏm anre stæfne · Sicut in celo ·

Swa þe on heofenu<m> · heahþrẏmnesse · æþele ⁊ ece a þanciað ·

Gewurðe þīn willa, swā þū waldend eart,
ēce geopenod geond ealle world,
and þū þe silf eart sōðfæst dēma,
rīce rædbora geond rūmne grund;
swā þīn hēahsetl is hēah and mære,
fæger and wurðlic, swā þīn fæder worhte,
æþele and ēce, þar ðū onsittest
on þīnre swīþran healfe: þū eart sunu and fæder
āna ægþer; swā is þīn æþele gecynd
micclum gemærsod, and þū monegum helpst,
ealra cyninga þrym, clypast ofer ealle;
bið þīn wuldorword wīde gehȳred
þonne þū þīne fyrde fægere geblissast;
sylest miht and mund micclum herige
and þē þanciað þūsenda fela,
eal engla þrym ānre stæfne.
Sicut in celo.
Swā þē on heofenum hēahþrymnesse,
æþele and ēce, ā þanciað

clæne ⁊ gecorene · cristes þegnas · singað ⁊ biddað · soðfæstne god
are ⁊ gifnesse · ealre þeode · þonne þu him tiðast tẏreadig cẏningc ·
swa þu eadmod eart ealre worlde · sẏ þe þanc ⁊ lof · þinre mildse ·
wuldor ⁊ willa · þu gewurðod eart · on heofonrice heah casere ·

Et in terra ·

⁊nd on eorðan ealra cẏninga · help ⁊ heafod · halig læce · reðe
⁊ rihtwis · rumheort hlaford · þu geæþelodest þe ealle gesceafta ·
⁊ tosẏndrodest hig · siððan on manega · sealdest ælce gecẏnd
agene wisan · ⁊ a þine mildse ofer manna bearn ·

Panem n<ost>r<u>m cotidianum ·

Swa mid sibbe sænst urne hlaf dæghwamlice duguðe þinre ·

clǣne and gecorene Crīstes þegnas,
singað and biddað sōðfæstne God
āre and gifnesse ealre þēode
þonne þū him tīðast, tīrēadig cyningc;
swā þū ēadmōd eart ealre worlde;
sȳ þē þanc and lof þīnre mildse,
wuldor and willa; þū gewurðod eart
on heofonrīce, hēah cāsere.
Et in terra.
And on eorðan, ealra cyninga
help and hēafod, hālig lǣce,
reðe and rihtwīs, rūmheort hlaford,
þū geæþelodest þē ealle gesceafta
and tōsyndrodest hīg siððan on manega;
sealdest ǣlcum gecynde āgene wīsan
and ā þīne mildse ofer manna bearn.
Panem nostrum cotidianum.
Swā mid sibbe sænst ūrne hlaf
dæghwāmlice duguðe þīnre;
rihtlice dǣlest

rihtlice dælest mete þinu<m> mannu<m> · ⁊ him mare gehætst
æfter forðsiðe · þines fæder rice · þ<æt> wæs on fruman · fægere
gegearwod · earda selost ⁊ ece lif · gif we soð ⁊ riht sẏmle gelæstað ·

Da nobis hodie ·

Sẏle us to dæg · drihten þine mildse · ⁊ mihta ⁊ ure mod gebig ·
þanc ⁊ þeawas on þin gewil · bewẏrc us on heortan · haligne gast
fæste on innan · ⁊ us fultu<m> sile · þ<æt> we moton wẏrcan willan þinne ·
⁊ þe betæcan tẏreadig cẏningc · sawle ure on þines silfes hand ·

Et dimitte nobis debita n<ost>ra ·

Forgif us ure sẏnna þ<æt> us ne scamige eft · drihten ure þonne þu
on dome sitst · ⁊ ealle men up ariseð · þe fra<m> wife · ⁊ fra<m> were ·
wurdon acænned · beoð þa gebrosnodon eft · ban mid þa<m> flæsce ·

mete þīnum mannum and him māre gehǣtst
æfter forðsīðe þīnes fæder rīce
þæt wæs on fruman fægere gegearwod,
earda sēlost and ēce līf
gif wē sōð and riht symle gelǣstað.
Da nobis hodie.
Syle ūs tō dæg, drihten, þīne
mildse and mihta and ūre mōd gebig,
þanc and þēawas, on þīn gewil;
bewyrc us on heortan hāligne gast
fæste on innan, and ūs fultum sile
þæt wē mōton wyrcan willan þīnne
and þē betǣcan, tȳrēadig cyningc,
sāwle ūre on þīnes silfes hand.
Et dimitte nobis debita nostra.
Forgif ūs ūre synna þæt ūs ne scamige eft,
drihten ūre, þonne þū on dōme sitst
and ealle men up ārīsað
þe fram wīfe and fram were wurdon ācænned;
bēoð þā gebrosnodon eft bān mid þām flǣsce

ealle ansunde eft geworden · þar we swutollice siððan oncnawað
eal þ<æt> we geworhton on worldrice · betere · ⁊ wẏrse · þar beoð buta
geara · ne magon we hit na dẏrnan · for ða<m> þe hit drihten wat ·
⁊ þar gewitnesse beoð wuldormicele · heofonwaru · ⁊ eorð
waru · helwaru þridde · þonne beoð egsa · geond ealle world
þar man us tẏhhað on dæg twegen eardas · drihtenes are
oððe deofles þeowet · swa hwaðer we geearniað her on life ·
þa hwile þe ure mihta mæste wæron ·

Sicut & nos dimittimus debitoribus n<ost>ris ·

Ac þonne us alẏsað lifigende god · sawle ure · swa we her gifað
earmon mannu<m> · þe wið us agilt ·
Et ne nos inducas in temtationem ·

And na us þu ne læt · laðe beswican · on costunga · cwellan ⁊
bærnan · sawla ure · þeah we sinna fela · didon for ure

ealle ansunde eft geworden;
þār wē swutollice siððan oncnāwað
eal þæt wē geworhton on worldrīce,
betere and wyrse, þār bēoð būta gēara;
ne magon wē hit nā dyrnan for ðām þe hit drihten wāt,
and þār gewitnesse bēoð wuldormicele,
heofonwaru and eorðwaru, helwaru þridde;
þonne bið egsa geond ealle world
þār man ūs tyhhað on dæg twēgen eardas,
drihtenes āre oððe dēofles þēowet,
swā hwaðer wē geearniað hēr on līfe
þā hwīle þe ūre mihta mǣste wǣron.
Sicut et nos dimittimus debitoribus nostris.
Ac þonne ūs ālyseð lifigende God
sāwle ūre swā wē forgifað
earmon mannum þe wið us āgilt.
Et ne nos inducas in temptationem.
And nā ūs þū ne lǣt lāðe beswīcan
on costunga cwellan and bærnan
sāwla ūre þēah wē sinna fela

disige · dæges ⁊ nihtes idele spræce · ⁊ unrihte weorc · þine bodu

[page 169]

bræcon · we þe biddað nu ælmihtig god · are ⁊ gifnes · ne læt
swa heanlice þin handgeweorc on endedæge eal forwurðan ·

S& libera nos a malo ·

Ac alẏs us of ẏfele · ealle we beþurfon godes gifnesse · we agẏlt
habbað · ⁊ swiðe gesingod · we ðe soðfæstan · god heriað · ⁊ lofiað ·
swa þu hælend eart cẏnebearn gecẏdd · cwẏcu<m> ⁊ deadum ·
æþele ⁊ ece ofer ealle þingc · þu miht on anre hand · eaðe
befealdan · ealne middaneard swilc is mære cẏningc ·

Amen· Sẏ swa þu silf wilt · soðfæst dema · we þe engla god
ealle heriað swa þu eart gewurðod · a on worlda forð ·

didon for ūre disige dæges and nihtes;
īdele sprǣce and unrihte weorc
þīne bodu brǣcon; wē þē biddað nū,
ælmihtig God, āre and gifnesse
ne lǣt swā hēanlice þīn handgeweorc
on endedæge eal forwurðan.
Sed libera nos a malo.
Ac ālys ūs of yfele; ealle wē beþurfon
Godes gifnesse; wē āgylt habbað
and swiðe gesingod; wē ðē, sōðfæstan God,
herìað and lofiað swā þū hælend
eart cynebearn gecȳdd cwycum and dēadum,
æþele and ēce ofer ealle þingc;
þū miht on ānre hand ēaðe befealdan
ealne middaneard: swilc is mǣre cyningc.
Amen
Sȳ swā þū silf wilt, sōðfæst dēma;
we þē, engla God, ealle heriað
swā þū eart gewurðod ā on worlda forð.

NOTES

7: MS ac hwar cymð heo nu: *a b-line is missing here, the result of eyeskip at the end of MS line 14 on page 167.*
17: MS ræcð: *this should read as* ræcað *to accord with its plural subject.*
34: MS sib and lufu: *these should be taken as* sibbe and lufe *to form correct accusatives: for a possible explanation of this reading, see the poem's Introduction.*
35: MS beorhtnys: *as with* sib and lufu, *this must be emended for case (accusative singular).*
47: MS þinre: *all previous editors other than Lumby emend this to* sinre*; however, see the poem's Introduction.* MS healf: *the line is already metrically problematic, so a dative inflection as an emendation is called for.*
48: MS æþela: *DOE does not record a masculine form of* gecynd, *so its adjective must be emended accordingly.*
73: MS ælce gecynd: *as the indirect object of* sealdest, *this noun phrase needs emending to dative; the MS reading* ælce *might suggest that the poet was thinking of the feminine form,* ælcre gecynde *(Dobbie's emendation), but elsewhere in the poem at line 27, we find the more common neuter form* gecynd, *so I emend to the neuter dative singular* ælcum gecynde.
78: rihtlice dælest: *previous editors consider the missing half-line here to be the b-line, with* rihtlice dælest *the a-line. I propose a missing a-line instead: because scribal eyeskip is most likely to occur at end-of-line breaks, the casualty should have appeared in the exemplar text as preceding, rather than following,* rihtlice dælest *(my line 78b), which is the first half-line to be copied onto line 15 of page 168 in the manuscript. Since a new verb (*dælest*) appears here, I am assuming a new clause as well, and would agree with earlier editors that the missing half-line was likely another noun phrase epithet for God.*
96: MS ariseð: *this verb must be emended to a plural form to agree with its plural subject,* men, *although the scribe or poet may have been thinking of humanity in a collective sense.*
98: MS gebrosnodon eft: o*ther editors delete* eft *after* gebrosnodon, *assuming that it creates an imperfect metre and is an eyeskip from two lines earlier. In reconstructing my half-lines 98a and 98b, I bear in mind that metre is 'loose' in this poem, retaining the a-line as* beoð þa gebrosnodon *and moving* eft *to the b-line where it helps to construct a plausible Type B line (instead of the Type A to be found in Ure and Dobbie): the final weak beat on the inflection of* flæsce *would be subsumed into the root of the word (see Type B b-line example given by Mitchell and Robinson's* A Guide to Old English, *p. 164).*
106: MS beoð egsa: *In the manuscript, this clearly (and erroneously) stands as a plural verb and a singular subject: most editors emend the verb, as here.*
112–13: MS us alysað lifigende god/ sawle ure: *editorial tradition assumes a third-person singular present verb since this is evidently a statement of faith ("The living God redeems us . . . ").*

113: MS swa we her gifað: *I emend to* forgifað *rather than to* her forgifað, *as this seems a case of substitution rather than expansion for metrical exigency: the correct form* forgif *has already been used appropriately in line 94, and on page 168, MS line 33 (four lines above the problematic reading) stands the phrase* her on life. *Like* for, her *is a three-letter word ending in 'r,' and its occurrence just above is in virtually the same position that* for *needs to be; both words are also on lines that are not only close together but lower down on an increasingly difficult part of the page to write on. These conditions could have caused the scribe's eye to substitute the one for the other.*
115: MS temtationem: *The scribe has accidentally dropped the 'p' from* temptationem.
120: *for whatever reason (perhaps metrical, or thematic to emphasize their pejorative meaning),* idele *and* unrihte *are apparently inflected as strong adjectives.*
122: MS gifnes: *this stands in the MS as a nominative where it should grammatically be either accusative or genitive, like* are *in the same line. Dobbie emends it to* gifnesse, *nineteenth-century editors leave it unchanged, and Ure presents it as* gifnes[se], *evidently unsure of a solution.*
125: MS Set: *The Latin for 'but,' usually* sed, *here* appears *as a green capital and the scribal ampersand abbreviation* (&) *creating the anomaly* Set *(see semi-diplomatic text). It was likely created by common scribal use of the ampersand for* et *('and'), with either an accidental or intended transfer of abbreviation from one conjunction to another.*

(c) *Junius Lord's Prayer*

The *Junius Lord's Prayer*, in Oxford, Bodleian Junius 121, is part of the so-called "Old English Benedictine Office," a companion piece to the *Old English Doxology* which precedes it and the *Baptismal Creed* poem which follows it, with only brief matter separating them. The Junius Old English liturgical poems are copied with their Latin source-text intercalations in red ink, and these are generally confined to line-ends where one petition or tenet of faith may occupy several lines in an attempt to preserve space. A single hand appears to have written both text and rubrics, and ascertaining which activity came first is by no means easy. The Junius 121 scribe inserts *þu,* mistakenly omitted from manuscript line 21 of folio 45v, so we may once again assume a text-to-text transmission rather than copying from dictation; we already know that a recension of the *Old English Doxology* at least a quarter century older than that in Junius 121 appears in Cambridge, Corpus Christi College 201, but it seems that the *Junius Lord's Prayer* certainly had at least one earlier exemplar as well. Since its manuscript was compiled in Worcester, where it remained until the sixteenth century, the *Junius Lord's Prayer* drew the attention of the Worcester Tremulous Hand[18] and acquired glosses in Latin for a number of its words: these appear in the semi-diplomatic text.

The *Junius Lord's Prayer* is to some degree midway in length between the other two, containing 46 verse lines, including its Latin, compared with the very brief 11 lines of Old English in the Exeter piece and the 137 verse lines in the Corpus poem. It also stands midway between the *Exeter Lord's Prayer* and the *Corpus Lord's Prayer* in terms of its sophistication: it is more than a simple, lightly ornamented articulation of the Latin original but far less than a creative series of digressions around the *Pater Noster* prayer. Dobbie refers to it as a "metrical paraphrase," considering it to be the best translation of the Latin liturgical texts that were turned to Old English verse, although his standards of excellence are nowhere set out.[19]

---

18 This term refers to the activities of a thirteenth-century scribe with distinctively shaky handwriting who glossed ca. 50,000 Old English words in at least twenty manuscripts; there was evidently an active interest in Old English and in preparing an alphabetical English-Latin word list during this period in Worcester; see Christine Franzen, *The Tremulous Hand of Worcester: A Study of Old English in the Thirteenth Century* (Oxford: Clarendon Press, 1991) 1–2.

19 Dobbie, ASPR VI, lxxvii.

While the *Corpus Lord's Prayer* concentrates on the use of the plural pronoun *we* to produce a constructed sense of community within the piece, the poet of the *Junius Lord's Prayer* begins by asking *frofres ic þe bidde* and only switches to a plural *we* thereafter. As such, it may be a junior attempt at composition or a moment of personal thought-gathering for the creation of a vernacular verse meditation.[20] It also has a less lexically textured syntax than other pieces; unlike the Corpus *Pater Noster* piece or the *Old English Doxology*, it does not rely on the pairing of substantives or verbs to structure its lines, and instead presents a simpler, more direct articulation of the poet's thoughts. Indeed, the Junius poem breaks the Latin of its original rather differently from the design of the *Corpus Lord's Prayer*: the first petition of the *Pater Noster* (*Sanctificetur nomen tuum*) is divided from the address to God (*Pater noster qui es in cęlis*) that opens the prayer, and both carry capitals to indicate two separate foci for the reader to pay attention to, but this is unlike the division in the *Corpus Lord's Prayer* of the address into two further units. Both poems separate the fifth petition, omitted entirely from the *Exeter Lord's Prayer*, into the plea for mercy (*Et dimitte nobis debita nostra*) and the promise of forgiveness to others (*Sicut et nos dimittimus debitoribus nostris*), but apart from this, the *Junius Lord's Prayer* presents its meditations petition by petition, according to their traditional divisions.

Both the *Corpus* and *Junius Lord's Prayer* poems preserve anachronistic detail by addressing Jesus Christ (despite the original prayer being ascribed to his ministry on earth), and Ure uses this detail in his argument for a common background lying behind the two pieces; however, similar anachronism appears in the *Kentish Great Miserere*, where King David is described as *Criste liofost* (line 3b: "most beloved by Christ") and, later, as praying to *helende Crist* (line 55), only two among a number of similar references. So the relationship between these two *Pater Noster* poems remains uncertain: Dobbie insists that they are not of common origin, while Ure believes they both come from "one school of (probably) monastic poets flourishing under the impetus given by the Benedictine revival."[21] I consider them different enough in both impulse and process to agree with Dobbie that they "were

20 I am grateful to Joyce Hill for this second suggestion to explain the first-person singular "lapse."

21 See Dobbie, ASPR VI, lxxiv, and Ure, *Benedictine Office*, 55.

from the beginning two separate translations . . . shown . . . by definite criteria of subject matter and style."[22]

Like the *Corpus Lord's Prayer* and the *Old English Doxology*, the *Junius Lord's Prayer* preserves the complete text of its Latin original but does not depart as radically as the other two poems do from its source-text; instead, its meditations return to recapture the essence of each Latin petition so that they may translate it effectively while at the same time demonstrating some awareness of scholarly commentary in their expansions. *Panem nostrum cotidianum da nobis hodie* is a good case in point: the *Junius Lord's Prayer* poet is evidently familiar with the theological implications of *panis* ("bread"), with reference both to the Eucharist, and to Christ as the "bread of heaven" who nourishes, heals, and sustains the Christian soul, because we are told that God sent bread *sawlum to hæle/ on middaneard manna cynnes/ þæt is se clæna Crist, drihten God* ("as salvation for souls onto the earth of the kin of men, that/which is the hallowed Christ, the lord God"; lines 21b–23).

This is, therefore, a relatively uncomplicated poem. It has few emendations and a text that is generally free from grammatical anomaly. As I note elsewhere,

> Far less sophisticated or broad-ranging in his approach and at best homiletic in his ornamentations, the *Junius Lord's Prayer* poet . . . espouses the orthodox position and never deviates from his Latin original in content, [though he] "errs" in his use of "ic." In so doing, he may be reflecting the older vernacular cultural tradition of narrative performance that regards the speaker of a poem as singular, despite authority or rationale for its pronoun.[23]

22 Dobbie, ASPR VI, lxxiv. See also Whitbread, "Old English Poems," 41, who seeks to separate the two *Pater Noster* poems.

23 Keefer, "'Ic' and 'We,'" 140.

SEMI-DIPLOMATIC TEXT

(folio 45r, line 10 – folio 45v, line 23)

Latin rubrics and capitals are in red. Glosses are by the Worcester Tremulous Hand.

Pater noster qui es in cęlis ·

Fæder manncẏnnes frōfres ic þe bidde ·

halig drihten · þu ðe on heofenu<m> eart · S<an>c<t>ificet<ur>

Þæt sẏ gehalgod · hẏgecræftu<m> fæst nom<en> tuum ·

eripie<n>s

þin nama nu ða · neriende crist · in urum

ferhðlocan · fæste gestaðelod · Adueniat

Cume nu to mannu<m> · mihta weal · regnu<m> tuu<m> ·

dend · þin rice to us · rihtwis dema · ⁊ ðin geleafa

in lifdæge · on urum mode · mære þurh

wunige · Fiat uoluntas tua sicut in cęlo &in t<er>ra ·

⁊ þin willa mid us · weorðe gelæsted on eardunge ·

eorðan rices · swa hluttor is in heofonwuldre ·

wẏnnum gewlitegod a to worulde forð ·

CRITICAL TEXT

Pater noster qui es in cęlis.

Fæder manncynnes,   frōfres ic þē bidde,

hālig drihten,   þū ðe on heofenum eart.

Sanctificetur nomen tuum.

Þæt sȳ gehālgod   hygecræftum fæst

þīn nama nū ðā,   neriende Crīst,

in ūrum ferhðlocan   fæste gestaðelod.

Adueniat regnum tuum.

Cume nū tō mannum,   mihta wealdend,

þīn rīce tō ūs,   rihtwīs dēma,

and ðīn gelēafa in līfdæge

on ūrum mōde   mǣre þurhwunige.

Fiat uoluntas tua sicut in cęlo et in terra.

And þīn willa mid ūs   weorðe gelǣsted

on eardunge   eorðan rīces,

swā hlūttor is   in heofonwuldre,

wynnum gewlitegod   ā tō worulde forð.

Panem n<ost>r<u>m cotidianum da nobis hodie ·

[folio 45v]

Sẏle us nu to dæge drihten gumena heofena
heahcẏning hlaf urne . þone ðu onsendest
sawlum to hæle on middaneard manna
cẏnnes þ<æt> is se clæna crist drihten god ·
Et dimitte nobis debita n<ost>ra ·

Forgẏf us gumena weard gẏltas ⁊ synna
⁊ ure leahtras alet lices wunda · ⁊ mandæda
swa we mildum wið ðe ælmihtigum gode oft
abẏlgeat. Sicut & nos dimittimus debitorib<us>: [offendim<us>]

i<n> t<er>ris
Swa swa we forlætað leahtras on eor n<ost>ris
illis
þan · þam þe wið us oft agẏltað · ⁊ him wom
dæde witan · ne þenceð · for earnunge ecan
lifes · Et nė nos inducas in temptationem ·

dolore
Ne læd þu us to wite · in wean sorge ne in cos
eripie<n>s
tunge · crist nerigende · þẏ læs we arlease

[offendim<us>]: this gloss stands in the left margin beside *abẏlgeat* which it translates.

Panem nostrum cotidianum da nobis hodie.
Syle ūs nū tō dæge,   drihten gumena,
heofena hēahcyning,   hlāf ūrne
þone ðū onsendest   sāwlum tō hǣle
on middaneard   manna cynnes
þæt is sē clǣna Crīst, drihten God.
Et dimitte nobis debita nostra.
Forgyf ūs, gumena weard,   gyltas and synna
and ūre leahtras ālēt,   līces wunda
and māndǣda,   swā wē mildum wið ðē,
ælmihtigum Gode,   oft ābylgeað.
Sicut et nos dimittimus debitoribus nostris.
Swā swā we forlǣtað   leahtras on eorþan
þām þe wið ūs   oft āgyltað
and him womdǣde   wītan ne þencað
for earnunge   ēcan līfes.
Et ne nos inducas in temptationem.
Ne lǣd þū ūs tō wīte   in wēan sorge
ne in costunge,   Crīst nerigende,
þȳ lǣs wē ārlēase   ealra þīnra mildsa

ealra þinra mildsa þurh feondscipe ·

fremde weorðan. Sed libera nos a malo ·

lib<er>a
⁊ wið ẏfele gefreo us eac nu ða · feonda

gehwẏlces we in ferhðlocan · þeoden engla

ðanc ⁊ wuldor · soð sigedrihten · secgað

þu
georne · þæs ðe, us milde mihtum alysdest

vinc<u>lis
fram hæftnẏde hellewites · AMEN ·

Weorðe þæt ·

þu: added as superscript with insertion mark after *ðe* .

þurh fēondscipe fremde weorðan.

Sed libera nos a malo.

And wið yfele gefrēo ūs ēac nū ðā
fēonda gehwylces; wē in ferhðlocan,
þēoden engla, ðanc and wuldor,
sōð sigedrihten, secgað georne
þæs ðe þū ūs milde mihtum ālȳsdest
fram hæftnȳde hellewītes.

AMEN. Weorðe þæt.

NOTES

28: MS abylgeat: *since the MS reading is unconventional for first plural (its subject is* we *and we find it so glossed in Latin), this verb is emended to* abylgeað.
32: MS þenceð: *since its subject is* we, *this verb is emended to display a plural ending.*

Baptismal Creed

The Old English *Baptismal Creed* poem follows the Junius text of the *Old English Doxology* and the *Junius Lord's Prayer* in what James Ure calls "the Old English Benedictine Office" as it is preserved in Oxford, Bodleian Junius 121. All three poems contain the Latin text of their originals, followed by an Old English verse meditation upon each discrete division, but, as we shall see, the *Baptismal Creed* differs substantially from the first two Junius 121 poems in its Latin. The Latin intercalations of the three Junius poems often appear jammed into the ends of lines, as if to save space: the *Baptismal Creed* is no exception, and on line 11 of folio 47r, two words—one Old English and one Latin—actually collide, with one letter superimposed onto another. It seems likely (although most unusual) that the rubricated Latin, reading *S<an>c<t>or<um com<m>u/ nionem*, was added first by the scribe over the ends of two lines (10 and 11),[1] not leaving enough space for the writing of the last word of the Old English for line 11, *⁊ ic gemænscipe mærre getreowe*. This last word then had to be split most awkwardly after "eo," which does not allow an easy division of two syllables; "-we" appears at the beginning of line 12, while the "o" of "getreo-" has been written on top of the first "n" of the Latin "-nionem." So the Latin was apparently copied first and the Old English then filled in, not always successfully, because the same scribe wrote both the Latin and Old English, switching between red and text ink as the need arose. Since this manuscript is from the very end of the Anglo-Saxon period and possibly even into the

1 Although he or she omits a majuscule "ƿ" to form the conjunction *ƿær* on folio 47r, manuscript line 17 (verse line 67).

early Anglo-Norman years, skill in page layout may not have been taught as well as in earlier generations.

Like the *Old English Doxology* and the *Junius Lord's Prayer*, the *Baptismal Creed* attracted glosses from the Worcester Tremulous Hand, and these are worth remarking upon for what they tell us of the use he made of the poem. This thirteenth-century scribe, whom Franzen assumes was involved in "reviving . . . the copying [and studying] of Old English manuscripts,"[2] mistook one Old English verb *([ge]byrgan*, "to taste") for another that is virtually identical in some inflected forms (*[ge]byrgan*, "to bury"), despite the scriptural context that ought to have been familiar here: verse line 32 refers to the burial of Christ's body by Joseph of Arimathea in his own tomb,[3] *þone geomormod Iosep byrigde* ("whom sorrowful Joseph buried"), but the Worcester Tremulous Hand glosses *byrigde* with the Latin infinitive *gustari*, literally "to be tasted" and evidently an error for *gustare*, "to taste."[4] This suggests that he was either unable to understand that the Old English poem was based on the baptismal Creed, despite its Latin intercalations, or was selecting individual words out of context (and in this case, got the wrong meaning [and voice] for his chosen lemma). The latter seems more likely, since he glosses the same word (*getreowe*) twice as Latin *credo* ("I believe") within five lines of text on folio 47r, one of these at the problematic collision between Latin and Old English, described above.

On first glance, the *Baptismal Creed* appears to be an expansion, as Dobbie suggests, of its Latin into Old English verse on the model of the longer Lord's Prayer poems or the *Old English Doxology*.[5] Ure generalizes his observations on the "Benedictine Office" poems such that "the treatment is the same in each case, the Latin being broken up into sections, each of which acts as a heading for a part of the poem."[6] These editors are short-sighted, however, because the piece is not an expansion of its Latin. While it contains Latin rubrics like the *Old English Doxology* and the two *Pater Noster* poems from Junius 121 and CCCC 201, the *Baptismal Creed* more readily resembles the *Kentish Great Miserere* in that its rubrics are incomplete, but there the like-

2 Franzen, *Tremulous Hand*, 183.

3 Matt. 27:57–60.

4 However, see the Introduction to *Vision of the Rood*, pp. 175-78, below.

5 Dobbie, ASPR VI, lxxii.

6 Ure, *Benedictine Office*, 49.

ness ceases. Line ends and vellum shortage govern the ungrammatical truncations in the Kentish poem's Latin (see below, pp. 130–31), but in most of the *Baptismal Creed*'s Latin statements, a deliberate division is made: the first half of each major Latin tenet of faith is present in Latin, but its second half is not. Thus we find *Credo in deum patrem omnipotentem* but not *creatorem caeli et terrae,* we find *Et in Iesum Christum filium eius unicum, dominum nostrum* but not *qui conceptus est de spiritu sancto Natus ex Maria virgine,* and so forth. This distinctive break, midway through the first four credal statements, creates an entirely unique effect in Old English liturgical poetry since it is an integral part of the poem's structure and almost certainly relies on the responsories of Church liturgy. These are a series of verses, primarily from the psalms but also taken from elsewhere in Scripture, chanted in turn by first one and then a second soloist, or by a choir and then a soloist, for use on special feast-days during the Mass or the Offices.[7]

The *Baptismal Creed* poem is not necessarily orthodox in this vernacular expression of the articles of faith. The second and longest responsory section bears on the annunciation, incarnation, and nativity narratives from the gospel by recreating *qui conceptus est de spiritu sancto, natus ex Maria virgine* to contain unusual language, unexpected imagery, and quite possibly a heretical ornamentation. The Virgin is initially described as *sanctan Marian* (line 15a), a Latinate construct rather than the Old English *halige,* likely selected for alliteration. Mary is then called *Ides unmæne* (line 16a), and is described in bridal terms: the poet tells us *Næs ðær gefremmed firen æt giftum, ac þær halig gast handgyft sealde,* "no sin was there committed at the marrying, but in that place the Holy Ghost gave the wedding gift" (lines 19–20). While the giving of wedding presents has a history that can certainly be traced back through the Germanic ancestors of the Anglo-Saxons, a configuration of Holy Spirit as gift-giver within a "wedding" context, based perhaps on a classical model or in patristic commentary, is not evident. This therefore may be an original image, making the poem even more interesting to study for the beliefs and cultural appurtenances that may have been blended within it.

7 See my "Worship the Lord in the Beauty of Holiness: Latin Prayer and Old English Liturgical Poetry," *On the Aesthetics of* Beowulf *and Other Old English Poems*, ed. John M. Hill (Toronto and London: U of Toronto P, 2010), 101–13.

However, the detail that is most fascinating, echoing a similarly problematic image in the *Corpus Lord's Prayer*, occurs in the very middle of this "nativity" section. The *Corpus Lord's Prayer* addresses God (lines 47b–48a) such that *Þu eart sunu and fæder/ ana ægþer*, while in *Baptismal Creed* (lines 16b–18) we are told of Mary that *heo þæt ærende onfeng freolice, and ðe fæder sylfne under breostcofan bearn acende,* "she accepted that task willingly, and Thee, the Father himself, bore as a child beneath her heart." As I have noted elsewhere, "[I]f we are to examine the echo another way, it more alarmingly begins to resemble one of the Modalistic Monarchianist heresies; Sabellianism would have the Triune God manifest to the human mind as one Being with different attributes, rather than as three Persons."[8] It is the *sylfne* that insists upon *ðe fæder* being accusative; since *sylfne* occurs in a line with an 'f'-alliteration, it has no metrical obligation, and if it were modifying another word, it would likely have stood closer to it. Thus, if *ðe fæder sylfne* must be accusative, then *bearn* is accusative in apposition to this phrase, and both are the direct object of the verb *acende,* suggesting that Mary bore, not a child *to* the Father, but the Father himself, as a child. This seems to be an ingenuous poetic creation, perhaps an attempt to describe Mary as *Theotokos* ("Christ-bearer"), which nevertheless misses its mark and verges on the heresy of Sabellius, which held that because God is One God, the Father Himself was born as the Son. The *Baptismal Creed* is therefore anything *but* a self-evident metrical expansion; sophisticated in design, it is a well-crafted and highly creative expression in two languages of the one liturgical recitation that was inextricably linked to the wellspring of the Christian faith, Holy Baptism. As such, it is mindfully and deliberately a credal piece, for the poet quotes the *Quicumque vult* or Athanasian Creed (see above, pp. 27–28 and below, 121) when describing the Holy Spirit: *Ne synd þæt þreo Godas, þriwa genemned, ac is an God, se ðe ealla hafað þa þry naman þinga gerynum,* "there are not three Gods, named as three, but there is one God, He who possesses all the three names, in the mysteries of existence" (lines 49–51).

The critical attention that this poem has attracted to date has been extraordinarily scanty. Dobbie describes it as a poem "in which the Latin text is enlarged upon," suggesting that "it introduces homiletic and explanatory material for which there is no warrant in the original text."[9] Ure sees the *Bap-*

8 Keefer, "'Ic' and 'We,'" 136 and n. 57.

9 Dobbie, ASPR VI, lxxii.

tismal Creed, together with the *Old English Doxology*, as losing "no opportunity . . . of introducing the essential points of faith and doctrine."[10] Kenneth Sisam connects the *Creed*'s stanzaic form and certain lexical terms with the *Seasons for Fasting* poem in CCCC 201, positing the same author for both.[11] However, while there are shared phrases to be found from one poem to another, this does not presume a common author nor even a common centre where they were composed: as the introductions to these liturgical poems indicate, such similarities are to be found very widely, and whether they indicate emulation or simply a common pool of popular metrical constructions cannot be ascertained with any ease.

---

10 Ure, *Benedictine Office*, 49–50.

11 Kenneth Sisam, *Studies in the History of Old English Literature* (Oxford: Oxford UP, 1953), 47–48.

SEMI-DIPLOMATIC TEXT

(folio 46r, line 10 – folio 47r, line 18)

Latin rubrics and capitals are in red. Glosses are by the Worcester Tremulous Hand.

C REDO IN DEUM PATREM

omnipotentem ·

Ælmihtig fæder · up on rodore · þe ða sciran

gesceaft · sceope ⁊ worhtest · ⁊ eorðan wang ·

ealne gesettest · ic þe ecne god ænne gecenne ·

lustum gelẏfe þu eart lifes frea · engla

ordfruma eorðan wealdend · ⁊ ðu gar —

secges · grundas geworhtest · ⁊ ða þu ma

nega canst · mærra tungla · Et in i<e>h<su>m xp<istu>m

filium eius unicum d<omi>n<u>m n<ost>r<u>m ·

e

I c on sunu þinne · soðne <u>gelẏfe</u> hælendne

cẏning · hider asendne · of ðam uplican

engla rice · þone gabriel godes ærendraca ·

S<an>c<t>a<m> marian · sẏlfre gebodode · ides unmæne

<u>gelẏfe</u>: here and on fol. 47r lines 8 and 13, what appears to be a horned "e" has been added above the "y" of *gelyfe*.

CRITICAL TEXT

Credo in deum patrem omnipotentem.
Ælmihtig fæder   ūp on rodore,
þe ðā scīran gesceaft   sceōpe and worhtest,
and eorðan wang   ealne gesettest,
ic þē ecne God   ǣnne gecenne,
lustum gelȳfe;   þū eart līfes frēa,
engla ordfruma   eorðan wealdend,
and ðū gārsecges   grundas geworhtest,
and þū ðā menigu canst   mǣrra tungla.
Et in Iesum Christum filium eius unicum dominum nostrum.
Ic on sunu þīnne   sōðne gelȳfe
hǣlendne cyning,   hider āsendne
of ðām ūplican   engla rīce,
þone Gabriel   Godes ǣrendraca
Sanctan Marian   sylfre gebodode;

[folio 46v]

heo þæt ærende · onfeng freolice · ⁊ ðe fæder

sẏlfne under breostcofan · bearn acende ·

næs ðær gefremmed · firen æt giftu<m> · ac þær

halig gast · handgẏft sealde · þære fæmnan

bosm · fẏlde mid blisse · ⁊ heo cuðlice cende

swa mærne · eorðbuendum engla scẏppend ·

se to frofre gewearð · foldbuendum ·

⁊ ẏmbe bethleem bodedan englas þ<æt> acenned

wæs crist on eorðan · Passus sub pontio pilato ·

Ða se pontisca pilatus weold under rom

warum · rices ⁊ doma · þa se deora frea

patib<u>lo
deað þrowade · on gealgan stah · gumena

gustari
drihten · þone geomormod · iosep bẏrigde ·

⁊ he of helle · huðe gefette · of þam susl

hofe · sawla manega · het ða uplicne eþel

ides unmǣne,   hēo þæt ǣrende
onfeng frēolice,   and ðē fæder sylfne
under brēostcofan   bearn ācende;
næs ðǣr gefremmed   firen æt giftum
ac þǣr hālig gāst   handgyft sealde,
þǣre fǣmnan bosm   fylde mid blisse
and hēo cūðlice   cende swa mǣrne
eorðbuendum   engla scyppend,
se tō frōfre gewearð   foldbuendum,
and ymbe Bethleem   bodedan englas
þæt acenned wæs   Crīst on eorðan.
Passus sub Pontio Pilato.
Đā sē pontisca   Pilatus weold
under Rōmwarum   rīces and dōma,
þā sē dēora frēa   dēað þrōwade;
on gealgan stāh   gumena drihten
þone gēomormōd   Iōsēp byrigde,
and hē of helle   hūðe gefette
of þām suslhofe   sāwla manega,
hēt ða ūplicne   ēþel sēcan.

secan · Tertia die resurrexit a mortuis ·

þæs þẏ ðriddan dæge þeoda wealdend · aras

rices frea · recen of moldan · ⁊ he · xl

daga folgeras sine · runum arette · ⁊ ða

his rice began · þone uplican eðel secan ·

cwæð þæt he nolde nænne forlætan · þe hi<m>

forð ofer þ<æt> · fẏlian wolde · ⁊ mid fæstum

sefan · freode gelæstan · Credo in sp<iritu>m s<an>c<tu>m

[folio 47r]

Ic haligne gast · hihte beluce · emne swa ecne

swa is aðor gecweden · fæder oððe freo

bearn · folca gereordum · ne sẏnd þ<æt> þreo

godas · þriwa genemned · ac is an god · se ðe

ealle hafað þa þrẏ naman · þinga gerẏnu<m>

soð ⁊ sigefæst · ofer side gesceaft wereda

wuldorgẏfa · wlanc ⁊ ece · S<an>c<t>am ęccl<esi>am catho

e
Eac ic gelyfe · þæt sẏn leofe gode · licam ·

Tertia die resurrexit a mortuis.
Þǣs þȳ ðriddan dæge   þēoda wealdend
ārās rīces frēa,   recen of moldan,
and he xl daga   folgeras sīne
rūnum ārētte,   and ðā his rīce began,
þone ūplican   ēðel sēcan;
cwæð þæt hē nolde   nǣnne forlǣtan
þe him forð ofer þæt   fylian wolde
and mid fæstum sefan   frēode gelǣstan.
Credo in spiritum sanctum
Ic hāligne gāst   hihte belūce
emne swā ēcne   swā is āðor gecweden,
fæder oððe frēobearn,   folca gereordum;
ne synd þæt þrēo Godas,   þriwa genemned,
ac is ān God   sē ðe ealle hafað
þā þrȳ naman   þinga gerȳnum,
sōð and sigefæst   ofer sīde gesceaft
wereda wuldorgyfa,   wlanc and ēce.
Sanctam ęcclesiam catholicam
Eac ic gelȳfe   þæt sȳn lēofe Gode

þe þurh ænne geþanc ealdor heriað · heo

fona heahcẏning · her for life · S<an>c<t>or<um> com<m>u

credo
⁊ ic gemænscipe mærne getreonionem ·

we · þinra haligra · her for life · Remissione<m>

Lissė ic gelyfe leahtra gehwẏlces · peccator<um>·

Carnis resurrẹctionem.

credo
⁊ ic þone ærest ealra getreowe · flæsces on fol

dan on þa forhtan tid · Et vitam ęt<er>nam ·

<Þ>ær ðu ece lif eallum dældest · swa her manna

gehwẏlc · metode gecwemað·

þe þurh ǣnne geþanc   ealdor heriað,
heofona hēahcyning,   hēr for līfe.
Sanctorum communionem
and ic gemǣnscipe mǣrne getrēowe
þīnra hāligra hēr for līfe.
Remissionem peccatorum
Lisse ic gelȳfe   leahtras gehwylces,
Carnis resurrectionem
and ic þone ǣrest   ealra getrēowe,
flǣsces on foldan   on þā forhtan tīd,
Et vitam ęternam
þǣr ðū ēce līf   eallum dǣlest,
swā hēr manna gehwylc   metode gecwēmað.

NOTES

9: MS ða þu manega: *many editors emend the MS reading to the noun* menigu (*'multitude'; ASPR VI, 78:* menegu), *assuming that the scribe "took the word to be a form of the adjective* manig,*" ASPR VI, 188). Leaving the form unemended makes for a clumsy construction since syntax requires an accusative substantive as the direct object of* canst, *and there are no attested feminine nouns on the* manig- *stem to account for* manega *as an accusative plural to fulfill this function. Emending to* menigu *requires that we assume* ða *to be a demonstrative agreeing with it: thus we must also invert the MS word order to read* þu ða menigu.
15: *I follow earlier editorial practice and anglicize the Latinate abbreviated 'Sanctam' of the MS to a weak Old English adjective.*

38: MS recen: *While ASPR VI emends to the adverbial form* recene *('quickly'), there is no reason why the adjective* recen (*'ready, prompt') cannot modify* frea *in the same line.*

67: MS ær: *It is evident that a coloured majuscule 'Þ' is missing from the gutter so that the conjunction* Þær *begins the new subordinate clause;* MS dældest: *since the clause containing this verb indicates future activity and not past actions,* dælest *is evidently the preferred form to be used for syntactic sense.*

Doxologies

(a) *Old English Doxology*

The *Old English Doxology* poem is unusual in the canon of Old English verse since it is preserved in more than one copy; the recensions found in Cambridge, Corpus Christi College 201 and Oxford, Bodleian Junius 121 are very close, so this edition follows not a single base text but the best readings from both, creating a composite critical text against which to compare both semi-diplomatic presentations. These two manuscripts differ minutely in their inclusion of the Latin original: both resolve the liturgical source to six divisions,[1] but where CCCC 201 has only the first word *Gloria* ("glory") on which to construct the initial Old English meditation, the Junius 121 scribe when acting as rubricator includes *patri* ("to the Father"), which is then repeated in the Latin of the second section on line 19 of folio 43v. As such, the Junius reading is likely an error.

Scribal punctuation in the two versions of the poem can be misleading, since it does not always mark caesuras or long line ends as it does in other poems of this genre. The Worcester Tremulous Hand scribe is active on the initial page of the Junius 121 *Old English Doxology*, where he attempts to gloss a full clause, its first two words in Middle English and its final two in Latin (OED *Sy þe wuldor and lof* = WTH *beo þe glorie laus*). He then adds only one more gloss to the page, most interestingly since it is at odds with the error he makes in understanding the context of the *Baptismal Creed*;[2] he glosses OE *feorh* ("soul"), part of a compound noun *feorhhyrde* ("soul-guardian"), with the Latin genitive plural *a<n>im<arum>* ("of souls"). Such

1 (i) *Gloria*; (ii) *Patri et Filio et Spiritui Sancto*; (iii) *Sicut erat in principio*; (iv) *Et nunc et semper*; (v) *Et in secula seculorum*; (vi) *Amen*.

2 See above, p. 84.

a translation is not incorrect, but neither would it have been evident to a non-Old English speaker, from the lack of morphological ending on *feorh*, the first element of the compound.[3] The genitive plural sense of *animarum* is therefore only remotely implicit here, and its gloss by the Tremulous scribe is an anomalous indication of familiarity that may be the result of his having used one of the glossaries compiled in the Anglo-Saxon period.

The *Old English Doxology* is structured in similar fashion to the *Corpus Lord's Prayer*, which stands immediately before it in CCCC 201: both poems rely throughout on the pairing of substantives (e.g. *CLP* 25b *þeaw and wisan; OED* 2a *wuldor and lof*) or finite verbs (e.g. *CLP* 60a *singað and biddað*; *OED* 30b *healdað and friðiað*) to pack semantic relevance into the relatively uncomplicated messages of their original liturgical sources. The *Old English Doxology* also repeats or varies constructions in related sections, such as the string *clæne and cræftig; þu gecyddest þæt* (lines 19 and 59); in each case the lines following are almost identical: *þa ðu, ece God, ana geworhtest* (line 20) and *þa ðu, mihtig God, man geworhtest* (line 60). In like manner, the a-line *þurh clæne gecynd*, which appears in lines 13 and 58, precedes a variant in the b-line: *cyning ofer ealle* or *þu eart cyning on riht*, respectively. Such a construction may have had a mnemonic function. Indeed, the poem repeats the noun *cræft* or its adjective *cræftig* four times, and the adjective *clæne* five times, creating a semantic resonance that connects one section of the poem (and thus its liturgical original) with another. As we see with the anachronistic use of Christ's name in the *Junius* and *Corpus Lord's Prayers* or the *Kentish Great Miserere*, the *Old English Doxology* also uses the terms *cristene* (lines 31b and 41b) and *Cristes* (line 63b), which form no part of the liturgical original but instead assume the culture of the Church as a given, safely established throughout Anglo-Saxon society by the time of this poem's composition. However, lexical, structural, and ideological similarities within the liturgical verse canon should not be taken to indicate a single author, a specific centre or even a common origin, but may instead be the result of shared metrical formulae that were useful in constructing poems of this kind.[4] Such formulae may have developed from the increased glossing activities that

---

3 There are three recorded occurrences of this word, the other two being in Bede: see *Dictionary of Old English in Electronic Form A-F*, ed. Angus Cameron, Ashley Crandell Amos, and Antonette di Paolo Healey (Toronto: Pontifical Institute Press, 2003).

4 Both Ure (*Benedictine Office*, 50–57) and, later, Whitbread ("Old English Poems," 37–40) seek to prove that the *Old English Doxology* and the *Corpus Lord's Prayer* were composed by the same poet.

accompanied renewed educational development during the Reform period, whereby Latin lemmata became so closely associated with their Old English translations within the liturgical or scriptural register—for instance, OE *wuldor* for Lat. *gloria*, OE *synn* or *leahtor* for Lat. *debitum,* OE *costung* for Lat. *temptatio*, and the like—that the semantic values of the Latin originals became transferred to the Old English equivalents, which were then used as common currency of understanding within the period.

We have seen elsewhere that Wulfstan translated the *Gloria Patri* as part of the liturgical materials necessary for every Christian soul to know, in English if not in Latin. The translation of this widely used closure formula into a free-standing vernacular metrical meditation is therefore important in understanding Wulfstan's attitude toward the *Gloria Patri*, calling into question Ure's contention that "the Gloria was not considered to be as necessary for the religious instruction of the laity."[5] It does not automatically follow that this poem was written for inclusion in the "Old English Benedictine Office," since it fits without issue into the larger number of pieces making up the metrical subgenre represented by this volume.

The *Old English Doxology* is very different from the *Titus Alphabet Doxology*, not only in length but in concept since it rehearses both sentences of its liturgical model,

> preserving seven pairs of half-lines for the Father, and six pairs for the Son and the Spirit, but seventeen pairs for *Sicut erat*, ten for *nunc et semper*, ten for *saecula saeculorum* and seven for 'amen': this makes a total of thirteen pairs of half-lines for the first sentence of the *Gloria Patri* but forty-four pairs for the second. In this we may be seeing some of the same attention to the eternal duration of God's glory rather than to ascribable Trinitarian glory itself that [can be seen] at the end of certain of the homilies.[6]

Like the *Corpus Lord's Prayer*, the *Old English Doxology* expands substantially on its liturgical original, but while the expansions are elegant, they are also orthodox. By way of example, the rubric *Sicut erat in principio* leads the poet to the events at the beginning of time as they affected humanity. God's creation of the world is the focus of lines 16–33, with the establishment of heaven and earth an example of God's generosity to his people, and the

5 Ure, *Benedictine Office*, 53.

6 Keefer, "In Closing," 230 and *passim*.

keeping holy of the seventh day of the week by men and women in favour with God (*þa þe cunnon cristene þeawas*, "those who know Christian customs," line 31) being humanity's reciprocal duty and expression of gratitude. This kind of expansion is logical and sensible, didactic in its sentiment, somewhat creative but in no way startlingly so, and ultimately not enterprising in the scope of its vision.

SEMI-DIPLOMATIC TEXT

(CCCC 201, page 169, line 10 – page 170, line 8)
Capitals alternate green and red.

[G]l<ori>a ·

Sẏ þe wuldor ⁊ lof · wide geopnod · geond ealle þeoda · þanc ⁊ willa ·

mægen ⁊ mildse · ⁊ ealles modes lufu · soðfæstra sib · ⁊ þines

silfes dom · world gewlitegod · swa þu wealdan miht · eall eorðan

mægen · ⁊ uplifte wind · ⁊ wolcna wealdest ealle on riht ·

Patri & filio & spiritui s<an>c<t>o ·

Ðu eart frofra fæder · ⁊ feorhhẏrda · lifes laððeow · leohtes

wealdend · asundrod fram sinnu<m> · swa þin sunu mære ·

þurh clæne gecẏnd · cẏninc ofer ealle · beald gebletsod ·

boca lareow · heah hige frofre · Sicut erat in principio ·

Swa wæs on fruman · frea mancẏnnes · ealre worlde · wlite

SEMI-DIPLOMATIC TEXT

(Junius 121, folio 43v, lines 13–23 – folio 44v, lines 1–12)
Capitals and rubrication are in red.
Glosses are by the Worcester Tremulous Hand.

beo þe glorie laus

G loria patri Sẏ þe wuldor ⁊ lof · wide

geopenod · geond ealle þeoda · þanc ⁊ wẏlla

mægen ⁊ mildse · ⁊ ealles modes lufu soð

fæstra sib · ⁊ ðines sẏlfes dom · worulde

gewlitegod · swa ðu wealdan miht · eall eorðan

mægen ⁊ uplẏfte · wind ⁊ wolcna · wealdest

eall on riht · Patri & filio & spiritui s<an>c<t>o ·

a<n>i<m>ar<um>
e

Þ u eart frofra fæder · ⁊ feorhhẏrde ·

lifes latteow · leohtes wealdend · asẏndrod

fram sẏnnum · swa ðin sunu mære · þurh

clæne gecẏnd cẏning ofer ealle · beald

[folio 44r]

gebletsod · boca lareow · heah hige frofre

⁊ halig gast · Sicut erat in principio

S wa wæs on fruman · frea mancẏnnes · ealre

---

feorhhẏrde: "e" is apparently written over the dotted "y" of this word in a hand that may be contemporary to the scribal hand.

CCCC 201

⁊ frofre · clæne ⁊ cræftig · þu gecẏddest þ<æt> · þa ðu ece god ana
geworhtest · þurh halige miht · heofonas ⁊ eorðan · eardas ·
⁊ uplẏft · ⁊ ealle þinc þu settest on foldan · swiðe feḷa cẏnna ·
⁊ tosẏndrodest hig · siððan on manega þu geworhtest · ece god
ealle gesceafta · on six dagu<m> · seofoðan þu gerestest · þa wæs
geforðod þin fægere weorc · ⁊ þu sunnan dæg silf halgodest ·
⁊ þu mærsodest hine manegum to helpe · þone hea an dæg ·
healdað ⁊ friðiað · ealle þa ðe cunnon · cristene þeawas ·
haligne heortlufan · ⁊ þæs hihstan gebod · on drihtenes
naman · se dæg is gewurðod. Et nunc & semper ·
And nu sẏmle þine soðan weorc · ⁊ þin micele miht manegu<m>
swutelað · swa þine cræftas hig cẏðað wide · ofer ealle world
ece standað · godes hand geweorc groweð swa þu hete ·
ealle þe heriað heriað · halige dreamas · clænre stæfne ·
⁊ cristene bec eal middaneard · ⁊ we men cweðað · on grunde

Junius 121

worulde wlite · ⁊ frofre clæne ⁊ cræftig ·
þu gecẏddest þ<æt> · þa ðu ece god ana gewrohtest ·
þurh halige miht · heofonas ⁊ eorðan ·
eardas ⁊ uplẏft · ⁊ ealle þing þu settest on
foldan · swẏðe feala cẏnna · ⁊ tosẏndrodost hig ·
sẏððon on mænego · þu gewrohtest ece god ·
ealle gesceafta · on sẏx dagum · ⁊ on þone
seofoðan þu gerestest · þa wæs geforðad þin
fægere weorc · ⁊ ðu sunnan dæg: sẏlf halgo
dest · ⁊ gemærsodest hine manegum to helpe
þone heahan dæg · healdað ⁊ freoðiaþ
ealle þa ðe cunnon cristene þeawas · haligne
heortlufan · ⁊ ðæs hehstan gebod · on driht
nes namon · se dæg is gewurðod. Et nunc & se<m>p<er> ·
⁊ nu ⁊ sẏmble · þine soðan weorc · ⁊ ðin mẏ
cele miht · manegum swẏtelað · swa þine
cræftas heo · cẏðaþ wide · ofer ealle woruld ·
ece standeþ · godes hand geweorc · groweð
swa ðu hete · ealle þe heriað · halige drea
mas · clænre stefne ⁊ cristene bec · eall

CCCC 201

her · gode lof ⁊ þanc · ece willa ⁊ þin agen dom ·

Et in s<e>c<u>la s<e>c<u>lorum ·

And on worlda world · wunað ⁊ rixað · cẏninc innan wuldre ·

⁊ his þa gecorenan · heah þrẏmnesse · halige gastas ·

wlitige englas · ⁊ wuldorgife · soðe sibbe · sawla þancung ·

modes mildse · þar is seo mæste lufu halig domes

[page 170]

heofonas sẏndon þurh þine ecan word æghwar fulle ·

swa sẏnd þine mihta ofer middaneard · swutole ⁊ gesẏne

þæt þu hig silf worhtest. Amen.

We þ<æt> soðlice secgað ealle þurh clæne gecẏnd · þu eart cẏninc

on riht · clæne ⁊ cræftig · þu gecẏddest þ<æt> · þa ðu mihtig god

man geworhtest · ⁊ him on dẏdest orð ⁊ sawle · sealdest word

⁊ gewitt · ⁊ wæstma gecẏnd · cẏddest þine cræftas · swilc is

cristes miht ·

[folio 44v]

Junius 121

middaneard · ⁊ we men cweþað · on grunde
her · gode lof ⁊ ðanc · ece willa · ⁊ ðin agen dom ·
Et in secula seculorum ·
⁊ on woruld a woruld wunað · ⁊ rixað cẏning
innan wuldre · ⁊ his þa gecorenan · heah
þrẏnnesse haliges gastes · wlitige englas ·
⁊ wuldorgẏfe · soðe sibbe · sawla þangung ·
modes miltse · þær is seo mæste lufu · halig
domas heofonas sẏndon · þurh þine ecan
æghwær fulle · swa sẏndon þine mihta ofer
middangeard · swutele ⁊ gesẏne þ<æt> ðu hẏ sẏlf
worhtest · A M E N ·
W e þæt soðlice · secgað ealle · þurh clæne gecẏnd ·
þu eart cẏning on riht · clæne ⁊ cræftig · þu ge
cẏddest þ<æt> · þa ðu mihtig god · man geworhtest ·
⁊ him on dẏdest · oruð · ⁊ sawul · sealdest word [flatu<m>]
⁊ gewitt · ⁊ wæstma gecẏnd cẏddest þine cræftas ·
swẏlc is cristes miht

[flatu<m>]: three small dots above *oruð* mark a *signe de renvoi* (scribal notation directing a reader to a gloss at a remove from the text it comments on), linking it to the left margin where the Worcester Tremulous Hand has written *flatu<m>* ("wind, air, breath").

CRITICAL TEXT

Gloria

Sȳ þē wuldor and lof   wīde geopenod

geond ealle þēoda,   þanc and willa,

mægen and mildse   and ealles mōdes lufu,

sōðfæstra sib   and þīnes sylfes dōm,

worulde gewlitegod;   swā þū wealdan miht

eall eorðan mægen   and ūplyfte,

wind and wolcna: wealdest eall on riht.

Patri et filio et spiritui sancto.

Þū eart frōfra fæder   and feorhhyrde,

līfes lātteōw,   lēohtes wealdend

āsyndrod fram synnum,   swā þīn sunu mǣre,

þurh clǣne gecynd   cyning ofer ealle,

beald gebletsod,   bōca lārēow,

hēah higefrōfer,   and hālig gāst.

Sicut erat in principio

Swā wæs on fruman   frēa mancynnes

ealre worulde   wlite and frōfre,

clǣne and cræftig;   þū gecȳddest þæt

þā ðū, ēce God,   āna geworhtest
þurh hālige miht   heofonas and eorðan,
eardas and ūplyft   and ealle þing;
þū settest on foldan   swȳðe fela cynna
and tosyndrodest hig   siððan on manega;
þū geworhtest, ēce God,   ealle gesceafta
on six dagum;   seofoðan þū gerestest;
þā wæs geforðad   þīn fægere weorc
and þū sunnan dæg   sylf hālgodest
and þū mǣrsodest hine   manegum tō helpe;
þone hēahan dæg   healdað and friðiað
ealle þā þe cunnon   crīstene þēawas,
hālige heortlufan   and þæs hēhstan gebod
on drihtenes naman: se dæg is gewurðod.
Et nunc et semper.
And nu and symble   þīne sōðan weorc
and þīn mycele miht   manegum swutelað,
swā þīne cræftas   hig cȳðað wide;
ofer ealle woruld   ēce standeþ
Godes handgeweorc,   grōweð swā þū hēte;

ealle þē heriað, heriað hālige drēamas
clǣnre stefne and crīstene bēc,
eall middaneard, and wē men cweþað
on grunde hēr, "Gode lof and þanc,
ēce willa and þīn āgen dōm."
Et in secula seculorum.
And on wor[u]lda wor[u]ld wunað and rīxað
cyning innan wuldre and his þā gecorenan,
hēahþrymnesse hāliges gāstes,
wlitige englas, and wuldorgyfe,
sōðe sibbe, sāwla þancung,
mōdes miltse; þǣr is sēo mǣste lufu:
hāligdōmes heofonas syndon
þurh þīne ēcan word ǣghwǣr fulle,
swā synd þīne mihta ofer middangeard
swutole and gesyne þæt þū hig sylf worhtest.
Amen.
We þæt sōðlice secgað ealle
þurh clæne gecynd: "þū eart cyning on riht,
clæne and cræftig; þū gecȳddest þæt

þā ðū, mihtig God,   man geworhtest
and him on dydest   oruð and sāwle,
sealdest word and gewitt   and wæstma gecynd;
cȳddest þīne cræftas.   Swylc is Crīstes miht.

NOTES

1: *Junius 121 inserts* patri *after* Gloria *but then repeats it in the next Latin inclusion at verse line 9:* Patri et filio et spiritui sancto.
2: MSS þe: *second-person singular pronouns vary in their scribal use of* 'þ' *and* 'ð'*; since the first use is* 'þ' *I default to that variant wherever it occurs in at least one of the MSS;* CCCC 201 geopnod: *a scribal error because we find the correct form in line 41 of* CLP.
5: silfes *CCCC 201.*
6: world: *CCCC 201.*
7: uplifte *CCCC 201.*
8: wind: *reads as if* windes*, genitive singular.*
10: feorhhyrda *CCCC 201.*
11: laððeow *CCCC 201, which might be the result of regional dialect.*
12: asundrod, sinnum *CCCC 201.*
13: cẏninc *CCCC 201.*
15: higefrofre *in both MSS is a shared error and needs emendation to a nominative form;* and halig gast *is missing from CCCC 201.*
18: ealre worulde: *I follow the Junius 121 spelling of* woruld *as the more commonly used form of the noun (CCCC 201 has* worlde*).*
20: MSS ðu: *here both MSS use* 'ð' *in the second-person singular pronoun (see note to line 2);* gewrohtest *Junius 121.*
22: þine *CCCC 201.*
23: swiðe *CCCC 201;* feala *Junius 121.*
24: and tosyndrodest hig siððan on manega: *this echoes line 72 of* CLP *and thus I retain the reading from CCCC 201;* tosyndrodost, siððon, mænego *Junius 121.*
25: gewrohtest *Junius 121; I prefer the CCCC 201 reading* geworhtest *throughout because this form appears in both MSS at line 60.*
26: syx *Junius 121;* and on þone/ seofoðan þu gerestest *Junius 121*: *this is more complete as a thought but creates a metrical anomaly with an unwieldy b-line; Ure and Dobbie nevertheless prefer it to the more metrically correct but abrupt half-line of CCCC 201 used here: the difficulty in Junius 121 comes at a MS line break where*

scribal error is more likely to occur, whereas the same section lies mid-line in CCCC 201 (see semi-diplomatic texts of each) and, while abrupt, is not incorrect. If taken as in the line from Junius 121, seofoðan *would of course be accusative; if taken as it reads in CCCC 201, it could be a genitive used adverbially as we see in* CLP 119.
27: geforðod *CCCC 201.*
28: MSS sunnan dæg: *other editors prefer to take this as the compound* sunnandæg *('Sunday'): here it remains two visually unconnected nouns* sunnan *and* dæg, *the way it stands in both MSS, to allow for the possibility of wordplay ('day of the sun/Son');* silf *CCCC 201.*
29: and þu mærsodest: *Junius 121 does not preserve this* þu.
30: heahan: *This word appears as* hea an *in CCCC 201, as though the scribe missed the* 'h' *mid-word and failed to notice it;* friðiað: *Junius 121 preserves this as* freoðiaþ.
32: halige: *both MSS read* haligne, *accusative masculine singular, to modify* heortlufan; *a shared error is always a matter of interest but this requires emendation since both elements of the noun,* heorte *and* lufu, *are feminine, ruling out the* '-ne' *inflection on the adjective;* hihstan *CCCC 201.*
33: drihtenes: *Junius 121 preserves the more common* dryhtnes, *but the CCCC 201 reading used here reflects the same form (*drihtenes are) *in line 108 of* CLP; namon *Junius 121.*
35: *in CCCC 201, the majuscule 'A' in* And *is coloured red, while in Junius 121, a red tironian nota* ⁊ *replaces* And*; CCCC 201 omits a second* and *or tironian nota to translate the second Latin* et, *while Junius 121, used here for this reading, adds a second nota for it;* symle *CCCC 201.*
36: micele *CCCC 201;* swytelað *Junius 121.*
37: hig: *Junius 121 reads* heo *for the nominative plural subject of* cyðað*; the CCCC 201 reading* hig *is less ambiguous to the eye;* cȳðaþ *Junius 121.*
38: woruld: *see note to line 18;* standað *CCCC 201 is likely an eyeskip error from* swutelað *above it.*
40: heriað: *CCCC 201 repeats* heriað *where Junius 121 has it only once; I include it as a solution to the lack of alliteration that caused earlier editors to replace* ealle *with adverbs beginning with 'h,' although removing strong stress from* ealle *would require that the terminal 'e' effectively be silent. This repetition may well not be a case of dittography, since words or whole verses in the Psalms are at times repeated for effect: see for example Ps 66:3 and 66:5, where the text of both verses in the* Romanum *and* Gallicanum *texts reads* confiteantur tibi populi deus, confiteantur tibi populi omnes, *glossed in Old English in most interlinear glossed psalters by variants on* we andettaþ þe folc god we andettaþ þe folc ealle *or left unglossed as obvious.*[9]

9 I take my evidence from Guido Oess's edition of the Arundel Psalter (London, BL Arundel 60), p. 113, a *Gallicanum* psalter likely coeval ("about the middle of the 11th century and certainly after 1012," p. 3) with the poems of CCCC 201. See Oess, *Der altenglischen Arundel-Psalter: Eine Interlinearversion in der Handschrift Arundel 60 des Britischen Museums* (Heidelberg: Carl Winter, 1910; repr. Amsterdam: Swets and Zeitlinger N.V., 1968).

41: stæfne *CCCC 201.*
42: cweðað *CCCC 201.*
43: ðanc *Junius 121.*
46: on wor[u]lda wor[u]ld: *Dobbie and Ure emend the problematic Junius 121 reading* on woruld a woruld *(the free-standing 'a' likely a confusion between the adverb* a *in the common phrase* a on worulda woruld *and the inflected genitive plural ending for* worulda*) to the preferable CCCC 201 one,* on worlda world, *but then silently alter the spelling to the Junius form* woruld. *My bracketing of the internal 'u' allows the textual evidence to stand more clearly.*
47: cyninc *CCCC 201*; MSS and his þa gecorenan: *early German editors emend for alliteration; Dobbie and Ure leave the reading intact and unexplained; for clearer syntax, I advise that the half-line be taken as if it reads* and þa his gecorenan; *the line is alliteratively deficient, but lexical emendation is too drastic a step when both versions read as they do.*
48: heahþrymnesse: *Junius 121 reads* heahþrynnesse, *rejected by Dobbie and Ure; since* heahþrymnesse *appears in* CLP 57 *in what I take to be the same grammatical form (dative singular), I have chosen the CCCC 201 reading. For the conventional explanation preferring this reading, see Whitbread, "Two Minor Old English Poems," 243, but see also Frank, "Late Old English* Þrymnys,*" for a more sophisticated historical explanation of the relationship between* þrymnys *and* þrynes; haliges gastes *Junius 121*: *adopted by Dobbie and Ure; this could be taken as a genitive singular where* haliges *borrows its ending from the noun it modifies, making for an easy translation when taken with* heahþrymnesse*; earlier German editors instead opted for the CCCC 201 reading* halige gastas *with the adjective assumed strong for a masculine nominative plural as in line 40 (*halige dreamas*)—here, 'spirits of holy[ness]'—modifying* gastas.
49: wuldorgife *CCCC 201.*
50: þancung: m*ost editors prefer this CCCC 201 reading over the Junius 121 word* þangung: *Ure notes, "The scribe of [Junius 121] has anticipated the 'g' after the 'n'" (p. 123).*
51: mildse *CCCC 201.*
52: haligdomes: *Junius 121 reads* haligdomas, *which Ure argues for as a late form of a genitive singular.*
53: word: *the Junius 121 scribe omits this word at the end of MS line 9 of folio 44v, evidently dropped in error on the move to line 10;* æghwar *CCCC 201.*
54: synd: *Junius 121 reads* syndon, *and thus Dobbie and Ure; CCCC 201's* synd *creates a less cluttered a-line with fewer weak beats, more in keeping with the general design of the poem's metre;* middaneard *CCCC 201.*
55: swutole: *Dobbie and Ure follow Junius 121's less common* swutele *as their base text;* þæt þu hig sylf worhtest: *as in line 37, I choose CCCC 201's* hig *over Junius 121's* hy, *this time for consistency, but retain Junius 121's* sylf. *Ure takes the clause as a relative one, commenting "[p]erhaps this is a case of 'þæt' as a generalized form of the*

relative" (p. 123) but it could as easily be subordinate with causality: "as thy powers over middle-earth are manifest and visible because thou thyself hast made them."

<u>58: cyninc</u> *CCCC 201.*

<u>60 MSS ð</u>: *see note to line 20.*

<u>61: orð</u> *CCCC 201*; <u>sawul</u> *Junius 121.*

<u>63: swilc</u> *CCCC 201.*

(b) *Titus Alphabet Doxology*

The book in which the *Titus Alphabet Doxology* is found was the private prayer-book of Ælfwine of Winchester when he was the dean of the New Minster but before he became its abbot (therefore written between 1023 and 1035).[10] It contains a variety of materials in addition to private devotions, many of which would have been of use to an eleventh-century monastery official either for personal study or public responsibilities: these include a calendar; the means by which to determine lucky and unlucky days; ways of calculating divisions of time, tides, and winds; and the dates on which the moveable feasts of Easter and the Lenten period preceding it were to fall each year. There are also texts for the interpretation of dreams and the meaning of thunder, as well as predictions for each day of a lunar month (called a "lunation"). Given its context of predictive material, the Alphabet that is closed by the three-line vernacular doxology poem of this volume is evidently the final element in the collection of prognostic texts.

The Alphabet letters proper of the Titus text are Roman orthographic forms only: no ash, thorn, eth or wyn, but including "k," "x," and "z," which were only rarely used in eleventh-century insular script, usually for foreign names, and "q," which was almost never used. As such, its original is obviously continental. Early German scholars regarded this text, transcribed and translated below, as a very early English translation of a type of alphabet from a common source, found in Latin and Middle High German in five manuscripts from the twelfth century and later, which was used to interpret dreams or foretell the future (known as "prognostication"). Beate Günzel, the most recent editor of Ælfwine's prayer-book, instead regards it as "advice for the life of a Christian"[11] and includes the *Gloria Patri* standing for the letter "z" as further support for her claim, but she does not attempt to explain why this final entry for the Alphabet is in verse rather than prose, or whether it is original to the Old English version of the Alphabet or borrowed from another source that is now lost. In a recent study, László Chardonnens describes the Alphabet as a "guest text," but sees its doxological conclusion as "an integral part of the Alphabet prognostic in as [*sic*] far as it constitutes the response to the letter."

10 Beate Günzel, ed., *Ælfwine's Prayerbook*, HBS 108 (Woodbridge: Boydell, 1993), 1–2.

11 See Günzel, *Ælfwine's Prayerbook*, 61–63, 62.

There has been no agreement about this text and its unusual conclusion, other than that it represents the "oldest alphabet prognostic hitherto."[12]

The Alphabet sentences in Cotton Titus D. xxvii appear as follows,[13] and an approximate translation for A–Y follows each entry. Their very vagueness is reminiscent of fortune-telling: when seeking the answer to a question, one opens a book (usually a service-book of importance like a psalter or gospel-book) and notes the first letter on the page that is evident. One then consults a list of prognostics such as these might be, to see what advice that letter brings with it. Its original is of course lost to us, but it must have been Latin in design, since the letter "Q" never appears in the alphabet used for writing Old English (Latin "qu," phonetic [kw], was rendered orthographically as "cw" in Old English).

A. *He gangeþ <ond> biþ his siðfæt gesund.* He will go and his travel will be safe.
B. *God þu fintst gyf ðu hit onginst, <ond> þe bið wel.* You will find God if you start it, and it will go well for you.
C. *Bliðnysse getacnaþ nis hit on þissum leohte.* C signifies joyfulness but not easily in these matters.
D. *Ne gewealdest þu þæs ðu wilt, ne þu hit æfre fintst.* You do not control that which you desire nor will you ever obtain it.
E. *Becume blisse ðe <ond> þu bist symble gesund.* Joy will come to you and you will be safe forever.
F. *Tacnað deaþ fram deaþe, on þyssum geare bide god Godes.* F signified death from death; in this year await good things from God.
G. *Þu scealt geðeon be þisse geþohtunge.* You will thrive by this counsel.
H. *Ðæt ðe ne biþ geseald, þenc þu on oðer.* That will not be given to you; consider something else.
I. *Ongin þæt þu wille, þæt þe bið geendod.* Begin what you want, and it will be completed by you.

12 László Sándor Chardonnens, *Anglo-Saxon Prognostics 900–1100* (Leiden: Brill, 2007), 57, 175; see pp. 174–80 for a broader discussion of the alphabet text.

13 Taken from Günzel, *Ælfwine's Prayerbook*, 121–22, and corrected against my own notes on the manuscript. I am very grateful to Roy Liuzza for translation advice and guidance within the field of prognostics; see also Roy Michael Liuzza, "Anglo-Saxon Prognostics in Context. A Survey and Handlist of Manuscripts," *ASE* 30 (2001): 181–230.

K. *Beorh þe, þæt þu ne gange on frecnysse*. Protect yourself, so that you do not go into danger.
L. *Hera þu God on ealle tid þines lifes*. Praise God at every occasion of your life.
M. *God þe gemiclað þæt ðe forð gespewð þæt þu don wilt*. God will strengthen you, so that henceforth what you desire to do will profit you.
N. *Hylt þu, ðæt to donne ne bið seald þinum dædum*. Stop: that which is to be done will not be through your actions.
O. *Ealle friðsumaþ God on eallum his mihtum*. Everything praises God in all his powers.
P. *Gyf þu riht nimst, nelt þu wifes wesan*. If you choose right, you will not desire to be married.
Q. *Forþam micel God is <ond> nergendlic swyðe <ond> þu fintst blisse*. Because God is powerful and a great Saviour, you will obtain joy.
R. *Forlæt al ða syn*. Abandon all sin.
S. *Þu bist hal gyf þu to Gode gehwyrfst; se sit hal <ond> mihtig*. You will be well if you turn to God; he is whole and powerful.
T. *Ne fyrhteð þa þe on synnum lyfiað <ond> yfel þencað*. Do not fear those who live in sin and think evil.
U. *Blisse ðe biþ geseald <ond> weg on geweald*. Joy be given to you and guidance into power.
X. *Blisse <ond> weg <ond> ece life*. Joy and guidance and eternal life.
Y. *Bycna sibbe and gesynta*. Y indicates peace and prosperity.

It is significant that the last entry, for "z," is a doxology. Thus the Alphabet acquires Christian closure through the inclusion of a formula that is appropriate to the ending of prayer, psalm, and hymn. At the same time, the doxology for "z" within itself becomes either a maxim, modelling a direction for the reader to a right way of thinking at the close of each daily task, or a prognostic solution that can never be inappropriate. The Alphabet Doxology itself ends with "amen," not part of the vernacular poem but clearly part of the concept of closure that is appropriate to vernacular liturgical verse, as we see with so many of the Old English pieces collected here.

SEMI-DIPLOMATIC

Z. wuldor sy ðe ⁊ wurðmýnte wereda driht[en]

fæder on soldan fægere gemæne

[fol 56v]

mid sylfan sunu ⁊ soðu<m> gaste. a m e n ::

CRITICAL

Wuldor sȳ ðē and wurðmynte, wereda drihten,

fæder in foldan, fægere gemǣne,

[fol 56v]

mid sylfan sunu and sōðum gāste. Amen.

NOTES

2 MS on soldan: *the insular tall "s" of* sy, *above this word, may account for the mis-copying of* soldan *for* foldan.
3 MS mid sylfan sunu: *ASPR VI assumes* sylfan *to be a weak adjective, either accusative or dative singular, but it might also be a levelled form of the strong dative singular* sylfum *("-um" > "-an"), not uncommon by the eleventh century. If so,* sunu *in the MS should be taken as the dative following* mid; *otherwise the construction may be assumed to be accusative, also acceptable after* mid.

Kentish Poems

The same tenth-century scribe has, with a significant number of mistakes,[1] copied out the two substantially different Kentish poems in this edition, separating them with a vernacular prose "Ages of the World," which also preserves a range of Kentish forms.[2] We must therefore assume that these three texts either were collected for their regional association by the London, BL Cotton Vespasian D. vi scribe or were already travelling together for that reason in its exemplar.

(a) *Kentish Hymn of Praise*

This poem has occasioned very little critical interest since the middle of the twentieth century,[3] which is unfortunate since it is a cleverly crafted piece[4] and a storehouse of liturgical sources that influenced its composition. Dobbie states that it has "no single source,"[5] and Greenfield and Calder, following

1 These include dropped letters or words corrected by insertion, dropped letters that the scribe didn't catch, and cancelled words: see notes to the semi-diplomatic texts.

2 Including number words (*fiorwertig, niogen, siofentig*, etc.), internal vowel shifts (*węron*), and inflectional endings (such as *templæs* or *ðanæ*): in the later tenth century, the vowels of morphological endings were evidently not uniformly pronounced as the universal unstressed vowel schwa [ə] in all regions of Anglo-Saxon England.

3 It was last edited by Dobbie, ASPR VI, pp. 87–88 in 1942; apart from a two-page note that identifies but does not expand upon only a few of its more obvious liturgical sources (Geoffrey Shepherd, "The Sources of the Old English *Kentish Hymn*," *MLN* 67 [1952], 395–97), no work has been done on it, other than by Keefer, since Dobbie's edition.

4 See Sarah Larratt Keefer, "*Techne* in the 'Kentish Hymn,'" *Essays in Medieval Studies: Proceedings of the Illinois Medieval Association* 6 (1989): 30–40.

5 Dobbie, ASPR VI, lxxx.

Shepherd, call it "a conflation and paraphrase of passages of the *Te Deum* and *Gloria [in Excelsis]*, presenting rather an exposition on the Trinity than a prayer for intercession and a confession of faith."[6] These two hymns certainly form the core of influence behind the *Kentish Hymn of Praise*, but the poet has a discernible agenda for their use: he or she concentrates not on humanity but on the first two Persons of God only. In order to maintain such a concentration on both Father and Son, all reference to the Holy Spirit is left out until the very end (line 42b), with attention instead lying on *weorada dryhten,* using *ðu*, *ðe* or *ðine* twenty-three times over against *we* and *us,* used only twice. Even time—eternity, ages of this world, the daily round of prayer—seems an unimportant detail within the verse. Apart from the opening lines, which invoke the hymn through the exhortation to mortal men and women, *wuton wuldrian . . . halgan hlioðorcwidum* ("Let us praise . . . with harmonious songs"), a focus on humanity is ignored in favour of a single-minded glorification of God.

We have seen that these two main liturgical influences on our poem would never have been found together in the same service at that time, since the *Gloria in Excelsis* was used for the Mass on Sundays and at high festivals, while the *Te Deum* was sung only at the close of the Night Office on feast-days (see above, pp. 29–30). It would seem, therefore, that the composer of the *Kentish Hymn of Praise* was familiar with the monastic Offices as well as with the liturgy of festal Mass, and was probably a monk or nun. Since Cotton Vespasian D. vi dates from the end of the tenth century and copying errors within this first poem confirm that the scribe was working from an exemplar, we can assume that the *Kentish Hymn of Praise* was composed in the first flush of the Benedictine Reform, sometime between 960 and 975, when the Rule of St Benedict was being learned (and indeed translated) throughout monastic establishments that were being revitalized or newly founded across Anglo-Saxon England. Therefore, in accordance with the teachings of the Rule on ownership and craftsmanship (see above, pp. 15–16), a piece such as the *Kentish Hymn of Praise* might have been inspired by a particular occasion where a Night Office concluding with the *Te Deum* might have been directly followed by a Mass containing the *Gloria in Excelsis*, such as the Nocturns and High Mass of Christmas.

---

6 Stanley Greenfield and Daniel Calder, *A New Critical History of Old English Literature* (New York: New York UP, 1986), 232.

The *Kentish Hymn of Praise* also contains reference to the Creeds known in Anglo-Saxon England, some of the tenets to which it refers being common to all three and others being specific to one. The first and second sections of the baptismal Creed, addressed to Father and Son, appear to have influenced phrasing in lines 3b (*lifs agend*), 14 (*an ece fęder, ælmehtig God*), 21a (*agenum fæder*), and 37b (*æce dryhten*), while Christ's ascension to God's right hand and role as final judge are echoed in lines 30–31a and 38–39a: it is noteworthy that *uiuos et mortuous* in the baptismal Creed is replicated exactly in *cwucra ge deadra* of line 39a. *Crucifixus* from the tenet of belief in Christ's death is mentioned only indirectly in the poem (lines 27b–28a), and faith in the Holy Spirit may be reflected in line 42b, *haliges gastes,* although this could have had its point of origin in a number of sources. By and large, the poet of the *Kentish Hymn of Praise* excludes a recital of Christ's life on earth and the final Creed declarations concerning the Church and its canon of belief; thus he or she chose to be selective in the statements of faith that were used, preferring a focus on the glory of God above, as we have seen, to a focus on the glorifying Church below.

To the baptismal Creed we should add the presence of the *Quicumque vult* (see above, pp. 27–28), also called the Athanasian Creed, since one of its unique elements does find expression in the *Kentish Hymn of Praise.* Its third verse reads, "Now this is the Catholic faith, that we worship one God in Trinity and Trinity in Unity," which is reinforced by its twenty-seventh and twenty-eighth verses, "Thus in all things, as has been stated above, both Trinity in unity and unity in Trinity must be worshipped. So he who desires to be saved should think thus of the Trinity."[7] These are clearly the source for lines 40–41 of the *Kentish Hymn of Praise*, *forðan ðu on ðrymme ricsast and on ðrinesse/ and on annesse ealles waldend* ("because you reign in glory and in Trinity and in unity, Lord of all"). The presence of these quotations from the Creeds must question Greenfield and Calder's rejection of this piece as a confession of faith; although not as overt in quoting the Creeds as we may see in some of these liturgical poems, the *Kentish Hymn of Praise* undoubtedly includes them in its liturgical background.

The last detail to be addressed has to do with the title of this piece. Its conventional editorial title is "Kentish Hymn," and this edition adds only the prepositional phrase "of Praise" to further refine it. But terminology that

7 Kelly, *Early Christian Creeds*, 17–19.

explains what is meant by "hymn" has a confusing history: in the third and fourth centuries, *psalmus* and *hymnus* were often used interchangeably for the Book of Psalms or for songs such as *Gloria in Excelsis* or *Te Deum.* Pieces that were written by individuals rather than being derived from scriptural originals were termed *psalmi idiotici*, "private hymns" (see above, p. 29), but while they were very popular and easily assumed into the liturgy, in the East they became the perfect medium for the conveying of heretical views to an unsuspecting laity. Not surprisingly, by the second half of the fourth century, most *psalmi idiotici* had been removed from the liturgy (the *Gloria in Excelsis* was at one stage banished in this fashion), and an orthodox resolve was taken to restrict the Greek Church to the Psalms of David alone.

In the seventh century, Isidore of Seville, whose work was known to Anglo-Saxon England, defined a hymn as having to adhere to two important criteria: *Si ergo et in laudem Dei dicitur et cantatur, tunc est hymnus.* It had thematically to consist of praise to God and the piece itself had to be sung. And by the time that the *Kentish Hymn of Praise* (by definition a *psalmus idioticus*) received its original editorial title more than a millennium later than Isidore, a "hymn" was understood to be a song designed for choir or congregation on specific occasions; it was not considered the same kind of piece as a "canticle," the designation given by the post-Reformation period in all Churches to songs assigned by tradition to use in the Mass or Office.[8] The unabashedly sentimental antiquarians of the Victorian period likely imagined Anglo-Saxons chanting their verse in some fashion, heroically if it were *Beowulf* and devoutly in the case of a poem like this, and such a belief most probably explains its editorial title, but modern scholarship underscores that it does not know the way in which Anglo-Saxon poetry was recited. Nevertheless, the title of the *Kentish Hymn of Praise* seems apt since the poem relies so substantially on *Gloria in Excelsis* and *Te Deum*, and because we must assume that it would have been made public when it was shared with the community of the monk or nun who wrote it.

8 These include the *Gloria in Excelsis*, *Sanctus*, and *Agnus Dei* in the Mass, and the *Te Deum*, *Benedictus*, *Benedicite*, *Nunc Dimittis*, and *Magnificat* from the Offices, or their Protestant counterparts, Morning and Evening Prayer.

SEMI-DIPLOMATIC TEXT

(London, British Library Cotton Vespasian D. vi,
folio 68v, line 11 – folio 69v, line 3)

Wuton wuldrian weorada dryhten halgan hlioðor

cwidu<m> · hiofenrices weard · lufian liofwendu<m> · lifęs

agend · ⁊ hi<m> simle sio sigefęst wuldor · uppe mid

h o

ænlum · ⁊ on eorðan sibb . gumena gewilcum godes wil

lan · we ðe heriað halgu<m> stefnum · ⁊ þe blætsiað

weorð lican

bilewitne fęder · ⁊ ðe þanciað þioda walden · ðines. wul

dordreames · ⁊ ðare miclan mægena gerena · ðe ðu god

dryhten gastes mæhtum · hafest on gewealdu<m> hiofen

⁊ eorðan · an ece fęder ælmehtig god · Ðu eart cyninga

[folio 69r]

n

cynigc cwicera gehwilces · Ðu eart sigefest sunu · ⁊

g

soð hęlend · ofer ealle gescęft an,la ⁊ manna · Ðu

dryhten god on dreamu<m> wunast · on ðære upplican

ænlum: "g" is missing but is not corrected; gewilcum godes: "h" and "o" added as superscripts without insertion marks.

ðines: *weorðlican* added as superscript with correction punctus after *ðines*.

cyningc: "n" added as superscript without insertion mark.

an,la: "g" added with insertion mark between "n" and "l".

CRITICAL TEXT

Wuton wuldrian weorada dryhten
hālgan hlīoðorcwidum, hiofenrīces weard
lufian līofwendum, līfęs āgend,
and him simle sīo sigefęst wuldor,
uppe mid ænglum, and on eorðan sibb
gumena gehwilcum goodes willan;
wē ðē heriað hālgum stefnum
and þē blætsiað, bilewitne fęder,
and ðē þanciað, þioda walden,
ðīnes weorðlican wuldordrēames
and ðāra miclan mægena gerēna
ðe ðū, God dryhten gāstes mæhtum
hafest on gewealdum hiofen and eorðan,
ān ēce fęder ælmehtig God.
Đū eart cyninga cyningc cwicera gehwilces.
Đū eart sigefest sunu and sōð hęlend
ofer ealle gescęft angla and manna.
Đū dryhten God on dreamum wunast

æðelan ceastre frea folca gehwæs swa ðu æt fru
man wære efeneadig bearn agenu<m> fæder · ðu eart
heofenlic lioht · ⁊ ðæt halige lamb · ðe ðy manscilde
middangeardes · for þinre arfęstnesse ealle to
wurpe fiond geflæmdest foll[c] generedes · blode
gebohtest bearn is.la[ræ] ða ðu ahofe ðurh ðæt
halige triow · ðinre ðrowuga[n] ðriostre senna
þ<æt> ðu on hæahsetle heafena rices · Sitest sige
hræmig on ða swiðran hand · ðinum god fæder
gasta gemyndig · Mildsa nu meahtig manna
cynne · ⁊ of leahtru<m> ales ðine ða liofan gescęft
⁊ us hale gedo heleða sceppe.d[n] niða nergend
for ðines naman are · ðu eart soðlice simle
halig · ⁊ ðu eart[ana], æce dryhten · ⁊ ðu ana bist

---

foll: "c" added as superscript without insertion mark.
is.la: "ræ" added as superscript with correction punctus between "s" and "l".
ðrowuga: "n" added as superscript without insertion mark.
sceppe.d: "n" added as superscript with correction punctus between "e" and "d".
eart: *ana* added as superscript with insertion mark after *eart*.

on ðǣre ūpplican æðelan ceastre,
frēa folca gehwæs, swā ðū æt fruman wǣre
efenēadig bearn āgenum fæder.
Ðū eart heofenlic līoht and ðæt hālige lamb
ðe ðū mānscilde middangeardes
for þinre ārfęstnesse ealle tōwurpe,
fīond geflǣmdest, follc generedes,
blōde gebohtest bearn Israēla.
Ðā ðū āhofe ðurh ðæt hālige trīow
ðīnre ðrōwunga ðrīostre senna
þæt ðū on hǣahsetle heafena rīces
sitest sigehrǣmig on ðā swīðran hand
ðīnum godfæder gāsta gemyndig.
Mildsa nū, meahtig, manna cynne
and of leahtrum alēs ðīne ðā līofan gescęft
and ūs hāle gedō, heleða sceppend,
nīða nergend, for ðīnes naman āre.
Ðū eart sōðlice simle hālig
and ðū eart āna ǣce dryhten
and ðū āna bist eallra dēma

eallra dema cwucra ge deadra crist nergend

forðan ðu on ðry<m>me ricsast ⁊ on ðrinesse

[folio 69v]

⁊ on annesse ealles waldend hiofena heahcyni^{n}c

haliges gastes fegere gefelled in fæder

wuldre :-

---

heahcynic: “n” added as superscript without insertion mark.

cwucra ge dēadra,   Crīst nergende,
forðan ðū on ðrymme rīcsast   and on ðrīnesse
and on ānnesse   ealles waldend
hiofena hēahcyninc   hāliges gāstes
fegere gefelled   in fæder wuldre.

NOTES

5: MS ænlum: *although the scribe has not corrected this reading as is done elsewhere, it is evident that the word intended is* ænglum (englum).
8: MS bilewitne: *accusative singular in concord with* þe, *even though a nominative would be expected in direct address.*
11: MS ðare: *some editors emend* ðare *to* ðinra *on the grounds that line 10 reads* ðines; *I emend it to the genitive plural demonstrative adjective* ðara, *which it more readily resembles, in concord with* mægena gerena.
23 MS ðe ðy: *obviously a scribal error for* ðe ðu *as in line 12, and emended as such.*
28a*: number concord seems lacking between* ðinre *(genitive singular) and* ðrowunga *(at first glance, genitive plural). I have left it unemended, as the second-person singular possessive adjective here may represent an underdeveloped articulation of the plural (the poet retaining something of the singular sense when forming such a possessive); however this noun phrase may instead represent one of two scribal errors, either* ðinra ðrowunga *or* ðinre ðrowunge; *or instead we might read* ðrowunga *as a genitive singular (see Dobbie, ASPR VI, 191).* 28b *presents more of a problem. Dobbie leaves it unemended, as here, but describes the difficulty succinctly: "Is* [ðriostre] *acc. sing., object of* āhofe, *with* senna *(for* synna*) gen. plur., 'the darkness of sins,' or is it gen. sing., with* senna *acc. plur., 'the sins of darkness'?" (ASPR VI, 190). He prefers the former interpretation but notes that* ðriostre *as any oblique form of* ðeostru *is unusual.*
30: MS sitest: *A punctus elevatus appears after* rices *and a majuscule 'S' begins* sitest, *here at what is effectively mid-clause, with MS layout disrupting syntax. I reluctantly revert to modern clausing and punctuation for this sentence.*
39: MS nergend: *Most editors emend to* nergende *(present participle) for metrical reasons. While it is grammatically acceptable, as we find in the noun phrase* niða nergend *(two common nouns linked by a genitive, 'redeemer of strifes,' at line 35a), its structure, consisting of a proper noun and a common noun in apposition to one another, is more awkward, and such a rhythm for a b-line is less likely: see KGM 169b. Such a slip can be accounted for by eyeskip, since* niða nergend *stands at the very end of folio 69r, MS line 15, exactly three lines above* crist nergend *at the end of MS line 18. For this reason, I follow the emendation to present participle as the more probable form.*

(b) *Kentish Great Miserere*

The *Kentish Great Miserere* is a very different kind of poem from the *Kentish Hymn of Praise*: it purports to derive from a single liturgical source, Psalm 50, whose *Romanum* Latin is intercalated into its text as we found with the *Pater Noster*, baptismal Creed, and *Gloria Patri* verse. Its poet has also constructed a narrative framework—the sin of King David in seducing Bathsheba and then sending her husband Uriah to certain death in the front lines of the battle—by which to contextualize the lengthy vernacular meditation. This narrative frames the actual confession of the king, which relies verse by verse on the Latin of the "Great Miserere" psalm, with the same words, *ðingode þioda aldor Dauid,* opening (lines 26–27a) and then closing (lines 166–67a) David's confession to God.

Once again we must assume that, like the *Kentish Hymn of Praise*, this poem was composed during the initial years of the Benedictine Reform period. Early in that period we find both *Romanum* and *Gallicanum* psalter-texts used side by side, with the *Gallicanum* predominating after 1000, so the inclusion by the poet of the *Romanum* and not the *Gallicanum* text would once again point to a date of composition relatively early in the Reform period. The presence of cancellation marks under *ðolienn* on folio 72v, manuscript line 3 shows that the scribe's eyes had been drawn back in his exemplar's text to *to ðolienne*, which he had copied into Vespasian D. vi in the previous line, when instead the inflected infinitive to be set down was *to healdenne* (see the note to the semi-diplomatic text, below). This confirms the existence of an earlier version of the poem than the one preserved for us today in Vespasian D. vi. And I have elsewhere rehearsed the evidence of this earlier exemplar to be seen at the scribe's page turn onto folio 71v, where he or she evidently compared the amount of vellum left (too little) and the remaining text (too much), and developed strategies to solve the dilemma:

> Cutting down his Latin rubrics to line-end was his primary method of compensating for this shortage. . . . Before his copying task was complete, the Vespasian D. vi scribe ultimately had to take a single extra sheet (fol. 73) on which to complete *Kentish [Great Miserere]*. By that time he was taking no chances, so on the recto side of the new sheet increased his number of lines from 17 to 21 as an additional space-saving measure.[9]

9 Sarah Larratt Keefer, "Respect for the Book: A Reconsideration of 'Form,' 'Content' and 'Context' in Two Vernacular Poems," *New Approaches to Editing Old English Poetry*, ed.

That the first strategy was to truncate the intercalated Latin rubrics of the poem tells us something interesting: not only did the original poem contain the full text of the Latin "Great Miserere" psalm, but the scribe assumed that the readers of his copy of the poem would be able to "fill in the blanks," suggesting that they knew the psalm's Latin by heart. We must therefore assume, at least for this witness of the poem, that the copying and reading environment was monastic.

The *Kentish Great Miserere* poet uses Latin *dominus* instead of Old English *dryhten* five times in the body of the poem: in lines 17b (*weorada dominus*), 90b (*bilwit dominus*), 109a (*aferre, domine*), 112b (*bilewit dominus*), and 160b (*mæhtig dominus*). Four of these are b-lines that serve to maintain the metrical rhythm, mere reinforcements of invocation to God; we might suspect at first that the vernacular alternative, *dryhten*, did not provide a metrical structure that met the poet's approval, but line 106b reads *weoruda dryhten*, so the choice of *dominus* for this very phrase in line 17b—and thence for the other three b-lines—is evidently more sophisticated than the simple need to meet metrical exigencies. The other use, in line 109 occurs in its a-line, *aferre, domine, [frea ælmeahtig]*, where the alliterator, such as it is, is "f"; *dryhten* would again have suited the metre here but the poet evidently preferred the Latinate to the vernacular address for God. Nor is the use of this word confined to King David's meditation on his sins and expression of contrition, so we cannot assume that it was intended to further characterize the king in any way. Its repetition may instead have been a conscious effort to capture the semantic import of the ritual address, used universally in formal prayer in the Latin liturgy, when addressing God (*deus* = "God") incarnate as Christ (*dominus* = "lord").

The *Kentish Great Miserere* poet had no more concerns about anachronism than we saw in the construction of the *Corpus* or *Junius Lord's Prayers*: although King David was the ancestor of the line from which Jesus of Nazareth was born, we are told in line 3 that the king was *cyninga cynost, Criste liofost* ("the keenest of kings, most beloved to Christ"), and Christ is invoked throughout the poem at lines 55, 61, 82, 99, 144 and 169. David's confession is made as much to *hælend min* (33a) or *dryhten weoruda* (38a, 106b), vernacular epithets for God the Son, as it is to *gasta sceppend* (42a) or

---

Sarah Larratt Keefer and Katherine O'Brien O'Keeffe (Woodbridge: Boydell, 1998), 21–44, 26; see also Sarah Larratt Keefer, *Psalm-Poem and Psalter-Glosses: The Latin and Old English Psalter-Text Background to "Kentish Psalm 50,"* American University Studies, Series VII: Theology and Religion, vol. 95 (New York: Garland, 1991), 22–26.

lifes liohtfruma (50a), vernacular epithets for God the Father. At lines 54–55 we hear the first of three direct addresses by David to the Son,[10] *Ic ðe, gasta breogo, helende Crīst, helpe bidde*, and we assume that the many second-person singular pronouns which follow are intended, in an extended example of anachronism, to invoke the second person of the Trinity and not the first.

The poet was a scholar familiar with some of the more arcane details of Latin church writing and also quite possibly a bishop. Careful reading of each meditation uncovers evidence to show that he was making use, not only of St Jerome's *Romanum* and *Gallicanum* versions of the Book of Psalms, but also of a scholarly recension of Jerome's third translation, the *Hebraicum*, known from ninth-century France as the "Theodulfian Hebraicum."[11] His Old English meditations quote from other psalms, perhaps to reinforce the centrality of King David as the speaker of the poem, but they also make reference to enough books from both Old and New Testaments to suggest that the poet had a substantial education in Holy Scripture, independent of whatever he might have acquired through performance in chapel or listening in refectory.[12]

Line 59, *ðæt ðu ne wilnast weora æniges deað* ("that thou willest not the death of any human"), could be taken together with the phrase from line 61, *cerrende Criste* ("turning to Christ"), as a reference to Ezekiel 18:32 ("for I do not desire the death of those who are to die, says the Lord God; turn yourselves and live"), but a closer parallel may be drawn. The *Great Miserere* psalm was sung as part of the Maundy Thursday reconciliation service; on this day in the week preceding Easter Sunday, those members of a parish who took on public penance during Lent were reunited with their ecclesiastical family under the direction of a bishop:

> The penitent should present himself in the bosom of the church, and whilst he lies completely prostrate on the ground, the bishop (*sacerdos*) should pray that he be reconciled as follows: first the antiphon is sung, 'Cor mundum crea in me, deus; spiri-

10 The others begin at lines 99 and 143.

11 Keefer, *Psalm-Poem and Psalter-Glosses*, 53; see also Sarah Larratt Keefer and David R. Burrows, "Hebrew and the Hebraicum in Late Anglo-Saxon England," *ASE* 19 (1990): 67–80, 70–76.

12 By way of examples, note *wynfęste getremed Hierusolimę*, lines 152–53, deriving from Isaiah 66: 10 and Zecharaiah 9: 9; and *lichaman . . . geðohtas*, line 44, deriving from Galatians 5:19 and 1 John 2:16.

tum rectum innoua in uisceribus,' then Ps. LI, followed by the Kyrie eleison, Pater noster and *preces* and then prayers asking for God's mercy towards the penitent.[13]

The Anglo-Saxon liturgy for reconciliation, which was also known in Germany, was substantially different from its continental counterpart. An examination of this liturgy, from a mid-tenth-century service-book used at the Anglo-Saxon monastic foundation at Fulda in Germany and from earlier tenth-century texts in a service-book likely from Glastonbury, shows that one of the prayers said by the presiding bishop at this reconciliation service on Maundy Thursday includes the sentence *uiuifica hunc famulum tuum .ill. quem tibi nullatenus mori desideras* ("revitalize this your servant [Name] whom you do not in any way wish to perish").[14] The close link between the recitation of the "Great Miserere" psalm and the bishop's inclusion of this statement suggests that the *Kentish Great Miserere* poet made a deliberate connection between David's penance and the rite of public reconciliation; and for him to have known this prayer in that context suggests that he was at the very least a priest and possibly even a bishop himself.

From the foregoing, we can see that the *Kentish Great Miserere* poet's voice remains quite audible throughout the poem. He constructs the piece with a narrative frame around it, introducing David as a warrior chief (*Dauid wæs haten diormod hæleð*, line 1) and his sin against God a compound one (of the flesh, through lust for Bathsheba—*þurh lichaman lene geðohtas . . . brohte to wife for gitsunga*, lines 15–24—and of the spirit, through his effective murder of Uriah—*he Uriam het aldre beneman*, line 21) in the first thirty lines. The voice of the poem is then given first to the familiar Latin of the psalm and then to David's impassioned confession, verse by verse: it is intensely intimate, using the first- and second-person singular pronouns *ic/me* and *þu/þe* that derive from their Latin originals *ego/me* and *tu/te* but moving well beyond the psalm's import in its delineation of the sinful human soul before its Creator. By doing this, the poet seems at first to stand as the dispassionate historian recording the events that led to the composition of the "Great Miserere"; however, his transition back to "objective narrator" at the

13 Hamilton, "Rites for Public Penance," 79. "Ps. LI" is here the "Great Miserere"; see p. 32, note 45, above.

14 Gregor Richter and Albert Schönfelder, eds., *Sacramentarium Fuldense Saeculi X* (Fulda: 1912; repr. HBS CI. Farnborough: St Michael's Abbey Press, 1972), 77; and Nicholas Orchard, ed., *The Leofric Missal*, HBS CXIV, 2 vols. (London: Boydell, 2002), II, 163–64.

poem's end never materializes: instead the voice that picks up the narrative after David's confession is that of a homilist whose tale of a king brought to his knees by sin is one from which all listeners may learn greater humility. We hear *swæ þingode þiode aldor* ("thus prayed the prince of the people," line 166) and *forðon he gebette balaniða hord* ("therefore he atoned for a multitude of evils," line 171; emphasis mine in both lines), which inevitably lead the poet to an invocation to God on behalf of himself and his audience: *forgef us, God mæahtig þæt we synna hord simle oferwinnan and us geearnian æce dreamas*, lines 174–76, where *us* and *we* seem to be a parochial or indeed a universal flock, the poet himself and the men and women for whom this poem was written.

SEMI-DIPLOMATIC TEXT

(folio 70r, line 10 – folio 73v, line 16)
Latin psalm-verses and sections are in red minium.

Dauid wæs haten diormod hæleð israela

brȩga æðelæ ⁊ rice cyninga cynost criste

liofost · wæs he under hiofenu<m> hearpera mærost

ðara we an folcu<m> gefrigen hæbben sangere he wæs

o
soðfæstest swiðe geðancol to ðingienne þi,dum

sinu<m> wið þane mildostan manna sceppend · wæs

se dryhtnes ðiowa dauid æt wige soð sigecem

pa · searocyne man casere creaftig þonn<e>

[folio 70v]

l
cu<m>burgebrec on gewinndagu<m> weorðan scoldan

hwȩðere him geiode swa ful oft gedeð þ<æt>te god

ferhte gylt gefræmmað · þurh lichaman

lene geðohtas · gelamp þ<æt> him mon ansende

saula neriend witgan mid wordu<m> weorada d<omi>n<u>s

⁊ secgan het selfu<m> gecyðan ymb his womdeda

þi,dum: “o” added as superscript with insertion mark between “i” and “d” of *þidum*.
cu<m>burgebrec: the scribe has first written *cūbur*, then added a correction punctus below the “r” and superscribed “l” above it.

CRITICAL TEXT

Dauid wæs hāten dīormōd hæleð,
Israēla brēga, æðelæ ond rīce,
cyninga cȳnost, Crīste līofost;
wæs hē under hiofenum hearpera mǣrost
ðara wē an folcum gefrigen hæbben;
sangere hē wæs sōðfæstest, swīðe geðancol
tō ðingienne þīodum sīnum
wið þane mildostan manna sceppend;
wæs se dryhtnes ðīowa Dauid æt wīge,
sōð sigecempa, searocyne man,
cāsere creaftig þonne cumbulgebrec
on gewinndagum weorðan scoldan;
hwęðere him geīode swā ful oft gedeð
þætte godferhte gylt gefræmmað
þurh līchaman lēne geðohtas:
gelamp þæt him mon ansende sāula neriend,
wītgan mid wordum, weorada dominus,
ond secgan hēt, selfum gecȳðan

waldendes doom þ<æt> se fruma wære his feores

sceldig forðam þe he uria<m> het aldre beneman

fromne ferdrinc · fere beserode · ⁊ him beza

be · brohte to wife · for gitsunga · þe he godes

eorre þurh his selfes weorc sona anfunde .

Him ða ðingode þioda aldor dauid georne ⁊ to dry

htne gebæd · ⁊ his synna hord selfa ontende

gyltas georne gode andhette weoruda dryht

ne ⁊ ðus wordu<m> spæc Miserere mei d<eu>s

secundu<m> magna<m> misericordiam tuam

t
Milsa ðu me meahta walden nu ðu wast manna

[folio 71r]

geðohtas help ðu hælend min handgeweorces þines

anes ælmehtig god eft<er> þinre ðara miclan mildhior

nesse :· Et secundu<m> multitudinem miserati

onem tuaru<m> dele iniquitate<m> meam -

t
Ond eac eft<er> menio milsa ðinra dryhten weoru

Milsa: "t" added as superscript with no insertion mark.
mildhiornesse: "t" omitted and uncorrected here.
milsa: "t" added as superscript without insertion mark.

ymb his womdēda waldendes doom
þæt se fruma wǣre his feores sceldig
for ðām þe he Ūriam hēt aldre beneman,
fromne ferdrinc, fēre beserode
ond him Bezabe brōhte tō wīfe
for gītsunge þe hē Godes eorre
þurh his selfes weorc sona anfunde.
Him ðā ðingode þīoda aldor
Dauid georne ond tō dryhtne gebæd,
ond his synna hord selfa ontēnde,
gyltas georne Gode andhette,
weoruda dryhtne, ond ðus wordum spæc.
Miserere mei deus secundum magnam misericordiam tuam:
"Miltsa ðū mē, meahta walden, nū ðū wāst manna geðohtas;
help ðū, hælend mīn, handgeweorces
þīnes ānes, ælmehtig God,
efter þīnre ðǣre miclan mildhiortnesse.
Et secundum multitudinem miserationem tuarum dele iniquitatem meam:
"Ond ēac efter menio miltsa ðīnra,

da · adilga min unriht to forgefenesse gaste minu<m>

amplius laua me ab iniustitia mea et a delicta mea

n
munda mæ :· aðweah me of se,nu<m> saule fra<m> wam

mum gasta sceppend geltas geclansa · þa ðe ic on

aldre æfre gefremede ðurh lichaman leðre ge

ðohtas :~ quoniam iniquitatem meam ego

agnosco et delictum meu<m> coram me est se<m>p<er>:~

n
forðan ic unriht min eal oncwawe ⁊ eac synna ge

hwær selfu<m> æt eagan firendeda geðrec beforan

standeð scelda scinað · forgef me sceppen min

lifes liohtfruma ðinre lufan blisse :~

Tibi soli peccaui et malu<m> coram te feci ut iusti

[folio 71v]

ficeris in sermonib<us>; tuis et uincas du<m> iudicaris

Nu ic anu<m> ðe oft syngode ⁊ yfela feola eac ge

fræmede gelta gra<m>hegdig · Ic ðe gasta breogo

helende crist helpe bidde ðæt me forgefene

---

se,nu<m>: "n" added as superscript with insertion mark between "e" and "n" of *senu<m>*.
oncwawe: The scribe has written *cwawe*; a hand perhaps contemporary has added a horizontal stroke through the descender of the first wyn and corrected the error by writing "n" above it in graphite.

dryhten weoruda,   ādīlga mīn unriht
tō forgefenesse   gāste mīnum.

Amplius laua me ab iniustitia mea Et a delicta mea munda mæ:

"Āðwēah mē of sennum,   sāule fram wammum,
gāsta sceppend,   geltas geclansa
þā ðe ic on aldre   æfre gefremede
ðurh līchaman   lēðre geðohtas.

Quoniam iniquitatem meam ego agnosco et delictum meum coram me est semper:

"Forðan ic unriht mīn   eal oncnāwe
ond ēac synna gehwǣr selfum æt ēagan,
firendēda geðrec   beforan standeð,
scelda scīnað;   forgef mē, sceppen mīn,
līfes līohtfruma,   ðīnre lufan blisse.

Tibi soli peccaui et malum coram te feci ut iustificeris in sermonibus; tuis et uincas dum iudicaris:

"Nū ic ānum ðē   oft syngode
ond yfela feola ēac gefræmede,
gelta gramhēgdig.   Ic ðē, gāsta breogo,
helende Crīst,   helpe bidde

gastes wunde an forðgesceaft feran mote

þy ðine wordcwidas weorðan gefelde · ðæt ðu ne

wilnast weora æniges deað · ac ðu synfulle sim

le lærdes ðæt hio cerrende criste herdon ⁊ hio<m>

lif mid ðe lansum[g] begȩton · swilce ðu æt dome

dryhten oferswiddes[t], ealra synna cynn sau

la neriend :- Ecce eni<m> in iniquitatibus :-

Ic on unrihtu<m> eac ðan in synnu<m> geeacnod wæs

ðu ðæt ana wast mæhtig dryhten hu me modor

gebær in scame ⁊ in sceldu<m> forgef me sceppend

min ðæt ic fra<m> ðæ<m> synnu<m> selfa gecerre þa ðy

mine ældran ær geworhtan · ⁊ ic selfa eac

sioððan beeode :- Ecce eni<m> ueritatem:-

[folio 72r]

ac ðu selua god soð an lufast þy ic ðe mid benum

---

lansum: "g" added as superscript without insertion mark.
oferswiddes: "t" added as superscript with insertion mark after "s".

ðæt mē forgefene gāstes wunde,
an forðgesceaft feran mōte,
þȳ ðīne wordcwidas weorðan gefēlde
ðæt ðū ne wilnast weora ǣniges dēað
ac ðū synfulle simle lǣrdes
ðæt hīo cerrende Crīste herdon
ond hīom līf mid ðē langsum begȩton,
swilce ðū æt dōme, dryhten, oferswīddest
ealra synna cynn, sāula neriend.
Ecce enim in iniquitatibus . . .
"Ic on unrihtum ēac ðan in synnum
geēacnod wæs; ðū ðæt āna wāst,
mæhtig dryhten, hū mē modor gebær
in scame ond in sceldum: forgef mē, sceppend mīn,
ðæt ic fram ðǣm synnum selfa gecerre,
þā ðe mīne ældran ǣr geworhtan
ond ic selfa ēac sioððan beēode.
Ecce enim ueritatem . . .
"Ac ðū, selua God, sōð ān lufast;
þȳ ic ðē mid bēnum biddan wille

biddan wille lifes ⁊ lisse liohtes aldor forðan ðu

me uncuðe eac ðan derne þinre snetera hord

a
selfa ontendes :~ asperies me ysopo et munda
bor:~

ðu me meahtig god milde ⁊ bliðe þurh ysopon

ealne ahluttra · þonn<e> ic geclænsod criste hero · ⁊

eac ofer snawe self scinende þinre sibbe lufan

sona gemete :~ Auditui meo dabis gaudium :~

Ontyn nu elmehtig earna hleoðor þ<æt> min gehernes

hehtful weorðe on gefean bliðse forðweard to

ðe · ðanne bioð on wenne waldend simle þa gebroce

nan ban bilwit d<omi>n<u>s ða þe on hænðum ær hwile wæron :~

auerte faciem tua<m> a peccatis meis et omnes :~

Ahwerf nu fra<m> synnu<m> saula neriend · ⁊ fra<m> misdedu<m>

minra gylta þine ansione ælmeahtig god · ⁊ ðurh

---

asperies: the letter "a" has been added by a contemporary hand above the "e" here.

līfes ond lisse,   līohtes aldor,
forðan ðū mē uncuðe   eac ðan derne
þīnre snetera hord   selfa ontēndes.
Asperies me ysopo et mundabor . . .
"Ðū mē, meahtig God,   milde ond blīðe,
þurh ysopon   ealne āhlūttra:
þonne ic geclænsod   Crīste hero
ond ēac ofer snāwe   self scīnende
þinre sibbe lufan   sōna gemēte.
Auditui meo dabis gaudium . . .
"Ontȳn nū, elmehtig ,   ēarna hlēoðor
þæt mīn gehērnes   hehtful weorðe,
on gefean bliðse   forðweard tō ðē;
ðanne bīoð on wenne,   waldend,   simle
þā gebrocenan bān,   bilwit dominus,
ðā þe on hænðum   ǣr hwīle wǣron.
Auerte faciem tuam a peccatis meis et omnes . . .
"Āhwerf nū fram synnum,   sāula neriend,
ond fram misdēdum   mīnra gylta
þīne ansīone,   ælmeahtig God,

miltsunga meahta þinra · ðu unriht min eall adilga :~

Cor mundu<m> crea in me d<eu>s et spiritu<m> rectu<m>

[folio 72v]

Æc ðu dryhten crist clęne hiortan in me mehtig

god modswiðne geðanc to ðolienne ðinne willan

⁊ to ðolienn healdenne halige domas · ⁊ ðu rihtne

gast rodera waldend · in ferðe minu<m> feste geniowa:~

Ne p<ro>icias me a facie tuae et spiritu<m> s<antu>m tuum:~

Ne aweorp ðu me weoruda dryhten fra<m> ansione

ealra þinra miltsa · ne ðane godan fra<m> me gast

haligne · aferre d<omi>ne frea ælmeahtig þinre arna

me. eal ne bescerwe :~ Redde mihi letitiam :~

Sæle nu bliðse me · bilewit d<omi>n<u>s þinre hælo heht

helm alwihta · ⁊ me lifgende liohtes hiorde gaste

ðine god selfa getreme ðæt ic aldorlice a forð

ðolienn: these cancellation marks below the repeated inflected infinitive *ðolienn(e)* show the scribe immediately aware of the slip; the correct inflected infinitive reading follows the cancellation. We cannot be certain whether the other slips here noted were corrected during this writing campaign or on subsequent reading.

s<antu>m: "c" added above the erroneous scribal abbreviation *sm* for *sanctum* without insertion mark.

ond ðurh miltsunga   meahta þīnra
ðū unriht mīn   eall ādīlga.
Cor mundum crea in me deus et spiritum rectum . . .
"Ǣc ðū, dryhten Crīst,   clęne hiortan
in mē, mehtig God,   mōdswīðne geðanc
tō ðolienne   ðīnne willan
and tō healdenne   hālige dōmas
ond ðū rihtne gāst,   rodera waldend,
in ferðe minum   feste genīowa.
Ne proicias me a facie tuae et spiritum sanctum tuum . . .
"Ne āweorp ðū mē,   weoruda dryhten,
fram ansione   ealra þinra miltsa,
ne ðane godan fram mē   gāst hāligne
āferre, domine,   frēa ælmeahtig,
þīnra ārna mē   eal ne bescerwe.
Redde mihi letitiam . . .
"Sæle nū bliðse mē,   bilewit dominus,
þīnre hælo heht,   helm alwihta,
ond mē, lifgende   līohtes hiorde,
gāste ðīne,   God selfa, getreme

sioððan to ðinu<m> willan weorðan mote :-

Doceam iniquos uias tuas et impii ad te :-

Simle ic ðine weogas wanhogan lærde ðæt hio

arlease eft gecerdan to hiora selfra saula

hiorde · god selfa · to ðe gastes mundberd ðurh

[folio 73r]

l

sibbe lufan seocan scodan :- libera me de sanguinib<us> :-

befreo me an ferðe fæder mancynnes fra<m> blodgete

⁊ bealaniðum god lifigende gylta geclansa helo

⁊ helpend · hiofenrices weard · ðanne tunge min

triowfest blissað for ðines selfes soðfestnesse :-

D<omi>ne labia mea aperies et os meum adnuntiauit:-

Ontyn nu waldend god weoloras mine swa min muð

sioððan mæhte ðine · ⁊ lof georne liodum to bliðse

soð sigedryhten seccende wæs :- q<uonia>m si uoluisses :-

[folio 73r]: lineation increases from 17 to 21 lines at this folio.
scodan: "l" added as superscript without insertion mark.
adnuntiauit: error for Ro/Ga *adnuntiabit*.

ðæt ic aldorlice   ā forð sioððan
tō ðīnum willan   weorðan mōte.
Doceam iniquos uias tuas et impii ad te . . .
"Simle ic ðīne weogas   wanhogan lǣrde
ðæt hīo ārlēase   eft gecerdan
tō hiora selfra   sāula hiorde,
God selfa, tō ðē,   gāstes mundberd,
ðurh sibbe lufan   sēocan scoldan.
Libera me de sanguinibus . . .
"Befrēo mē an ferðe,   fæder mancynnes,
fram blōdgete   ond bealaniðum,
God lifigende,   gylta geclansa,
hēlo ond helpend,   hiofenrīces weard;
ðanne tunge mīn   trīowfest blissað
for ðīnes selfes   sōðfestnesse.
Domine labia mea aperies et os meum adnuntiauit . . .
"Ontȳn nū, waldend God,   weoloras mīne
swā mīn mūð sioððan   mæhte ðīne
ond lof georne   līodum tō bliðse,
sōð sigedryhten   seccende wæs.

Ic ðe onsegednesse sona brohte . weoruda dryhtne

ðer ðu wolde swa · ða ðu þ<æt> ne lufedest lifes bretta

ðæt ic ðe bernelac bregan moste deadra neata

dryhtne to willan :~ Sacrificiu<m> d<e>o sp<iritu>s contrib<u
latus:~>

ac ðe micle ma mehtig dryhten lifiende crist

r
liicweðe bið se gehnysta gast hiorte geclansod · ⁊

geeadmeded ingeþancum ða ðu ælmæhtig æfre

tate:~
ne æwest :~ Benigne fac d<omi>ne in bona uolun

Gedoo nu fræmsume frofre ðine to ðinu<m> godan

gastes willan ðætte sione dun sigefest weorðe

⁊ weallas sion wynfęste getremed hierusolimę

god lifiende :~ Tunc acceptabis sacri [..]

[folio 73v]

Swa þu frea meahtig anfehst siþðan · liofwende

---

liicweðe: "r" added as superscript without insertion mark.
[folio 73v]: lineation once again increases from 21 to 23 lines on this folio.

Quoniam si uoluisses . . .

"Ic ðē onsegednesse   sōna brōhte,
weoruda dryhtne,   ðēr ðū wolde swā;
ðā ðū þæt ne lufedest,   līfes bretta,
ðæt ic ðē bernelāc   brengan mōste
dēadra nēata,   dryhtne tō willan.

Sacrificium deo spiritus contribulatus . . .

"Ac ðē micle mā,   mehtig dryhten,
lifiende Crīst,   liicwerðe bið
sē gehnysta gāst,   hiorte geclansod
ond geēadmēded   ingeþancum;
ðā ðū, ælmæhtig,   ǣfre ne ǣwest.

Benigne fac domine in bona uoluntate . . .

"Gedoo nū fræmsume   frōfre ðīne
tō ðīnum gōdan   gāstes willan
ðætte Sione dūn   sigefest weorðe
ond weallas Sion   wynfęste getremed,
Hierusolimę,   God lifiende.

Tunc acceptabis sacri [..] . . .

"Swā þū, frēa mieahtig,   anfehst siþðan

lac lioda þ^{r}ine hælend manna · hio ðæt halige cealf
on wigbed þin willu<m> asettað liohtes aldor · forgef me
lifigende meotod mancynnes · mæhtig d<omi>n<u>s · ðæt
ða sorhfullan saule wunde · þa ðe ic on ælde · ł on
giogeðe in flæ^{s}chaman gefręmed hæbbe leahtra
hegeleasra mid lufan þinra gastæ forgeofene glid<an>
mote :~ Swæ þingode þiode aldor dauid to dryhtne
deda gemyndig þ<æt> hine męhtig god mannu<m> to fro
fre ðæs cynedomes crist neriende · waldende god
weorðne munde · forðon he gebette balaniða
hord mid eaðmede ingeþance · ða ðe he on ferðe
gefręmed hebbe hæfde · gastes wunde · forgef us

þine: "r" added as superscript without insertion mark.
ł: the MS preserves the scribal abbreviation ł for *uel* ("or") rather than the word itself.
flæchaman: "s" added as superscript without insertion mark.
hæfde: the scribe first wrote *hebbe*, then added cancellation marks below and seems to have smudged the word in an attempt at erasure; the correct form *hæfde* is written after the error.

līofwende lāc   līoda þīnra,
hælend manna: hīo ðæt hālige cealf
on wīgbed þīn   willum āsettað,
līohtes aldor;   forgef mē, lifigende
meotod mancynnes,   mæhtig dominus,
ðæt ðā sorhfullan   sāule wunde
þā ðe ic on ælde   uel on giogeðe
in flǣschaman   gefręmed hæbbe
leahtra hegelēasra,   mid lufan þīnre
gāstæ forgeofene   glīdan mōte."
Swǣ þingode   þīode aldor,
Dauid tō dryhtne,   dēda gemyndig,
þæt hine mę̄htig God   mannum tō frōfre
ðæs cynedōmes,   Crīst neriende,
waldende God, weorðne munde;
forðon hē gebētte   balanīða hord
mid ēaðmēde   ingeþance,
ðā ðe hē on ferðe   gefręmed hæfde,
gāstes wunde;   forgef ūs, God mæahtig,

god mæahtig þ<æt> we synna hord simle oferwinnan ·

⁊ us geearnian æce dreamas · an lifigendra lan

des wenne amen :~

þæt we synna hord   simle oferwinnan
ond ūs geearnian   ǣce drēamas
an lifigendra landes wenne.
Amen

NOTES

24: MS gitsunga: *this needs to be emended to a dative singular after* for.
35: MS ðara: *Dobbie rightly notes that while the MS reading (genitive plural demonstrative adjective) makes no sense, a dative singular feminine demonstrative adjective does, and is "supported by Psalms 108: 25, line 4 and Psalm 113: 10, line 1 in the Paris Psalter" (ASPR VI, 191). I follow his emendation here.*
44: MS lichaman leðre: leðre *is a comparative form of the adjective* lað *describing the weak masculine noun* lichaman, *and as such we would expect to find it declined weak, providing the form* leðran *for an oblique case instead. The word stands penultimate on its MS line, and apart from its being an error in the scribe's copy-text which he did not catch, we cannot account for this form unless the repeated inflectional ending* -an *had been rejected as unappealing by the original poet. I leave it unemended.*
54: MS gelta gramhegdig: *in this phrase governed by* feola *and the genitive which parallels* yfela *in the line above, we would expect to find the adjective* gramhegdig *reflecting the case (genitive plural) of the noun it modifies. Since it does not carry an inflectional ending, we can only assume that it is intended to be genitive plural.*
63: MS oferswiddest: *it has been editorial custom to regularize the 'dd' to 'ðd' to make this verb conform to the model of* oferswīðan; *although it may a scribal error, on the page it looks quite intentional, with both 'd's shaped with exactly the same ductus. I have retained it as perhaps a regional feature of the scribe's own pronunciation.*
71: MS þa ðy: *as in line 43 above,* þa ðe *introduces a relative clause whose referent,* synnum, *governs the sense of lines 71–72; it is emended accordingly.*
74: MS selua: *seeing* selfa *spelled instead with a 'u' and showing an orthographic awareness of difference for the voicing of the labiodental fricative [f] > [v] between two voiced sounds (here [l] and the vowel [ə]) is an anomaly, especially when we consider that all the other spellings of this word in the poem use orthographic 'f'.*
78: MS þinre snetera: *although the evidently plural form of* snetera *can be explained as collective (i.e. wisdoms = wisdom) as found in the Glossary (see CHM,* snyttru, *p. 313), it is modified by a genitive singular possessive adjective.*

88: MS bliðse: *this word is not agreed upon by earlier editors: some take it as third-person singular present of* bliðsian/blissian *whose subject is* gehernes, *while others prefer it as a noun, dative singular of* bliðs/bliss, *with* gefean *as a genitive singular.*
110: MS þinre: *this must be emended to* þinra *for concord with* arna, *the noun it modifies.*
129: MS tunge . . . triowfest: *since* tunge *is most commonly assumed a feminine noun, we would expect to find the weak adjective* triowfest *that modifies it, inflected for nominative as* triowfestu; *this is however later Anglo-Saxon verse, and either the poet felt the terminal syllable '-u' interfered with the structure of his line, or this may be regarded as one of several admittedly rare but attested instances of the noun being inflected as masculine.*
135: MS seccende: *Like some of the earlier editors, I prefer to leave this unemended, but it is clear that it is the present participle of* secgan, *used here with* wæs *to indicate continuity, a departure from the Latin perfect verb* adnuntiauit, *which itself is an interesting error.*
140: MS bregan: *this verb should read* brengan *("bring") to translate* dedissem *('give') of the complete psalm-verse, and is emended as such.*
156: MS þinre: *this possessive adjective needs to be emended to* þinra *to agree with* lioda, *the genitive plural noun that it modifies, since the plural pronoun* hio *of the next line confirms that it is plural and not singular that drives the sense of* liod *here.*
164: MS þinra: *emendation (this time to singular from plural) must be made to preserve concord between* lufan *(dative singular) and its possessive adjective.*
175 oferwinnan: *a modal auxiliary, like* magan *or* motan, *inflected as a plural subjunctive, is to be understood for this infinitive.*

Ah, Beloved Lord

Ah, Beloved Lord, re-titled from its ASPR title "Prayer," has no single liturgical source and seems to draw from a number of disparate influences (epithets for God that resonate with litanies, echoes of the Nicene Creed, and substantial confessional material). Yet despite its use of the first-person singular pronoun, it is a piece given to aphorism, deliberately structured for rhetorical effect on its audience. As such, it resembles a prayer less than it does a homily or exhortation, and has been re-titled accordingly, using its incipit. It remains to us in two unrelated manuscripts. The earlier witness is London, Lambeth Palace 427, an interlinear glossed Gallican psalter, where we find the poem's first fifteen pairs of half-lines added in a later eleventh-century hand to a space at the bottom of folio 183v, following a partially glossed confessional prayer at the end of the Psalter proper. Its only complete version stands on the first three pages of the fire-damaged twelfth-century British Library fragment Cotton Julius A. ii, folios 136–44, where it was evidently to be foregrounded in the collection that the complete book was to contain: the accompanying texts are a dialogue and riddle-like sayings that belong to the genre of wisdom literature, not unlike the prose texts of chronology and measurement that appear in London, BL Cotton Vespasian D. vi and Titus D. xxvii.

Ah, Beloved Lord starts a new page at the top of folio 136r with what must once have been a glorious blue-green capital ash (Æ); its internal sections are set off with elegant coloured capitals of red minium (lead), yellow, blue, and green; and it contains two red ornamental division *notae* (ꝸ) indicating where words from one line have been added at the end of the next line, which itself is carrying text. We find blank space following the poem to the page end on 137r. *Ah, Beloved Lord* was edited first by Francis Junius in 1655. Since then it had been largely ignored until Barbara Raw's discussion of it in 1978. Although Greenfield and Calder describe it as a "79-line poem in which the speaker rather tearfully and melodramatically beats his breast,"[1] Raw is more perceptive: "[T]he meaning is conveyed through a series of oppositions, and this is reflected in the syntax, with its parallels and variations" which "provide a structure for the poem as a whole." Raw's awareness of "this patterned kind of writing," and the use of "rhetorical device" and "encomiastic verse" technique indicates a more sophisticated construct than Greenfield and Calder's survey would have us believe the piece to be.[2] Dobbie notes that it has "an effect of studied unity" that serves to reinforce the poem's "craftedness."[3]

We can easily link *Ah, Beloved Lord* to the rest of the liturgical poetry canon in Old English through common vocabulary and phrasing. But when we turn to Cotton Julius A. ii, its complete manuscript witness, we find substantial differences from other liturgical verse in layout and design. It contains no intercalated Latin and thus no self-referential indication of primary or even secondary influence on its composition. More importantly, the way in which it has been preserved on the page demonstrates deliberate lexical choice through repetition intended to affect the structure of the piece: twinned or contrasted phrases and expressions are physically placed in exactly the same location (initial, medial or terminal) on their respective manuscript lines. Such a layout has in part been achieved through the use of the division *notae*, which allow for the interruption of one manuscript line at its outer edge by text from the previous line. This pattern of identically located words and phrase constructions holds true with astonishing consistency for related word-pairs (such as *deoflon* and *drihtne* in initial positions), for the repeated phrases *dæiges* ⁊ *nihtes* or *hafað* ⁊ *sceawað* at the ends of their manuscript lines, or for the repeated phrase *on eorðan her* in the centres of theirs. It also holds true for the entire sections concerning *earming* and *eadig*, each begun with a red "S" and ending with space to the line-end. The poet apparently constructed this piece with its written form—how it would look on the page—already in mind and thus a major influence on its structure. This may have had something to do with its metrical composition, but while many of these balanced phrases create half-lines and thus fall in with modern editorial convention (two indented half-lines with blank space for the caesura) surprisingly consistently, we must remember that modern editorial convention was unknown in the Anglo-Saxon period.

---

1 Greenfield and Calder, *New Critical History*, 235.

2 Barbara Raw, *The Art and Background of Old English Poetry* (London: Edward Arnold, 1978), 121–24.

3 Dobbie, ASPR VI, lxxxvii.

We do not know how the poet instructed a scribe to write down this piece, or if he or she served as its first copyist. If we are correct in assuming "text-consciousness" at work in the poem from its inception, then we must also assume that each written recension of it must have preserved something of this inherent impulse. Therefore it seems relatively certain that the Anglo-Norman scribe of Julius A. ii was not responsible for discovering the poem's structure and initiating the related layout for it on its manuscript lines. It seems unlikely in any case; *Ah, Beloved Lord* is missing two half-lines, and the Julius A. ii scribe either was responsible for losing them or was working from a flawed exemplar. That the latter is more likely the case can be seen from a comparison with the *Corpus Lord's Prayer* on the pages of CCCC 201, since the shape of the text on the page is frequently predetermined by the shape of an exemplar text from which it was copied. Two half-lines are also missing from the *Corpus Lord's Prayer*, but each instance coincides with a line-end in the manuscript, and from this physical evidence we can infer simple eyeskip as the cause (see p. 55 above for a discussion of these missing lines), with the lines more likely than not present in the exemplar text. Dobbie assumes the half-lines lost from *Ah, Beloved Lord* to have been 25b and 77b, but there is no easy way of explaining the first missing half-line as the fault of the scribe, since its location falls part of the way through a scribal line in Cotton Julius A. ii; however, its omission affects the balance of phrase locations on the manuscript lines (see note to line 25b in the critical text below). The second missing half-line is perhaps an error by the Julius copyist, but when added to all the other evidence it seems probable that the exemplar for Julius A. ii was missing these lines as well. Therefore, what stands in the pages of Julius A. ii is perhaps an attempt at xerographic (or identical) replication of the exemplar text's layout, which may even provide the form of a still-earlier recension, carefully preserved from book to book, its lineation copied exactly. If this is indeed the case, it enables us to gain access, albeit in a mirror darkly, to an earlier copy of a piece in yet another physical witness, adding to the fragment in Lambeth 427 to suggest that more than one version of this poem was made before the twelfth century.

Whoever composed *Ah, Beloved Lord*, then, seems to have thought in terms of spatialization on a page, and of how to construct lexical contrasts and balances to display them to their best advantage physically on manuscript lines. Modern readers assume "text-consciousness" as a precondition of communications in an age ruled by the universally visual and literate, so that as we write, we think in terms of actualized "texts" rather than of oral "tellings." Katherine O'Brien O'Keeffe points out that "the physical evidence of the writing of [Old English] poetic works—their irregular spacing of free morphemes, highly individual and sporadic capitalization and punctuation, and copying of verse without regard to length of line—argue that the visual conventions which provided necessary information for the reading of contemporary verse in Latin . . . were unnecessary in Old English."[4] What she says holds true for most of the Old English verse canon; however, it is only partially accurate when we look at the complete copy of *Ah, Beloved Lord* in Julius A. ii representing a more sophisticated conceptualization—perhaps the result of an environment of literacy influencing its composition—where its visual presentation seems to have been part of its plan.

The extreme sensitivity to layout evident in this poem has gone unremarked upon until now. Dobbie and Raw (who I assume was using ASPR volume VI) ignore scribal clues in the manuscript witness and create a text that is different from the one in Julius A. ii. On folio 136v, we have three coloured capital "N"s, one yellow, one red, one blue, and each introducing its own clause. Clearly a conscious contrast is intended for the reading audience. Yet in Dobbie we find the second clause, *Ne mage we næfre asæcgan* (verse line 33a) uncapitalized and wholly subordinated to the first. Raw follows his punctuation and layout, going so far as to suggest that the first *Ne mæg þe aherian* and the third, *Ne þeah engla werod* (lines 30a and 35a), are parallels, referring to men and angels; she regards the second clause that was capitalized in the manuscript, *Ne mage we næfre asæcgan*, instead as the counterpart of *ne magon hy næfrę areccean* (line 37a), an observation reinforced by the fact that the b-line of each ends with *ne þæt soðe* (or *gerim*) *witan/wytan* (lines 33b and 37b). Such perception is valuable, but when we take manuscript evidence into account, it is surely not enough. Clues to another structure that has been obscured by editorial decision remain in the manuscript; by their removal from a critical edition, another interpretation has been overlooked.

Ne mage we næfre asæcgan was deliberately placed so that a red minium capital *N* could be drawn in the capital gutter. This in turn was only possible because manuscript line 3 on folio 136v where it appears has been disrupted: instead of running over onto the beginning of the line, *middangeard* from the previous manuscript line (2) is brought down to manuscript line 3's end, where the first of the two ornamental *notae* stands as divider between the two parts, leaving the beginning of the line free for the red capital "N" and this clause. The disruption also has the salutary effect of placing *ne þæt soðe witan*

4 Katherine O'Brien O'Keeffe, *Visible Song: Transitional Literacy in Old English Verse,* CSASE 4 (Cambridge: Cambridge UP, 1990), 21–22.

(verse line 33b) at the beginning of manuscript line 4. When we look to see where its lexical counterpart noted by Raw (*ne þæt gerim wytan*, verse line 37b) appears, we find it at the beginning of scribal line 7. This balance too has been constructed spatially as a result of the disruption at manuscript line 3, and so we have to assume that the poet—and perhaps several generations of scribes, ending with the xerographic efforts in Julius A. ii—intended three and not two capital "N"s, as we find in the manuscript, for a reason. Thus we must take seriously *Ne mage we næfre asecgan* as a separate element, and the central one, of three distinct sections.

Ah, Beloved Lord is an intriguing poem. Like "Cædmon's Hymn," the earliest Old English verse composition to list names of God for humanity to praise, this piece presents a complex list of divine epithets that recall litanies invoking the individual persons of the Trinity before listing those saints whose favour the supplicant was asking for; such epithets for God were "used for a variety of liturgical purposes, both public and private."[5] Many of these epithets for God appear in other related liturgical or religious poems of the pre-Conquest period, raising interesting questions about shared cultural aesthetics. *Ah, Beloved Lord* also presents aphoristic statements in its opening section: *Se byð earming þe* ("Wretched is he who . . .," verse line 11), *Se byð eadig, se þe* ("Blessed is he, the one who . . .," line 16), *wa him þære mirigðe* ("Woe [be] to him for that pleasure," line 13), or *wel him þæs geweorkes* ("Joy [be] to him because of this work," line 18). Some of these are echoed in other liturgical poems (see *Corpus Lord's Prayer*, line 19, *wel bið ðam þe wyrcð willan þinne*, "joy be to that one who does thy will") and raise questions about the didactic tone of such statements and the influence of homiletic writing and thought on such a piece.

5 Michael Lapidge, ed., *Anglo-Saxon Litanies of the Saints*, HBS 106 (Woodbridge: Boydell, 1991), 2. See also pp. 2–13 for a good background to the function of litanies within the Christian Church.

SEMI-DIPLOMATIC TEXT

(Lambeth Palace 427, folio 183v, lines 8–17)

The first letter "E" is a red capital; the subsequent capitals are black with red or ochre dots in the curves or spaces of each letter.

Eala drihten leof eala dema god · geare me ece waldend.

Ic wat mine sauwle synnum forwundod. Ge hæl

þu hẏ heofona drihten · ⁊ gelacna þu heo lifes al

dor · forþon ðu eþest miht ealra læc a ðara þege

wurde side oððe wide Eala frea brihta folces

scẏppend. gemilda þin mod me to gode . Syle

ðine are þinum earminge. Se bið earming þe on

eorðan her dæges ⁊ nihtes deoflu<m> compað ⁊ his

willan wyrcð þa him þære myrigðe. þonne hand

lean hafað ⁊ s̆ceawað butan he þæs yfles ær geswice·

SEMI-DIPLOMATIC TEXT

(London, British Library, Cotton Julius A. ii,
folio 136r, line 1 – folio 137r, line 14)

Capitals in blue, green, yellow, and, more commonly, red minium. Two ornamental *notae* mark text brought down from the previous line. There was extensive damage done to this manuscript by the fire of 1731 which devastated Sir Robert Cotton's library.

Æla drihten leof . æla dema god . geara

me . ece waldend. ic wat mine saule . sẏn

num forwundod . gehæl þu hẏ . heofena drihten.

⁊ gelacna þu hẏ. lifes ealdor . forþan ðu eðest

miht. ealra læca. ðæra þe gewurde: side oððe wẏde.

Æla frea beorhta. folkes scippend. gemilsa þẏn

mod. me to gode. sile þẏne are. þẏne earminge.

Se bẏð earming. þeo on eorðan her. dæiges ⁊ nihtes.

deoflon campað. ⁊ hẏs willan wẏrcð. wa him þære

mirigðe. þonne he ða handlean. hafað ⁊ sceawað.

bute he þæs ẏfeles ær geswẏce.

CRITICAL TEXT

Ǣlā, drihten lēof, ǣlā dēma God:
geara mē, ēce waldend;
ic wāt mīne sāule synnum forwundod;
gehǣl þū hȳ, heofena drihten,
and gelācna þū hȳ, līfes ealdor,
forþān ðū ēðest miht ealra lǣca
ðǣra þe gęwurde, sīde oððe wȳde.
Ǣlā, frēa beorhta, folkes scippend:
gemilsa þȳn mōd mē tō gōde,
sile þȳne āre þīnum earminge.
Se byð earming þe on eorðan hēr,
dæiges and nihtes, dēoflon campað,
and hys willan wyrcð; wā him þǣre mirigðe
þonne he ðā handlēan hafað and scēawað
būte hē þæs yfeles ǣr geswȳce.

Se bẏð eadig. se þe on eorðan her. dæiges ⁊ nẏhtes
drihtne hẏræð. ⁊ a hẏs willan wẏrcð. wel hẏm þæs
geweorkes. ðonne he ða handlean. hafað ⁊ sceawað .
gẏf he ealteawne. ende gedreogeð.

Æla leohtes leoht. æla lẏfes wẏnn. getiþa me. tirea
dig kẏning. þonne ic minre sawle. swegles bẏdde.
ece are. þu eart eaðe god. hæfst ⁊ waldest. ana ofer
ealle . eorðan ⁊ heofonas . sẏddra gesceafta.

Ðu eart soð meotod. ana ofer ealle . eorðbugende.
swilce on heofonum up. þu eart hælend god.

[folio 136v]

Ne mæg þe aherian. hæleða ænig. þeh us geso[mni]e
geond sidne grund. men ofer moldan. geond ealne

Ne mage we næfre asæcgan. ꝥ middaneard.
ne þæt soðe witan. hu þu æðele eart. ece drihten.

Se byð ēadig, se þe on eorðan hēr,
dæiges and nyhtes drihtne hȳræð
and ā hys willan wyrcð; wel hym þæs geweorkes
ðonne he ðā handlēan hafað and scēawað,
gyf he ealtēawne ende gedrēogeð.
Ǣlā lēohtes lēoht, ǣlā lȳfes wynn:
getīþa mē, tīrēadig kyning,
þonne ic mīnre sāwle swegles bydde
ēce āre; þū eart ēaðe God,
hæfst and waldest
āna ofer ealle eorðan and heofonas
sȳddra gesceafta. Ðū eart sōð meotod
āna ofer ealle eorðbūgende,
swilce on heofonum up þū eart hælend God.
Ne mæg þē āherian hæleða ǣnig,
þēh ūs gesomnie geond sīdne grund
men ofer moldan geond ealne middaneard.
Ne mage wē nǣfre āsæcgan ne þæt sōðe witan
hū þū æðele eart, ēce drihten.

Ne þeah engla werod. up on heofenum. snotra tosom
ne. sæcgan ongunnon. ne magon hẏ næfre areccean
ne þ<æt> gerim wẏtan. hu þu mære eart. mihtig drihten
ac is wunder mẏcel. wealdend engla. gif þu hit sẏlf
a wast. sigores ealdor. hu þu mære eart. mihtig ⁊
mægenstrang. ealra kẏninga kẏning. crist lifiend
ealra worulda scippend. wealdend engla. ealra duge
þa duguð. drihten hælend .

Ðu eart se æðela. þe on ærdagum. ealra femnena wẏn.
fægere akende. on bethlee<m> ðære bẏrig. beornum to
frofre. eallu<m> to are. ẏlda bearnu<m>. þa<m> þe gelẏfað.
on lẏfiendne god. ⁊ on þ<æt> ece leoht. uppe on roderu<m>.

[Ð]ẏn mægen ẏs swa mære. mihtig drihten. swa þæt
ænig ne wat. eorðbuende. þa deopnesse. drihtnes mih
ta. ne þ<æt> ænig ne wat. engla hades. þa heahnisse. heo

Ne þēah engla werod ūp on heofenum
snotra tōsomne sæcgan ongunnon,
ne magon hȳ næfre āreccean ne þæt gerīm wytan
hū þū mære eart, mihtig drihten;
ac is wunder mycel, wealdend engla,
gif þū hit sylfa wāst, sigores ealdor,
hū þū mære eart, mihtig and mægenstrang
ealra kyninga kyning, Crīst lifiende,
ealra worulda scippend, wealdend engla,
ealra dugeþa duguð, drihten hælend.
Ðū eart se æðela þe on ærdagum
ealra fēmnena wyn fægere akende
on Bethleem ðære byrig beornum tō frofre,
eallum tō āre ylda bearnum,
þām þe gelȳfað on lyfiendne God
and on þæt ēce lēoht ūppe on roderum.
Ðȳn mægen ys swā mære, mihtig drihten,
swā þæt ǣnig ne wāt eorðbūendra
þā dēopnesse drihtnes mihta,
ne þæt ǣnig ne wāt engla hādes

Ic þe andette. ælmihtig god. Ꝺ fena kẏninges.

þæt ic gelẏfe on þe. leofa hælend. þæt þu eart se mic

cla . ⁊ se mægenstranga . ⁊ se eadmoda ealra goda. ⁊

[folio 137r]

se ece kẏning. ealra gesceafta. ⁊ ic eom se litla for

þe ⁊ se lẏðra man. se her sẏngige. swiðe genehhe. dæ

ges ⁊ nihtes. do swa ic ne sceolde. hwile mid weorce. hwi

le mid worde. hwile mid geþohte. þearle scẏldi. inwit

niðas: oft ⁊ gelome.

Ac ic þe halsige nu. heofena drihten. ⁊ gebidde me to þe

bearna selost. þæt ðu gemilsige me. mihtig drihten .

heofena heahkẏning. ⁊ se halga gast. ⁊ gefẏlste

me. fæder ælmihtig. þ<æt> ic þinne willan gewẏrcean mæ

ge. ær ic of þẏsu<m> hlænan. lẏfe gehweorfe.

þā hēahnisse heofena kyninges.
Ic þē andette, ælmihtig God,
þæt ic gelȳfe on þē, lēofa hǣlend,
þæt þū eart se miccla and se mægenstranga
and se ēadmōda ealra goda
and se ēce kyning ealra gesceafta,
and ic eom se lītla for þē and se lyðra man,
se hēr syngige swīðe genehhe,
dæges and nihtes, dō swā ic ne sceolde:
hwīle mid weorce, hwīle mid worde,
hwīle mid geþōhte, þearle scyldi,
inwitnīðas oft and gelōme.
Ac ic þē hālsige nū, heofena drihten,
and gebidde mē to þē, bearna sēlost,
þæt ðū gemilsige mē, mihtig drihten,
heofena hēahkyning, and se hālga gāst,
and gefylste mē, fæder ælmihtig,
þæt ic þīnne willan gewyrcean mæge
ǣr ic of þysum hlǣnan lȳfe gehweorfe.

Ne forweorn þu me. wuldres drihten. ac getẏþa
me. tẏreadig kẏning. læt me mid englu<m>. up siðian.
sittan on swegle. herian heofonas god haligu<m> reor
de. a butan ende. amen.

Ne forweorn þū mē, wuldres drihten,
ac getȳþa mē, tȳrēadig kyning;
lǣt mē mid englum up siðian,
sittan on swegle,
herian heofonas God hāligum reorde
ā būtan ende. amen.

NOTES

1: Lamb. 427 MS Eala: *Lambeth 427's* Eala *rather than the twelfth-century* Ӕla *most probably represents the spelling of the original poem; however, since the complete piece lies in the twelfth-century book, I preserve the spelling of the latter, odd as it may seem to the eye.*
10: Jul. A.ii MS þyne: *I prefer the unambiguous dative singular of Lamb. 427,* þinum, *rather than changing both forms to an artificial one* (þynum) *as in ASPR VI, 94. Nevertheless the Julius A. ii reading is likely a copying error, the scribe writing* þyne *a second time instead of* þynum.
11: Jul. A.ii MS þeo on: *Julius A. ii has a superfluous 'o' in this phrase.*
12: Jul. A. ii MS deoflon: *this is a late reading of the dative plural where the '-um' inflection has levelled to '-on'; while we have evidence for such levelling as early as the beginning of the eleventh century, the reading from Lamb. 427 is* deoflu<m>. *ASPR VI emends to dative singular* deofle *on the grounds that* hys, *line 13, refers to the devil, singular.*
14: he ða: *these two words are missing in Lamb. 427, evidently dropped by eyeskip at the end of MS line 9 of the poem fragment, when the scribe copied* handlean *where* he ða *should first have appeared.*
15: Lamb. 427 MS butan: butan *is the more widely used form of the conjunction, but* bute *is an acceptable reading and needs no emendation.*
25: *A half-line is missing here, most probably the b-line; the omission comes toward the end of folio 136r, MS line 18, just before the phrase* ana ofer ealle. *Interestingly, the dropped half-line of verse pulls the spatialized pairing of words or phrases (see above, p. 158) out of visual balance, since this* ana ofer ealle *ought to stand three or four words in toward the centre of a line as it does on MS line 20, just below, and the*

addition of a half-line of verse at the end of MS line 18 would have moved it to precisely the right place.

42: MS lifiend: *this present participle missing its terminal 'e' occurs at the very end of line 10 on folio 136v, and I have emended it accordingly. However the terminal 'd' has a 'flag' at the end of its ascender; it is impossible to tell, given the damage to the MS, if this was intended as some kind of abbreviation indicating 'e'.*

52: MS eorðbuende: *Dobbie does not emend this reading, which appears lexically and morphologically to be nominative or accusative plural; taken with* ænig, *which governs the singular verb* wat, *its form should more correctly be genitive plural, both to construct the partitive genitive that logic requires here and to reflect the partitive genitive found in the parallel construction of line 54. It is possible that this reading was somehow carried forward from line 28,* eorðbugende, *where it is accusative plural.*

73: MS hlænan: *earlier editors including Dobbie have emended this adjective to its more common form* lænan, *which we might expect in a line with 'l' alliteration;* þis læne lif, *'this transitory life,' is a "very common homiletic phrase, rather old-fashioned [even] in [Wulfstan's] time" (Bethurum,* Homilies of Wulfstan, *342) and is found both in this eleventh-century piece and in "Vision of the Rood," which belongs at its latest possible date to the end of the tenth century (see p. 37). I find* hlænan *an interesting enough lexical relic which might point to regional dialect that I have left it unchanged.*

76: up siðian: *Dobbie assumes a missing half-line at 77b, but it is more likely that eyeskip accounts for a dropped half-line between* up siðian *at the very end of MS line 12 on folio 137r, and* sittan on swegle *which begins MS line 13. I therefore posit a lost half-line that would fill 77a and consist of an infinitive (governed by* læt *in line 76a) and a short prepositional phrase or an adverb.*

Vision of the Rood

Nine of the poems in this edition are new to the classroom setting, but this tenth is one of the crown jewels of Anglo-Saxon verse, widely anthologized for student use for as long as Old English has formed part of university curricula. As one of the first "dream" or "vision" poems in the English language, it is unique as a magnificently crafted and conceptualized piece of Anglo-Saxon writing, since its central import is an account of the crucifixion of Christ as narrated by the Rood (OE *rod*, "cross") on which he suffered. It remains in a single copy only on the pages of an Anglo-Saxon collection of homilies and religious verse that found its way to Vercelli in Italy. The catalogued canon of published scholarship on this piece totalled 136 books and articles between 1972 and 2004 alone, and at least 15 studies proposing liturgical influences on it have appeared in the last 35 years.

Its traditional editorial name, "Dream of the Rood," will likely be irreplaceable for these reasons, although scholars have contended for some time with the fact that the nameless Visionary to whom the Rood speaks is not apparently asleep: while he or she tells us that *swefna cyst*, "the best of dreams," came as a miracle (line 1), the noun *swefn* can also mean "vision," and the Visionary takes pains to point out that the miracle occurred during the night *syðþan reordberend reste wunedon*, "after speech-bearers [i.e. human beings] were occupied with rest" (line 3). In like manner, at the close of the Rood's speech, we hear of no awakening by the Visionary, only that *Gebæd ic me þa to þan beame bliðe mode elne mycle þær ic ana wæs mæte werede*, "with joyful mind and great zeal I prayed for myself then to the Tree where I was alone with little company" (lines 122–25; emphasis mine); here the Visionary is repeating the Rood's description of Christ's body in the tomb from line 69b, where, *mæte werede* ("devoid of company," the *litotes,* or understatement, being repeated), the Saviour "rests," neither sleeping nor dead but in a condition of liminality that the Rood, who had seen only the corpses taken down after execution, could not comprehend. The Visionary is therefore presumed to be in a similarly liminal state, which is not a dreaming sleep for the duration of the miracle since he or she is already *þær ic ana wæs mæte werede*, "where I was alone with little company." Early editors Dickins and Ross note that "[it] is entirely different from any other in which a dream is described."[1] It is for these reasons that I prefer the title "Vision of the Rood."

In 1919, Howard Patch examined the liturgical influences on this poem in a study that was surprisingly inconclusive; however, it marked the start of a trend by liturgical scholars to push back the boundaries of understanding the liturgical inspiration that lay behind such a remarkable piece. Over the last thirty years, Éamonn Ó Carragáin has been the foremost investigator in this regard, proposing early Roman forms and services influencing its composition, and linking *Vision of the Rood* through liturgy with the brief lapidary poem carved in runes on the side of the Ruthwell Cross which shares its language.[2] While *Vision of the Rood* contains no intercalated Latin text and depends on no single liturgical source, it overtly quotes a section of the baptismal Creed at lines 97b–109, and scholars have found it a treasure-house of references to the rituals of Holy Week leading up to Easter Sunday. Most recently, investigations of it have centred on the baptismal liturgy of Holy Saturday and on the Veneration of the Cross of Good Friday afternoon.[3]

A singular hallmark of this poem is polysemy, a device whereby the poet uses a word with several discrete meanings in such a way that all of them might apply simultaneously *in potentia* to the context. A good example of this occurs with the verb *byrigde* in line 101—*Deað he þær byrigde*—which can mean, at the same time, "there he tasted death" and "there he buried [i.e. destroyed] death."[4] This example of polysemy draws its effect from gospel

1 Bruce Dickins and Alan S.C. Ross, eds., *The Dream of the Rood* (London: Methuen, 1934; repr. 1965), 18.

2 A good compendium of Ó Carragáin's scholarship on this poem is his 2005 volume, *Ritual and the Rood: Liturgical Images and the Old English Poems of the* Dream of the Rood *Tradition.*

3 See Elaine Treharne, "'Hiht wæs geniwad': Rebirth in *The Dream of the Rood*," *The Place of the Cross in Anglo-Saxon England*, ed. Catherine E. Karkov, Sarah Larratt Keefer, and Karen L. Jolly, Publications of the Manchester Centre for Anglo-Saxon Studies 4 (Woodbridge: Boydell, 2006), 145–57; and Keefer, "Revisiting Good Friday."

4 See the translation "error" made by the Worcester Tremulous Hand in *Baptismal Creed* when glossing this word, pp. 84 and 90, above.

references to Christ, who used the phrase "tasting death" when describing those who serve God,[5] together with a clause from the Preface to the Mass for Easter Sunday which reads *qui mortem nostram moriendo destruxit et uitam resurgendo reparauit*, "who by dying has destroyed our death and by arising, has restored life."[6] The poet was well-enough versed in scriptural teachings and the liturgy of the Church to be able to construct such a "loaded" reference. Elsewhere I have more fully described the polysemy inherent in the thematic make-up of the *Vision of the Rood*:

> But within this exterior and fictional superimposition lie a considerable number of binary pairs, all belonging to the same conclusion that "either/and" brings with it: that both alternatives must be true. . . . In line 4b, *syllicre treow* (a more rare tree), that odd comparative adjectival form accompanying the neuter noun, creates a split-second echo whereby, were the noun *treow* feminine, "faith," instead of neuter, "tree," the accompanying adjective with its "re" ending could be plausibly feminine as well . . . the verb *beran* (carry, bear) begins a progressive development in polarities: in this half of the poem we see the Rood bear Christ so that both are buried in death, but in the second half, the faithful must ultimately bear "on their breasts the best of signs," in *breostum . . . beacna selest*, either as the spiritual faith (semantic of the feminine noun *treow*, "belief") in the Redeemer and His Redemption, and as the physical emblem of that faith (semantic of the neuter noun *treow*, "tree"). . . . In line 30a, the Rood is cut off from its *stefn*, "root," but that act engenders another process by which, like the grieving disciples of lines 70–1, it finds a *stefn*, "voice," with which to relate and witness.[7]

Where *Vision of the Rood* has punctuation (described as "vary[ing] strangely . . . with no consistency in [its] use"),[8] its puncti are on the line rather than *elevati*, and for the most part they indicate syntax rather than line end or caesura, but even then they are inconsistent. Capitals are infrequent and may simply be larger forms of a minuscule letter, such as the large "a" on folio 104v, manuscript line 15, or the large "h" on the same folio five lines further

5 Matthew 16:28; see also Mark 8:39; John 8:52.

6 Richter and Schönfelder, *Sacramentarium Fuldense*, 88. See also Orchard, *Leofric Missal*, II, 176. Both of these service-books are from the same century as the *Vision of the Rood*'s manuscript witness.

7 Sarah Larratt Keefer, "'Either/And' as 'Style' in Anglo-Saxon Christian Verse," *Anglo-Saxon Styles*, ed. Catherine E. Karkov and George H. Brown (Binghamton: SUNY P, 2003), 179–200, 185–86.

8 Krapp, ASPR II, xxx.

down. I have tried to follow these manuscript indicators when constructing sentence breaks in the critical text of this poem—even though such practice has resulted in five new sentences starting with *Ac*, "however" (verse lines 11, 43, 115, 119 and 132)—since ignoring evidence of this kind, which lies much closer to the date of composition than modern editions can hope to do, can obscure meaning, as we saw in *Ah, Beloved Lord*. At least one half-line and possibly a longer section of the poem are missing at verse line 76, but we have no idea of the extent of the loss. Scholars believe that the text was missing from the exemplar for the Vercelli copy as well, in part because of the location of the evident omission in its manuscript witness, mid-page on folio 105v, partway through manuscript line 14, where there is no good reason for eyeskip to have occurred.

Metrically, *Vision of the Rood* is particularly interesting for the significant number of hypermetric lines it contains.[9] Scholars have debated over which lines to include in this group (some are only potentially hypermetric) and over what the significance of their construction might have been, but nothing in any way conclusive has been agreed upon. Different editorial conventions have presented the poem's hypermetric lines visually in different ways: the majority of twentieth-century editors simply make them longer to create "wrap-around," but I prefer to follow the model of decreasing the left margin so that the lines are more visible to the reading eye.[10]

9 Old English half-lines that are expanded so as to include an extra series of drop-lift relations; each hypermetric half-line will generally contain an extra lift and several extra drops.

10 Used by Mitchell and Robinson in *A Guide to Old English*, 258–63, and thus made popular to a generation of Old English students and instructors.

SEMI-DIPLOMATIC TEXT
(folios 104v, line 7 – folio 106r, line 32)

Hwæt ic swefna cẏst secgan wylle hæt me gemætte

to midre nihte syðþan reordberend reste wunedon.

þuhte me þæt ic gesawe syllicre treow on lyft

lædan leohte bewunden beama beorhtost eall þæt

beacen wæs begoten mid golde gimmas stodon fægere

æt foldan sceatum . swylce þær fife wæron uppe

on þam eaxlegespanne beheoldon þær engel dryht

nes ealle fægere þurh forðgèsceaft ne wæs ðær huru

fracodes gealga . ac hine þær beheoldon halige gastas

men ofer moldan ⁊ eall þeos mære gesceaft :,

Syllic wæs se sigebeam ⁊ ic synnu<m> fah forwunded

mid wommu<m> geseah ic wuldres treow . wædum geweor

ðode wynnu<m> scinan gegyred mid golde gimmas hæfdon

bewrigene weorðlice wealdes treow:, hwæðre ic

þurh þæt gold ongytan meahte earmra ærgewin

CRITICAL TEXT

Hwæt, ic swefna cyst   secgan wylle,
hwæt mē gemǣtte   tō midre nihte
syðþan reordberend   reste wunedon;
þūhte mē þæt ic gesāwe   syllicre trēow
on lyft lǣdan   lēohte bewunden,
bēama beorhtost: eall þæt bēacen wæs
begoten mid golde,   gimmas stōdon
fægere æt foldan scēatum,   swylce þǣr fīfe wǣron
uppe on þam eaxlegespanne;   behēoldon þǣr engel dryhtnes ealle
fægere þurh forðgesceaft,   ne wæs ðǣr hūru fracodes gealga.
Ac hine þǣr behēoldon   hālige gāstas,
men ofer moldan   and eall þēos mǣre gesceaft.
Syllic wæs se sigebēam and ic synnum fāh,
forwunded mid wommum;   geseah ic wuldres trēow
wǣdum geweorðod   wynnum scīnan,
gegyred mid golde: gimmas hæfdon
bewrigene weorðlīce   wealdendes trēow.
Hwæðre ic þurh þæt gold ongytan meahte

þæt hit ærest ongan swætan on þa swiðran healfe
eall ic wæs mid surgum gedrefed. Forht ic wæs for
þære fægran gesyhðe geseah ic þæt fuse beacen .
[folio 105r]
wendan wædum ⁊ bleom hwilum hit wæs mid wætan bestemed . beswyled
mid swátes gange. hwilum mid since gegyrwed . hwæðre ic þær
licgende lange hwile. beheold hreowcearig . hælendes treow .
oððæt ic gehyrde þæt hit hleoðrode ongan þa word sprecan
wudu selesta þæt wæs geara iu . ic þæt gyta geman . þæt ic wæs
aheawen holtes on ende astyred of stefne minu<m> genaman
me ðær strange feondas geworhton him þær to wæfersyne
heton me heora wergas hebban . bæron me ðær beornas
on eaxlum . oððæt hie me on beorg asetton gefæstnodon me
þær feondas genoge . geseah ic þa frean mancynnes efstan
elne mycle . þæt he me wolde on gestigan . þær ic þa ne dorste
ofer dryhtnes word bugan oððe berstan . þa ic bifian geseah
eorðan sceatas ealle ic mihte feondas gefyllan hwæðre

earmra ǣrgewin, þæt hit ǣrest ongan
swǣtan on þā swīðran healfe; eall ic wæs mid sorgum gedrēfed.
Forht ic wæs for þǣre fægran gesyhðe; geseah ic þæt fūse bēacen
wendan wǣdum and blēom: hwīlum hit wæs mid wǣtan bestēmed,
beswyled mid swātes gange. Hwīlum mid since gegyrwed.
Hwæðre ic þǣr licgende lange hwīle
behēold hrēowcearig hælendes trēow
oððæt ic gehȳrde þæt hit hlēoðrode;
ongan þā word sprecan wudu sēlesta:
“þæt wæs geāra iū — ic þæt gȳta geman —
þæt ic wæs āhēawen holtes on ende,
āstyred of stefne mīnum: genāman mē ðǣr strange fēondas,
geworhton him þǣr tō wǣfersȳne, hēton mē heora wergas hebban;
bǣron mē ðǣr beornas on eaxlum oððæt hīe mē on beorg āsetton;
gefæstnodon mē þǣr fēondas genōge; geseah ic þā frēan mancynnes
efstan elne mycle þæt hē mē wolde on gestīgan;
þǣr ic þa ne dorste ofer dryhtnes word
būgan oððe berstan þā ic bifian geseah
eorðan scēatas; ealle ic mihte
fēondas gefyllan hwæðre ic fæste stōd.

ic fæste stod . Ongyrede hine þa geong hæleð þæt wæs god
ælmihtig strang ⁊ stiðmod . gestah he on gealgan heanne
modig on manigra gesyhðe . þa he wolde mancyn lysan .
bifode ic þa me se beorn ymbclypte . ne dorste ic hwæðre
bugan to eorðan feallan to foldan sceatu<m> . ac ic sceolde fæste
standan. Rod wæs ic aræred . ahof ic ricne cyning heofona
hlaford . hyldan me ne dorste . þurh drifan hi me mid
deorcan næglu<m> . on me syndon þa dolg gesiene opene inwid
hlemmas . ne dorste ic hira nænigu<m> sceððan bysmeredon hie
unc butu ætgædere eall ic wæs mid blode bestemed . begoten of
þæs guman sidan . siððan he hæfde his gast onsended . feala
ic on þam beorge gebiden hæbbe wraðra wyrda . geseah ic weruda
god þearle þenian þystro hæfdon bewrigen mid wolcnum
wealdendes hræw . scirne sciman sceadu forð eode . wann
under wolcnum weop eal gesceaft cwiðdon cyninges fyll
crist wæs on rode hwæðere þær fuse feorran cwoman to

"Ongyrede hine þā geong hæleð þæt wæs God ælmihtig,
strang and stīðmōd; gestāh hē on gealgan hēanne,
mōdig on manigra gesyhðe, þā hē wolde mancyn lȳsan;
bifode ic þā mē se beorn ymbclypte: ne dorste ic hwæðre būgan tō eorðan,
feallan tō foldan scēatum. Ac ic sceolde fæste standan.
"Rōd wæs ic āræred; āhōf ic rīcne cyning,
heofona hlāford; hyldan mē ne dorste;
þurhdrifan hī mē mid deorcan næglum: on mē syndon þā dolg gesiene,
opene inwidhlemmas; ne dorste ic hira nǣnigum sceððan;
bysmeredon hīe unc būtū ætgædere; eall ic wæs mid blōde bestēmed,
begoten of þæs guman sīdan siððan hē hæfde his gāst onsended.
"Feala ic on þām beorge gebiden hæbbe
wrāðra wyrda: geseah ic weruda God
þearle þenian; þȳstro hæfdon
bewrigen mid wolcnum wealdendes hrǣw,
scīrne scīman; sceadu forð ēode,
wann under wolcnum; wēop eal gesceaft,
cwīðdon cyninges fyll: Crīst wæs on rōde;
hwæðere þǣr fūse feorran cwōman

þam æðelinge ic þæt eall beheold . Sare ic wæs mid gedrefed

hnag ic hwæðre þam secgu<m> to handa eaðmod elne mycle

genamon hie þær ælmihtigne god ahofon hine of ðam

[folio 105v]

hefian wite forleton me þa hilderincas standan steame

bedrifenne eall ic wæs mid strælum forwundod . aledon hie

ðær limwerigne gestodon him æt his lices heafdu<m> beheoldon hie

ðær heofenes dryhten ⁊ he hine ðær hwile reste meðe æfter

ðam miclan gewinne. Ongunnon him þa moldærn wyrcan

beornas on banan gesyhðe curfon hie ðæt of beorhtan stane

gesetton hie ðær on sigora wealdend ongunnon him þa sorh

leoð galan earme on þa æfentide þa hie woldon eft siðian

meðe fram þam mæran þeodne reste he ðær mæte weorode

hwæðere we ðær reotende gode hwile . stodon on staðole syððan

up gewat hilderinca . hræw colode fæger feorgbold þa us

man fyllan ongan . ealle to eorðan þæt wæs egeslic wyrd

bedealf us man on deopan seaþe hwæðre me þær dryhtnes

þegnas freondas gefrunon gyredon me golde ⁊ seolfre .

tō þām æðelinge; ic þæt eall behēold.
Sāre ic wæs mid sorgum gedrefed; hnāg ic hwæðre þām secgum tō handa
ēaðmōd elne mycle; genāmon hīe þǣr ælmihtigne God,
āhofon hine of ðām hefian wīte; forlēton mē þā hilderincas
standan stēame bedrifenne; eall ic wæs mid strǣlum forwundod;
Ālēdon hīe ðǣr limwērigne, gestōdon him æt his līces hēafdum,
behēoldon hīe ðǣr heofenes dryhten and hē hine ðǣr hwīle reste,
mēðe æfter ðām miclan gewinne. Ongunnon him þā moldærn wyrcan
beornas on banan gesyhðe; curfon hīe ðæt of beorhtan stāne,
gesetton hīe ðǣron sigora wealdend, ongunnon him þā sorhlēoð galan
earme on þā ǣfentīde; þā hīe woldon eft sīðian
mēðe fram þām mǣran þēodne; reste hē ðǣr mǣte weorode;
hwæðere wē ðǣr rēotende gōde hwile
stōdon on staðole: stefn up gewāt
hilderinca, hrǣw cōlode
fæger feorgbold; þā ūs man fyllan ongan
ealle tō eorðan: þæt wæs egeslic wyrd;
bedealf ūs man on dēopan sēaþe; hwæðre mē þǣr dryhtnes þegnas,
frēondas gefrūnon . . .
gyredon mē golde and seolfre.

Nu ðu miht gehyran hæleð min se leofa þæt ic bealuwara

weorc gebiden hæbbe sarra sorga is nu sæl cumen þæt me

weorðiað wide ⁊ side menn ofer moldan ⁊ eall þeos mære

gesceaft . gebiddaþ him to þyssu<m> beacne on me bearn godes

þrowode hwile forþan ic þrymfæst nu . hlifige under

heofenu<m> . ⁊ ic hælan mæg . æghwylcne anra þara þe him bið

egesa to me iu ic wæs geworden wita heardost . leodum la

ðost ær þan ic him lifes weg rihtne gerymde reordbe

rendu<m> hwæt me þa geweorðode wuldres ealdor ofer holm

wudu heofonrices weard, swylce swa he his modor eac

marian sylfe ælmihtig god . for ealle menn geweorðode

ofer eall wifa cynn . Nu ic þe hate hæleð . min se leofa .

þæt ðu þas gesyhðe secge mannu<m> onwreoh wordu<m> þæt hit is

"Nū ðū miht gehȳran,   hæleð mīn se lēofa,
þæt ic bealuwara weorc   gebiden hæbbe,
sārra sorga: is nū sǣl cumen
þæt mē weorðiað   wīde and sīde
menn ofer moldan and eall þēos mǣre gesceaft
gebiddaþ him tō þyssum bēacne;   on mē bearn Godes
þrōwode hwīle;   forþan ic þrymfæst nū
hlīfige under heofenum   and ic hǣlan mæg
ǣghwylcne ānra   þāra þe him bið egesa tō mē;
iū ic wæs geworden   wīta heardost,
lēodum lāðost   ǣr þan ic him līfes weg
rihtne gerȳmde   reordberendum;
hwæt, mē þā geweorðode   wuldres ealdor
ofer holtwudu,   heofonrīces weard,
swylce swā he his mōdor ēac, Marīan sylfe,
ælmihtig God,   for ealle menn
geweorðode   ofer eall wīfa cynn.
"Nū ic þē hāte,   hæleð mīn se lēofa,
þæt ðū þās gesyhðe   secge mannum,
onwrēoh wordum   þæt hit is wuldres bēam

wuldres beam se ðe ælmihtig god on þrowode. for man

cynnes manegu<m> synnu<m> . ⁊ adomes ealdge wyrhtu<m> deað he

þær byrigde hwæðere eft dryhten aras mid his miclan

mihte mannu<m> to helpe he ða on heofenas astag . hider

eft fundaþ on þysne middangeard mancynn secan on

[folio 106r]

domdæge dryhten sylfa ælmihtig god ⁊ his englas mid . þæt he

þonne wile deman se ah domes geweald anra gehwylcu<m> swa he

him ærur her on þyssum lænum life geearnaþ . ne mæg þær

ænig unforht wesan . for þam worde . þe se wealdend cwyð . fri

neð he for þære mænige hwær se man sie se ðe for dryht

nes naman deaðes wo,de [l] biteres onbyrigan swa he ær on

ðam beame dyde . ac hie þonne forhtiað · ⁊ fea þencaþ hwæt hie to

criste cweðan onginnen . Ne þearf ðær þonne ænig unforht

---

wo,de: a gap is left where there is an erasure, and then an "l" is superscribed above *wode* with an insertion mark like a comma below.

se ðe ælmihtig God   on þrōwode
for mancynnes   manegum synnum
and Adomes   ealdgewyrhtum;
dēað hē þǣr byrigde,   hwæðere eft dryhten ārās
mid his miclan mihte   mannum tō helpe;
hē ðā on heofenas āstāg;   hider eft fundaþ
on þysne middangeard   mancynn sēcan
on dōmdæge   dryhten sylfa,
ælmihtig God   and his englas mid,
þæt hē þonne wile dēman,   se āh dōmes geweald,
ānra gehwylcum   swā hē him ǣrur hēr
on þyssum lǣnum   līfe geearnaþ;
ne mæg þær ǣnig   unforht wesan
for þām worde   þe se wealdend cwyð:
frīneð hē for þǣre mænige   hwǣr se man sīe
se ðe for dryhtnes naman   dēaðes wolde
biteres onbyrigan   swā hē ǣr on ðām bēame dyde.
Ac hīe þonne forhtiað   and fēa þencaþ
hwæt hie tō Crīste   cweðan onginnen.
Ne þearf ðǣr þonne ǣnig   anforht wesan

wesan þe him ær in breostu<m> bereð beacna selest.. Ac ðurh

ða rode sceal rice gesecan of eorðwege æghwylc sawl seo þe

mid wealdende wunian þenceð ge bæd ic me þa to þan beame

bliðe · mode elne mycle þær ic ana wæs mæte werede wæs

modsefa afysed on forðwege feala ealra gebad langung

ic
hwila is me nu lifes hyht þæt, þone sigebeam secan mote

ana oftor þonne ealle men well weorþian me is willa to ðam

mycel on mode ⁊ min mundbyrd is geriht to þære rode ·

Nah ic ricra feala freonda on foldan   ac hie forð heonon

gewiton of worulde dreamum sohton him wuldres cyning

lifiaþ nu on heofenu<m> mid heahfædere wuniaþ on wuldre ⁊ ic wene

me daga gehwylce hwænne me dryhtnes rod ꝥe ic her on eor

þæt,: an insertion mark follows *þæt*, and *ic* is included above in superscription.
foldan: the gap after foldan marks an erasure.
ꝥe: the MS appears to have the scribal abbreviation for *þæt* (a thorn with a stroke running through its ascender) and then "e", as though the scribe had anticipated the next clause as subordinate rather than relative after the relative particle *þe*.

þe him ǣr in brēostum bereð bēacna selest.
Ac ðurh ðā rōde sceal rīce gesēcan
of eorðwege ǣghwylc sāwl,
sēo þe mid wealdende wunian þenceð."
Gebæd ic mē þā tō þān bēame blīðe mōde
elne mycle þǣr ic āna wæs
mǣte werede; wæs mōdsefa
āfȳsed on forðwege; feala ealra gebād
langunghwīla; is mē nū līfes hyht
þæt ic þone sigebēam sēcan mōte
āna oftor þonne ealle men,
well weorþian; mē is willa tō ðām
mycel on mōde and mīn mundbyrd is
geriht tō þǣre rōde. Nāh ic rīcra feala
frēonda on foldan. Ac hīe forð heonon
gewiton of worulde drēamum sōhton him wuldres cyning,
lifiaþ nū on heofenum mid hēahfædere,
wuniaþ on wuldre and ic wēne mē
daga gehwylce hwænne mē dryhtnes rōd
þe ic hēr on eorðan ǣr scēawode

ðan ær sceawode on þysson lænan life gefetige ⁊ me þon<ne> gebring<e>

þær is blis mycel dream on heofonu<m> þær is dryhtnes folc ge

seted to symle þær is singal blis ⁊ he þon<ne> asette þær ic

syþþan mot wunian on wuldre well mid þam halgu<m> dreames

brucan si me dryhten freond se ðe her on eorþan ær þrowode

on þa<m> gealgtreowe for guman synnu<m> he us onlysde ⁊ us lif

forgeaf heofonlicne ham hiht wæs geniwad mid bledu<m> ⁊ mid blisse

þa<m> þe þær bryne þolodan · se sunu wæs sigorfæst on þa<m> sið

fate mihtig ⁊ spedig · þa he mid manigeo com gasta weorode

on godes rice anwealda ælmihtig englu<m> to blisse. ⁊ eallu<m> ðam

halgu<m> þam þe on heofonu<m> ær wundedon on wuldre þa heora

wealdend cwom ælmihtig god þær his eðel wæs :~

on þysson lǣnan līfe gefetige
and mē þonne gebringe þǣr is blis mycel,
drēam on heofonum, þǣr is dryhtnes folc
geseted tō symle, þǣr is singāl blis;
and mē þonne āsette þǣr ic syþþan mōt
wunian on wuldre, well mid þām hālgum
drēames brūcan; sī mē dryhten frēond,
se ðe hēr on eorþan ǣr þrōwode
on þām gealgtrēowe for guman synnum;
hē ūs onlȳsde and ūs līf forgeaf,
heofonlicne hām; hiht wæs genīwad
mid blēdum and mid blisse þām þe þǣr bryne þolodan;
se sunu wæs sigorfæst on þām sīðfate,
mihtig and spēdig þā hē mid manigeo cōm
gāsta weorode on Godes rīce,
anwealda ælmihtig, englum tō blisse
and eallum ðām hālgum þām þe on heofonum ǣr
wunedon on wuldre, þā heora wealdend cwōm,
ælmihtig God, þǣr his ēðel wæs.

NOTES

2: MS hæt: *the poem's opening word* Hwæt *(an interjection) is written with a very large insular* 'h' *and its second letter, the rune* 'wyn' *(* ƿ *), is enclosed in this large 'h's inverted bowl: the scribe may have written the second* hwæt *(a pronoun), once again omitting its wyn.*
3: reste wunedon: *some early editors questioned whether* reste *should be taken as a dative singular ('dwelt in rest') or as an accusative singular ('occupied their bed'): both are possible.*
9: MS eaxlegespanne: *some editors emend to* eaxlgespanne; *Krapp (ASPR II, p. 61) does not, and DOE allows for both possibilities; I have left it unemended.*
15: MS geweorðode: *Krapp (ASPR II, 61) leaves this unchanged, but here I follow more recent editors who emend it as a singular form of a past participle.*
17: MS bewrigene: *as with* geweorðod *in line 15, this remains unchanged in ASPR II (61), but many modern editors apparently see no good grammatical reason for assuming the terminal 'e' to be an inflection, and emend it accordingly back to an uninflected form. However, DOE preserves the MS reading, perhaps assuming it to be a masculine accusative singular, and therefore I leave it unaltered;* MS wealdes: *leaving this word unemended disrupts both the metre and sense of its line, and Dickins and Ross rightly note (p. 23) that in the scribe's exemplar text this might have read* wealdēdes (*with the suspension mark indicating a missing 'n'); it would be easy to read such a word as* wealdes, *which would account for the error. With other editors, I therefore emend the word to read* wealdendes, *which fulfils metrical exigency and makes good sense.*
20: MS surgum*: this reading is clearly a scribal error and needs emendation to* sorgum. *The same word is omitted from an identical phrase at the end of MS line 30 on folio 105r (verse line 59); using the construction here allowed the emendation to be made in the later line.*
23b: *although this is an unlikely new sentence as it lacks a finite verb, consistency in adhering to MS evidence (the capital 'H') requires that we read this as a new thought (although see line 38 where a similar construction does not carry a capital 'h' for* hwæðre*) and therefore that we understand the verb* wæs *in order to complete the clause.*
40: *I am not convinced that 40b carries three strong beats to make this line hypermetric, and have laid it out accordingly.*
47: MS nænigum: *some editors emend this to* ænigum *to provide for alliteration; however this is a hypermetric line in whose b-line the first strong stress falls on the verb* dorste, *which has no comparable alliterator in the a-line, so there is no standardization to its design. It seems plausible that the intensity of the double negative* ne . . . nænigum *derives either from the exemplar used by the Vercelli scribe or from a scribal reflex to intensify the obedient refusal of the Rood—a retainer who does not question his lord's authority—to destroy those crucifying Christ.*

59: MS mid [sorgum] gedrefed: *The emendation adding* sorgum *to this clause is a logical one: it completes the syntax, balances the alliteration, and echoes line 20b; since the word was dropped at the end of MS line 30, folio 105r, it is doubtless a scribal error.*
65: MS moldærn: *most editors emend this reading to* moldern, *but CHM (p. 240) includes it as a neuter noun form so I have left it unaltered.*
68: *I am not convinced that this line is hypermetric, and have laid it out accordingly.*
70: MS reotende: *Early editors emended this to* geotende *('dripping,' from* geotan, *'to pour') for alliteration; modern editors (including Krapp, ASPR II, 63) emend it to* greotende *('weeping') for the same reason. However* rēotan *is a viable Old English verb, in no way rarely used and more or less synonymous with* greotan, *so I prefer to leave the reading unemended since it provides, if not received metrical proficiency, at least good sense.*
71: MS syððan: *this word makes no sense where it is, since a substantive is needed to account for the possessive* hilderinca *and be the subject of* gewat, *rather than a conjunction or an adverb. Both Krapp, and Dickins and Ross, add* stefn *to the line so that it reads* syððan stefn up gewat, *but because the poem has just moved back from a lengthy hypermetric section to much shorter, metrically dramatic and terse lines as the Rood concludes its narrative of the crucifixion proper, the additional strong syllable seems jarring.* Syððan*'s position as the last word of its line on folio 105v (MS line 10) may have something to do with the error:* siðian *stands two lines above, and one might conjecture the* 's' *of* stefn *initially written, then an eyeskip upwards to MS line 8 catching the prominent 'ð' of* siðian, *and the pen returning to line 10 to produce not* stefn *but* syððan *(Krapp reconstructs it as scribal omission rather than scribal error). I therefore follow this logical but more radical emendation (most recently adopted by Mitchell and Robinson, 261) of completely replacing* syððan *with* stefn.
76: frēondas gefrūnon: *at least a half-line and possibly more of the poem is missing at this point. The missing part belongs in the middle of MS line 14, folio 105v, and may have been omitted from the exemplar as well.*
91: MS holmwudu: *most modern editors (excluding Krapp) emend this to* holtwudu *on the grounds that it is a hapax legomen ('ghost word,' unattested elsewhere) and that* holmwudu *('sea-wood'? 'wood up on a hill'?) makes less sense than the better-attested* holtwudu *('trees of the forest'). Again, this word stands at the very end of its line (MS line 23 of folio 105v) and could readily be the result of eyeskip leading to an anomalous form, so I emend in the interest of the best sense of the text.*
101: byrigde: *see Introduction, p. 176 note 4, above.*
117: MS unforht: *likely an eyeskip from the earlier* unforht *('unafraid'), nowhere near it on its line but used recently enough to stay in the memory, especially if the scribe were sub-vocalizing while copying, since it makes no sense in this context.* Anforht *('terrified'), similar in form but opposite in meaning, is the customary emendation here.*

<u>118</u>: *this may refer to the wearing of a carved or ornate cross around the neck or to receiving the sign of the cross traced in consecrated oil ('chrism') on the breast at baptism.*
<u>122</u>: *even though there is no decisive punctuation or large letter in the MS to mark a division, it is here that the Rood ceases its narrative and the Visionary once again takes it up, so I have begun with a new capital for a new sentence.*
<u>142: MS he</u>: *Krapp and other modern editors emend to* me, *although Dickins and Ross do not ("this is not necessary: there is a change of subject,* he *referring to* Dryhtnes *of l. 140," p. 34). DOE notes "with accusative object (unless otherwise indicated)" and sense 1.a makes provision for reflexive use: "to seat oneself." Therefore, although there is no ready evidence for the mistake in the manuscript, I emend accordingly to* me.

Bibliography

PRIMARY SOURCES: VERSE-TEXT EDITIONS

Dickins, Bruce, and Alan S.C. Ross, eds. *The Dream of the Rood*. London: Methuen, 1934. Repr. 1965.

Günzel, Beate, ed. *Ælfwine's Prayerbook*. HBS 108. Woodbridge: Boydell, 1993.

Krapp, George P., and Elliott van Kirk Dobbie, eds. *Anglo-Saxon Poetic Records: A Collective Edition*. 6 vols. New York: Columbia UP, 1931–53.

Lindelöf, U., ed. *Der Lambeth-Psalter*. Helsinki: Acta Societatis Scientiarum Fennicae 43, 1914.

Lumby, J.R., ed. *Be Domes Dæge, De Die Judicii: An Old English Version of the Latin Poem Ascribed to Bede*. O.S. EETS 65, 1876. Repr. Woodbridge: Boydell, 1964.

Muir, Bernard James, ed. *The Exeter Anthology of Old English Poetry*. Exeter: U of Exeter P, 1994. 2nd ed. 2000. 2 vols.

Pulsiano, Phillip, ed. *Glossed Texts, Aldhelmiana, Psalms*. ASMMF 4. Tempe, AZ: ACMRS, 1996.

Robinson, Fred C., and Eric G. Stanley, eds. *Old English Verse Texts from Many Sources: A Comprehensive Collection*. EEMF 23. Copenhagen: Rosenkilde and Bagger, 1991.

Sisam, Celia, ed. *The Vercelli Book: A Late Tenth Century Manuscript Containing Prose and Verse*. EEMF 19. Copenhagen: Rosenkilde and Bagger, 1987.

Thorpe, Benjamin, ed. and trans. *The Homilies of the Anglo-Saxon Church: The First Part, Containing the Sermones Catholici or Homilies of Ælfric*. New York: Johnson Reprint Corporation, 1971. Orig. publ. London, 1846. 2 vols.

Ure, James, ed. *The Benedictine Office: An Edition of the Old-English Text*. Edinburgh: Edinburgh UP, 1957.

SECONDARY RESOURCES

Bately, Janet. "Lexical Evidence for the Authorship of the Prose Psalms in the Paris Psalter." *ASE* 10 (1982): 69–95.

Batiffol, Pierre. *History of the Roman Breviary*. Trans. A.M.Y. Baylay. London: Longman, 1898.

Bethurum, Dorothy, ed. *The Homilies of Wulfstan*. Oxford: Clarendon Press, 1957.

Birch, W. de Grey, ed. *An Ancient Manuscript of the 8th or 9th Century*. London: Simpkin and Marshall, 1889.

Brown, George H. *The Dynamics of Literacy in Anglo-Saxon England*. Toller Memorial Lecture. Manchester: Manchester Centre for Anglo-Saxon Studies, 1995.

Cabrol, F. *Le livre de la prière antique*. Paris: H. Oudin, 1900. Trans. anon. by a Benedictine of Stanbrook as *Liturgical Prayer*. Westminster, MD: The Newman Press, 1950.

Chardonnens, László Sándor. *Anglo-Saxon Prognostics 900–1100*. Leiden: Brill, 2007.

Colgrave, Bertram, and R.A.B. Mynors, eds. and trans. *Bede's Ecclesiastical History of the English People*. Oxford: Oxford UP, 1969.

Crawford, S.J., ed. *The Old English Version of the Heptateuch*. EETS 160. London, 1922; repr. 1969.

Cross, F.L., ed. *The Oxford Dictionary of the Christian Church*. London: Oxford UP, 1958.

Crotty, Richard, trans. *Rule of St. Benedict*. Nedlands: U of Western Australia P, 1963.

Dictionary of Old English: A to G on CD-ROM. Ed. Angus Cameron, Ashley Crandell Amos, and Antonette di Paolo Healey. Toronto: Pontifical Institute of Mediaeval Studies for the Dictionary of Old English Project, 2008.

Dix, Dom Gregory. *The Shape of the Liturgy*. London: Dacre Press, 1945.

Duchesne, L. *Origines du culte chrétien*. Paris: Thorin et Fils, 1898.

Duffield, Samuel W. *The Latin Hymn-writers and their Hymns*. New York: Funk and Wagnall, 1889.

Frank, Roberta. "Late Old English *Þrymnys* 'Trinity': Scribal Nod or Word Waiting to be Born." *Old English and New: Studies in Language and Linguistics in Honor of Frederic G. Cassidy*. Ed. Joan H. Hall, A.N. Doane, and Dick Ringler. New York: Garland, 1992. 97–110.

Franzen, Christine. *The Tremulous Hand of Worcester: A Study of Old English in the Thirteenth Century*. Oxford: Clarendon Press, 1991.

Gatch, Milton McC. *Preaching and Theology in Anglo-Saxon England*. Toronto: U of Toronto P, 1977.

Greenfield, Stanley, and Daniel Calder. *A New Critical History of Old English Literature*. New York: New York UP, 1986.

Hamilton, Sarah. "Rites for Public Penance in Late Anglo-Saxon England." *Liturgy of the Late Anglo-Saxon Church*. Ed. H. Gittos and M. Bradford Bedingfield. HBS Subsidia 5. Woodbridge: Boydell, 2005. 63–103.

Jones, Christopher A., ed. *Ælfric's Letter to the Monks at Eynsham*. CSASE 24. Cambridge: Cambridge UP, 1998.

Karkov, Catherine E. "Abbot Ælfwine and the Sign of the Cross." *Cross and Cruciform in the Anglo-Saxon World*. Ed. Sarah Larratt Keefer, Karen L. Jolly, and Catherine E. Karkov. Morgantown: West Virginia UP, 2010. 105–32.

Keefer, Sarah Larratt. *The Old English Metrical Psalter: An Annotated Set of Collation Lists with the Psalter-Glosses*. Garland Reference Library of the Humanities 189. New York: Garland, 1979.

—. "*Techne* in the 'Kentish Hymn.'" *Essays in Medieval Studies: Proceedings of the Illinois Medieval Association* 6 (1989): 30–40.

—. *Psalm-Poem and Psalter-Glosses: The Latin and Old English Psalter-Text Background to "Kentish Psalm 50."* American University Studies. Series VII: Theology and Religion, vol. 95. New York: Garland, 1991.

—. "Manuals." *The Liturgical Books of Anglo-Saxon England*. Ed. R.W. Pfaff. Old English Newsletter Subsidia 23. Kalamazoo, MI: Medieval Institute Press, 1995. 99–110.

—. "Respect for the Book: A Reconsideration of 'Form,' 'Content' and 'Context' in Two Vernacular Poems." *New Approaches to Editing Old English Poetry*. Ed. Sarah Larratt Keefer and Katherine O'Brien O'Keeffe. Woodbridge: Boydell, 1998. 21–44.

—. "'Either/And' as 'Style' in Anglo-Saxon Christian Verse." *Anglo-Saxon Styles*. Ed. Catherine E. Karkov and George H. Brown. Binghamton: SUNY P, 2003. 179–200.

—. "'Ic' and 'We' in Eleventh-Century Old English Liturgical Verse." *Unlocking the Wordhord: Anglo-Saxon Studies in Memory of Edward B. Irving, Jr.* Ed. Mark C. Amodio and Katherine O'Brien O'Keeffe. Toronto: U of Toronto P, 2003. 123–46.

—. "In Closing: Amen and Doxology in Anglo-Saxon England." *Anglia* 21 (2003): 210–37.

—. "The Veneration of the Cross in Anglo-Saxon England." *Liturgy of the Late Anglo-Saxon Church*. Ed. H. Gittos and M. Bradford Bedingfield. HBS Subsidia 5. Woodbridge: Boydell, 2005. 141–82.

—. "Revisiting Good Friday, Nones: The Veneration of the Cross and *The Dream of the Rood*." *Poetry, Place and Gender: Studies in Medieval Culture in Honor of Helen Damico*. Ed. Catherine Karkov. Kalamazoo, MI: Medieval Institute Press, 2009. 38–59.

—. "Worship the Lord in the Beauty of Holiness: Latin Prayer and Old English Liturgical Poetry." *On the Aesthetics of* Beowulf *and Other Old English Poems*. Ed. John M. Hill. Toronto and London: U of Toronto P, 2010. 103–13.

Keefer, Sarah Larratt, and David R. Burrows. "Hebrew and the Hebraicum in Late Anglo-Saxon England." *ASE* 19 (1990): 67–80.

Kelly, J.N.D. *Early Christian Creeds*. Harlow: Longman, 1950. 3rd ed. 1972.
—, ed. and trans. *Rufinus: A Commentary on the Apostles' Creed.* London: Longman, 1955.
Ker, Neil R. *Catalogue of Manuscripts Containing Anglo-Saxon*. Oxford: Clarendon Press, 1957. Repr. 1990.
Knowles, Dom David. *The Monastic Order in England.* 2nd ed. Cambridge: Cambridge UP, 1966.
Lapidge, Michael, ed. *Anglo-Saxon Litanies of the Saints.* HBS 106. Woodbridge: Boydell, 1991.
Liuzza, Roy Michael, ed. *The Old English Version of the Gospels*. 2 vols. Early English Text Society 304 and 314. Oxford: Oxford UP, 1994–2000.
—. "Anglo-Saxon Prognostics in Context. A Survey and Handlist of Manuscripts." *ASE* 30 (2001): 181–230.
Logeman, H., ed. *The Rule of St Benet*. London: Trübner, 1888.
Mitchell, Bruce, and Fred C. Robinson. *A Guide to Old English.* 6th ed. Oxford: Blackwell, 2001.
Muir, Bernard James, ed. *A Pre-Conquest English Prayer-Book*. HBS 103. Woodbridge: Boydell, 1988.
Ó Carragáin, Éamonn. *Ritual and the Rood: Liturgical Images and the Old English Poems of the* Dream of the Rood *Tradition*. London: British Library Publications; Toronto: U of Toronto P, 2005.
—. "Sources or Analogues? Using Liturgical Evidence to Date 'The Dream of the Rood.'" *Cross and Cruciform in the Anglo-Saxon World*. Ed. Sarah Larratt Keefer, Karen L. Jolly, and Catherine E. Karkov. Morgantown: West Virginia UP, 2010. 136–65.
Oess, Guido, ed. *Der altenglischen Arundel-Psalter: Eine Interlinearversion in der Handschrift Arundel 60 des Britischen Museums.* Anglistische Forschungen 30. Heidelberg: Carl Winter, 1910. Repr. Amsterdam: Swets and Zeitlinger N.V., 1968.
O'Keeffe, Katherine O'Brien. *Visible Song: Transitional Literacy in Old English Verse*. CSASE 4. Cambridge: Cambridge UP, 1990.
—. "Texts and Works: Some Historical Questions on the Editing of Old English Verse." *New Historical Literary Study: Essays on Reproducing Texts, Reproducing History*. Ed. J.N. Cox and L.J. Reynolds. Princeton: Princeton UP, 1993. 54–68.
Orchard, Nicholas, ed. *The Leofric Missal*. HBS CXIV. 2 vols. London: Boydell, 2002.
Patch. Howard. "Liturgical Influence in *The Dream of the Rood*." PMLA 34 (1919): 233–57.
Raw, Barbara. *The Art and Background of Old English Poetry.* London: Edward Arnold, 1978.
Richter, Gregor, and Albert Schönfelder, eds. *Sacramentarium Fuldense Saeculi X.* Fulda: 1912. Repr. HBS CI. Farnborough: St Michael's Abbey Press, 1972.

Scragg, D.G. "Towards a New Anglo-Saxon Poetic Records." *New Approaches to Editing Old English Verse*. Ed. Sarah Larratt Keefer and Katherine O'Brien O'Keeffe. Cambridge: Brewer, 1998. 67–77.

Shepherd, Geoffrey. "The Sources of the Old English *Kentish Hymn*." *MLN* 67 (1952): 395–97.

Sisam, Celia, and Kenneth Sisam, eds. *The Salisbury Psalter*. EETS 242. London: Oxford UP, 1959.

Sisam, Kenneth. *Studies in the History of Old English Literature*. Oxford: Oxford UP, 1953.

Symons, Dom Thomas, ed. *Regularis Concordia: The Monastic Agreement of the Monks and Nuns of the English Nation*. London: Nelson, 1953.

Thorpe, Benjamin, ed. and trans. *The Homilies of the Anglo-Saxon Church*. 2 vols. London: Ælfric Society, 1846. Repr. 1971.

Treharne, Elaine. "'Hiht wæs geniwad': Rebirth in *The Dream of the Rood*." *The Place of the Cross in Anglo-Saxon England*. Ed. Catherine E. Karkov, Sarah Larratt Keefer, and Karen L. Jolly. Publications of the Manchester Centre for Anglo-Saxon Studies 4. Woodbridge: Boydell, 2006. 145–57.

Weber, Robert, ed. *Biblia Sacra iuxta Vulgatam Versionem*. 2 vols. Stuttgart: Deutsche Bibelgesellschaft, 1969. Repr. 1983.

Whitbread, Leslie. "Notes on Two Minor Old English Poems." *Studia Neophilologica* (1951): 96–102. Repr. *English Language Notes* IV.4 (June 1967): 241–43.

—. "The Old English Poems of the *Benedictine Office* and Some Related Questions." *Anglia* 80 (1967): 37–49.

Withers, B.C., and R. Barnhouse, eds. *The Old English Hexateuch: Aspects and Approaches*. Kalamazoo, MI: Richard Rawlinson Center in association with Medieval Institute Publications, 2000.

Appendix A: How Old English Poetry Functions

There are a number of excellent comprehensive introductions to Old English verse available to the student today, but to provide background to this edition, the following summary may be helpful.

Old English poetry does not rhyme, but instead follows a common model of rhythm and alliteration, shared by many of the Germanic-speaking cultures in the north-west of early medieval Europe and known as the "Germanic alliterative long-line." It is, however, important to remember that this notion of "line" is a modern one, born of our familiarity with conventional page-layout for Old English verse, since we have already learned that in its manuscripts it was set down in what appear to be "prose blocks." Because many such metrical compositions were stories in all likelihood originally oral in nature, they were based on the natural rhythms of speech itself. Over the generations these became formulaic and structural, partly to distinguish them as ritualized language of performance, and partly to make them easier to remember for performative purposes.

By the time Old English poetry was committed to writing, it was made up of short text sections consisting of two "half-lines" (the first conventionally called the "a-line" or "on-verse," the second the "b-line" or "off-verse") separated by a caesura, generally the result of a clause boundary or similar syntactic break:

```
 / x   x  /  x     /  x x  x / x
Fæder manncynnes,     frofres ic þe bidde,

 / x  /  x    /  x  x  /  x x  x
halig drihten,   þu ðe on heofenum eart.
```

Since Germanic verse is composed of sound alliteration and distinctive rhythmic patterns, a basic fact to remember is that each pair of Old English half-lines is bound together by shared alliteration but does not have to reflect identical rhythms in its "a" and "b" sections. Every half-line generally contains two strong beats ("lifts") interspersed with an unprescribed number of weak beats ("drops"); within each pair of half-lines that make up the "long-line" from which early Germanic prosody gets its name, at least one and often both lifts of the a-line are expected to alliterate with the first lift of the b-line, while its second lift frequently stands independent of the alliterative pattern. This does not of course form an absolute standard, but only an empirical model. Lifts lie on the stressed long-vowel syllable of substantive words (nouns, adjectives, some pronouns), or on the root syllable of a verb that is inflected or carries some form of prefix and thus gives weight to words with semantic import.[1] However, despite useful comparison with similar Germanic verse of the same period from Iceland and the continent, we can only assume, from the comparatively small extant canon of Old English poetry, the degree to which these assumptions are correct: there are no contemporary treatises on Anglo-Saxon theories of vernacular metre available to us. So it is important to remember that, while scholars have tried to posit "models" of rhythm (such as Sievers's Five Types, described below), we find substantial deviation in metre from poem to poem and must admit that our understanding of Anglo-Saxon prosody is far from complete.

Alliteration can occur in several different ways in Old English verse: where "G" and "H" stand for alliterating lifts, and both "Y" and "Z" indicate lifts that do not alliterate, the four strong-beat patterns in a long-line can sound:

> G G G Y, where both lifts of the a-line alliterate with the first lift of the b-line (considered a "classical" model);
>
> G H G H, or its variant, G H H G, where double alliteration appears in the line (found both in verse assumed to be early and in verse that is manifestly late);
>
> Y G G Z, where the second lift of the a-line and first lift of the b-line alliterate only;

1 Lifts may also lie on a syllable made up of a short vowel followed by two consonants (such as *dryht-* in *dryhten*, found throughout the liturgical verse canon); and a substantive word accented within its half-line but consisting of two short syllables can apparently count as a long syllable (these are always obvious within their metrical context) and are known as "resolved stress."

G Y G Z, where the first lift of the a-line and first lift of the b-line alliterate only (these last two are often found in verse from later Anglo-Saxon England, and therefore appear frequently in the poetry of this volume).

Even a design as open-ended as this may be helpful to the source-scholar engaged in a comparison of a poem's lexicon with a possible influence, in predicting whether a poet's choice of words was determined by their initial sounds (i.e. whether the need for each of them to alliterate played a role in their selection).[2]

Alliterating sounds used by Anglo-Saxon poets could include vowels (any vowel can alliterate with any other vowel), common consonants ("t" alliterates with "t," "w" with "w" and so forth), or common sounds. By way of example for this last possibility, the single sound "sh" ([š] or [ʃ], an unvoiced sibilant) is rendered orthographically in both Old and Modern English by not one but two letters, in Old English these being "s" and "c": *scip* is pronounced (and means) "ship" in Old English, and we would expect to find this sound, if used as an alliterator, matched with words beginning, not with "s" but with "sc" instead. "Hr" is another example of a common sound (as in *hrim*, "rime-frost," where Modern English has lost the initial "h"), but here we frequently find it alliterated with both "r" and "h" alone, as well as with "hr" itself; the tendency has been to suggest that such instances are the result of late composition, but we cannot be certain, so it is worthwhile not to assume any hard-and-fast rules.

We must also remember that orthographic "c" and "g" in Old English will be enunciated differently, depending on the vowel that follows them. In most cases when in front of "e" and "i," orthographic "c" is sounded as "tch" (unvoiced affricate [č] or [ʧ]), and orthographic "g" is sounded as "y[u]h" (semi-vowel or glide [j]). When in front of "a," "o," "u," and "y," orthographic "c" is sounded like "k" (unvoiced velar stop [k]) and orthographic "g" like "g" (voiced velar stop [g]). However, since manuscripts held no indication of vowel length or consonant phonology, we will at times find alliteration apparently assumed between the two kinds of "c" or of "g," as we found with "hr" alliterating with "h" or "hr" or "r". This is a phenomenon known as "scribal alliteration," where we presume that either the unknown composer of the poem was thinking of letters and not sounds in words needed for alliteration (and so was thinking in terms of the text inscribed in letters on a page for the eyes,

2 See the discussion of alliterative restriction in Keefer, *Old English Metrical Psalter*, 49–51.

rather than the phonemes constructing a composition for the ears), or the scribe engaged in the act of copying may have augmented the poem with lines that alliterated at least to the eye, even if not to the ear. It is again usually considered a mark of later composition, but since the manuscript witnesses for virtually the entire canon of Old English poetry belong to the mid-tenth century at the earliest, such a consideration must once more be taken as inconclusive.

Old English verse is made up of rhythm in half-lines (the lifts and drops in relation to one another), as well as the alliteration that binds each half-line pair together. This rhythm, when combined with its accompanying alliteration, creates a "sound-track" to enhance the meaning of words being used, intensifying phonology for sound-effect, and speeding or slowing the movement of the line toward or against a dramatic conclusion. The German scholar Eduard Sievers is credited with identifying five "types" of metrical model for the Old English half-line and gives his name to their classification. All depend to some degree on the rise and fall of human speech, though the imposition of structural formulation would enhance that speech by ritualizing it. To generalize within a fairly complex subject, we distinguish these five general patterns of rhythm by the letters A–E. The first three, most commonly found in the canon of liturgical poetry, are constructed of lifts and drops only, while the last two, which have subsets within them, allow for "half-lifts," also called "secondary stress" and common in spoken English wherever compound words are used: in the expression "an e-mail," the word "an" would represent a lack of stress or drop, the stressed syllable "e-" (which stands for "electronic") is of paramount importance because it distinguished the kind of mail concerned, and thus would carry the main stress or lift, while the word "-mail" takes more emphasis than "an," but less than "e-", so it nicely represents a half-lift for our purposes here.

Sievers's Types

Type A (falling stress): lift – drop – lift – drop, or / x / x. Each "drop" may represent more than one unstressed syllable. One or even two extra weak syllables can at times precede the first lift in an A-Type pattern, a construction known as "anacrusis," which occurs only in the first half-line, or a-line, of a pair.

Type B (rising stress): drop – lift – drop – lift, or x / x /. These are often used for dramatic effect in the b-line at the end of a half-line pair where the alliteration binding the two verses ends. The first drop may contain up to five syllables, but the second must have only one or two.

Type C (clashing stress): drop – lift – lift – drop, or x / / x. These can slow the pace of a line or foreground important details. The second lift can be a short syllable, since it needs to be articulated immediately after the first stress, which would most likely be long. As with the B-Type, the first drop may have up to five syllables, but the last drop at the long-line's end must have only one.
Type D^1 and D^2: D^1: lift – lift – half-lift – drop, or / / \ x; D^2: lift – lift – drop – half-lift, or / / x \. This type is often made up of two words, the first with two short syllables and the second with three syllables, but it can also contain up to three drops between the first and second lifts. As with the C-Type, its last drop must consist of only one syllable.
Type E: lift – half-lift – drop – lift, or / \ x /, something like a mirror image of D-Type since it can be made up of two words, the first a tri-syllabic word and the second with two short syllables; its drop may contain only one or two syllables at most.

I borrow a mnemonic from the great Old English grammarian Bruce Mitchell, with affectionate gratitude, as its alliteration enables the student to remember the appropriate letter pertaining to each type:

A	Anna angry	/ x / x	falling - falling
B	And Byrhtnoth bold	x / x /	rising – rising
C	In keen conflict	x / / x	clashing
D^1	Ding down strongly	/ / \ x	falling by stages
D^2	Deal death to all	/ / x \	broken fall
E	Each one with edge	/ \ x /	fall and rise.[3]

Bearing Sievers's Five Types in mind, it is helpful to imagine a poem in Modern English using "classical" Old English structure (as it is understood from poems like *Beowulf* that may be earlier than the mid-tenth century). Lines from such a piece might run something like this:

/ x / x	/ x x / x
Gold and green in	grass-covered meadow
x x x / / x	x x / x x /
Under the high heavens	in the heat and the rain

3 Mitchell and Robinson, *A Guide to Old English*, 165.

In the first line, "g" is the alliterator that binds the half-lines to one another (the final lift falls on "m" in the second half-line), with both sides following a strong-weak pattern, identified as Type A by Sievers. It is not iambic metre because there is no limit to the number of weak beats allowed between strong ones. In the second line, we have an "h" alliterator, but each half-line presents a different rhythm: "under the high heavens" brings its alliterating lifts together one after another, "high heav-," with the weak beats, "under the" and "-ens" on either side of them, in what Sievers called Type C, or "clashing stress." In the b-line, "in the heat and the rain" looks a little like an example of trochaic metre, weak-strong, with the nouns "heat" and "rain" carrying the stresses. However, we have already seen that there is no single prescribed number of weak beats to precede the strong beats in most Old English rhythmic patterns as there would be in a proper line of trochaic metre.

Then there are the two other types to be found in Old English alliterating half-lines: these are Types D (D^1 used here) and E, which include not only lifts and drops but half-lifts as well: we have seen that tri-syllabic compound words used either at the end of a half-line (Type D) or the beginning of a half-line (Type E) often account for these patterns. In Modern English, equivalent but non-alliterating examples of each might be

/ x / \ x / \ x /
Gather blackberries, wild-rose and mint.

A note must be added on the subject of Old English half-lines that are expanded so as to include an extra series of drop-lift relations, because *Vision of the Rood* is one of the more celebrated of Old English poems with such "hypermetric" lines. Scholars are divided as to what the additional beats might mean or how they developed, but each hypermetric half-line will generally contain an extra lift and will certainly contain several extra drops.

Glossary

All substantives are shown as nominative and indicate grammatical gender if nouns. Verbs are shown in their infinitive forms. Verbs or nouns with variant "ge-" prefix are located below by their root (thus **gewlitegod** is to be found under "w" for **(ge)wlitigian**). Commonly found lexical variants are indicated in parentheses to the headword if the presence or absence of one or more consecutive letters is the issue (i.e. **up(pe)**) or standing next to the headword before its entry where variance is due to dialect (i.e. **stæfn, stefn).** Inflected forms and specific usages are generally keyed to the texts by superscribed line number in this edition, using the Text Key below; '*etc*' assumes that the reader can extrapolate correctly. "Æ/æ" appears after "A"; "Đ/ð" and "Þ/þ" are to be found after "T."

Abbreviations

pro = pronoun	adj = adjective	adv = adverb	prep = preposition
conj = conjunction	vb = verb	interj = interjection	
1 = first person	2 = second person	3 = third person	
n(om) = nominative	a(cc) = accusative	g(en) = genitive	d(at) = dative
i(nst) = instrumental			
masc = masculine	fem = feminine	neut = neuter	
sg = singular	pl = plural		
pres = present tense	pret = preterite (past) tense		
imp = imperative	subj = subjunctive		
p ptc = past participle	pres ptc = present participle		
inf = infinitive	infl inf = inflected infinitive		
comp = comparative	superl = superlative	uninfl = uninflected	rel = relative
subst = substantive	poss = possessive	fig = figuratively	
erron = erroneously	w = with		

Text Key

ASPR Title	*Edition Title*	*Abbrev.*
Lord's Prayer I	Exeter Lord's Prayer	ELP
Lord's Prayer II	Corpus Lord's Prayer	CLP
Lord's Prayer III	Junius Lord's Prayer	JLP
Creed	Baptismal Creed	BC
Gloria I	Old English Doxology	DOX
Gloria II	Titus Alphabet Doxology	TAD
Kentish Psalm 50	Kentish Great Miserere	KGM
Kentish Hymn	Kentish Hymn of Praise	KHP
Prayer	Ah, Beloved Lord	ABL
Dream of the Rood	Vision of the Rood	VR

ā: adv. *forever, always*. **ā on worlda forð** *world without end*
ābūgan: vb. *bow, do reverence*. **ābūgað** 3pl pres CLP[12]
ābylgan: vb. *offend*. **ābylgeað** 1pl pres JLP[28]
ac: conj. *but, however, nevertheless*
ācennan, acæennan: vb. *bring forth, bear (a child), produce*. **ācende** 3sg pret BC[18] **ācænned, akende** p. ptc CLP[97] ABL[46]
ādȳlgian, ādlegian: vb. *blot out, destroy*. **ādīlga** imp sg KGM[38, 97]
Adom: proper name. *Adam*. **Adomes** gsg VR[100]
āf(i)erran: vb. *remove, take away*. **āferre** imp sg KGM[109]
āfȳsan: vb. *drive, impel, fill with longing*. **āfȳsed** p ptc VR[125]
āgan: vb. *own, possess*. **āh** 3sg pres VR[107]
āgen: adj. *own*. CLP[18] DOX[44] **āgenum** dsg KHP[21] **āgene** apl CLP[73]
āgend: noun, masc. *master, owner, lord*. asg KHP[3]
āgyltan: vb. *offend, sin*. **āgyltað** 3pl pres JLP[31] **āgilt** 3pl pres CLP[114] **āgylt** p ptc CLP[127]
āh: see **āgan**
āhēawan: vb. *fell, cut down*. **āhēawen** p ptc VR[29]
āhebban: vb. *raise, lift up*. **āhof** 1sg pret VR[44] **āhofe** 2sg pret KHP[27] **āhofon** 3pl pret VR[61]
āherian: vb. *praise*. ABL[30]
āhlūttrian: vb. *cleanse, purify*. **āhlūttra** imp sg KGM[81]
āhwæðer: pron/conj. *one or the other, either*. BC[47]
āhweorfan: vb. *turn away*. **āhwerf** imp sg KGM[93]
akende: see **ācennan**

ālǣtan, ālētan: vb. *forgive, pardon.* **ālēt** imp sg JLP[26]
aldor(lice): see **ealdor(lice)**
ālecgan: vb. *lay down.* **ālēdon** 3pl pret VR[63]
ālētan: see **ālǣtan**
ālȳfan, ālīefan: vb. *grant, allow.* **ālȳf** imp sg CLP[31]
ālȳsan, ālīesan: vb. *redeem, set free.* **ālȳsdest** 2sg pres JLP[44] **ālyseð** 3sg pres CLP[112] **ālȳse, alēs** sg pres subj CLP[8] KHP[33]
(e)al(l)wihta: noun, fem/neut pl gen only. *(of) all creatures.* KGM[113]
amen: closure marker for prayers; in Hebrew *so may it be*
an: see **on**
ān: adj. *one, single, alone, only.* **āna** CLP[48] DOX[20] VR[123, 128] *etc* **ǣnne** asg BC[5, 56] **ānes** gsg KGM[34] **ānre** dsg CLP[13, 55] **ānum** dsg KGM[52] **ānra** gpl VR[86, 108]
ān: adv. *only.* KGM[74]
and: conj. *and*
andettan: vb. *confess, acknowledge.* **andette** 1sg pres ABL[56] **andhette** 3sg pret KGM[29]
anfehst: see **onfōn**
anfindan: see **onfindan**
anforht: adj. *terrified.* VR[117]
angel: see **engel**
ānnes: noun, fem. *unity, one-ness.* **ānnesse** dsg KHP[41]
ansendan: see **onsendan**
ansīon, ansīen: noun, fem/neut. *face, countenance.* **ansīone** asg KGM[95]
ānsund: adj. *whole, sound.* **ansunde** npl CLP[99]
anwealda: noun, masc. *ruler.* VR[153]
ār: noun, fem. *mercy.* **āre** asg CLP[4, 108] ABL[10] ABL[24] asg/gsg CLP[61] dsg ABL[48] KHP[35] **arna** gpl KGM[110]
ārǣran: vb. *raise, lift up, build, spread.* **ārǣred** p ptc ELP[5] VR[44]
āreccean, āreccan: vb. *declare, express.* ABL[37]
ārētan: vb. *gladden, comfort.* **ārētte** 3sg pret BC[40]
ārfæstnes, ārfęstnes: noun, fem. *mercy, grace, goodness.* **ārfęstnesse** dsg KHP[24]
ārīsan: vb. *arise, rise up.* **ārīsað** 3pl pres CLP[96] **ārās** 3sg pret BC[38] VR[101]
ārlēas: adj. *wicked.* **ārlēase** npl JLP[37] KGM[120]
āsæcgan, āsecgan: vb. *express, narrate, declare.* ABL[33]
āsendan: vb. *send forth.* **āsendne** p ptc BC[12]
āsettan: vb. *set up, set oneself.* **asette** sg pres subj VR[142] **āsettað** 3pl pres KGM[158] **āsetton** 3pl pret VR[32]

āstīgan: vb. *ascend.* **āstāg** 3sg pret VR[103]
āstyrian: vb. *remove.* **āstyred** p ptc VR[30]
āsyndrian: vb. *distance, sever, divide.* **āsyndrod** p ptc DOX[12]
āðor: see **āhwæðer**
āðwēan: vb. *cleanse, wash away.* **āðwēah** imp sg KGM[41]
āweorpan: vb. *cast away.* **āweorp** imp sg KGM[106]

ǣcan, īecan: vb. *increase, fulfil.* **ǣc** imp sg KGM[99]
ǣce: see **ēce**
ǣfentīd: noun, fem. *evening.* **ǣfentīde** asg VR[68]
ǣfre: adv. *ever*
æfter, efter: prep w dat. *according to, after*
ǣghwǣr: adv. *everywhere*
ǣghwæðer: pron, adv. *either, both.* **ǣgþer** CLP[48]
ǣghwilc: adj. *each, every.* VR[120] **ǣghwylcne** asg VR[86] **ǣghwilcum** dsg CLP[18]
ǣgþer: see **ǣghwæðer**
ǣlā: interj. *oh, ah.* ABL[1, 8, 21]
ǣlc: adj. *every, all, each.* erron. **ǣlce** dsg CLP[73] **ǣlcere** dsg CLP[25]
ælde: see **ieldo**
ældor: see **ealdor**
ælmihtig: adj. *almighty.* VR[39, 153] **ælmehtig** KHP[14] **ælmeahtig** KGM[95, 109] **elmehtig** KGM[86] **ælmihtigne** asg VR[60] **ælmihtigum** dsg JLP[28]
ængel: see **engel**
ǣnig: pro. *any, anyone.* VR[110, 117] ABL[30] **ǣniges** gsg KGM[59]
ǣnne: **seen**
ǣr: adv. *first of all, earlier.* CLP[5] **ǣr hwīle** *before* KGM[91.]
ǣr: conj. *before.* ABL[73] **ǣr þan** *before* VR[88]
ǣrdæg: noun, masc. *past time, former day(s).* **ǣrdagum** dpl ABL[45]
ǣrende: noun, neut. *errand, message, mission.* asg BC[16]
ǣrendraca: noun, masc. *messenger.* BC[14]
ǣrest, ǣrist: noun, masc. *arising, resurrection.* BC[64]
ǣrest: adv. *first, initially.* VR[19]
ǣrgewinn: noun, neut. *ancient strife, torment long ago.* asg VR[19]
ǣrur: adv. *earlier.* VR[108]
æt: prep w dat. *at, near, in, on.* BC[19] VR[63]
ætgadere: adv. *together.* VR[48]
æðele: adj. *noble.* ABL[34] CLP[48] **æþela** ABL[45] **æðelæ** KGM[2] **æþelan, æðelan** asg CLP[6, 46] dsg KHP[19]

(ge)æðelian: vb. *make noble, make renowned.* **geæþelodest** 2sg pret CLP[71] **geæþelod** p ptc CLP[29]
æðeling: noun, masc. *prince, nobleman.* **æðelinge** dsg VR[58]
ǣwan: vb. *despise.* **ǣwest** 2sg pres KGM[147]

(ge)bād: see **(ge)bīdan**
balanīð, bealunīð: noun, masc. *malice, wickedness.* **balanīða** gpl KGM[171] **bealaniðum** dpl KGM[126]
bān: noun, neut. *bone.* CLP[98] npl KGM[90]
bana: noun, masc. *slayer.* **banan** gsg VR[66]
(ge)bæd: see **(ge)biddan**
(ge)bær, bǣron: see **(ge)beran**
(ge)bærnan: vb. *kindle, burn, consume.* CLP[117]
bēacen: noun, neut. *sign, beacon.* VR[6] **bēacne** dsg VR[83] **bēacna** gpl VR[118]
beald: adj. *brave, strong.* DOX[14]
bealuware: noun, masc (pl). *those who dwell in evil.* **bealuwara** gpl VR[79]
bēam: noun, masc. *tree.* VR[97] **bēame** dsg VR[114, 122] **bēama** gpl VR[6]
bearn: noun, masc. *child, offspring.* VR[83] apl KHP[26] **manna bearn** *children of men* CLP[74] **bearnum** dpl ELP[3] ABL[47]
bēc: see **bōc**
bedealfan: vb. *bury.* **bedealf** 3sg pret VR[75]
bedrīfan: vb. *sprinkle.* **bedrifenne** p ptc asg VR[62]
beēode: see **begān**
befealdan: vb. *fold up, envelop.* CLP[132]
beforan: adv. *openly, at hand.* KGM[48]
befrēogan: vb. *liberate.* **befrēo** imp sg KGM[125]
begān: vb. *commit, perform.* **beēode** 1sg pret KGM[72]
bēgen: numerical adj. *both.* **būta** CLP[102] **būtū** acc dual VR[48]
begēotan: vb. *cover [with], pour.* **begoten** p ptc VR[7, 49]
begę̄tan, begietan: vb. *acquire, attain.* **begę̄ton** 3pl pres (subj?) KGM[62]
beginnan: vb. *begin.* **began** 3sg pret BC[40]
behealdan: vb. *behold, see, watch.* **behēold** 1sg pret VR[25, 58] **behēoldon** 3pl pret VR[9, 11, 64]
belūcan: vb. *embrace, enclose, surround.* **belūce** 1sg pres BC[46]
bēn: noun, fem. *prayer, supplication.* **bēnum** dpl KGM[75]
benēman, benǣman: vb. *deprive of, rob of.* KGM[21]
bēon/wesan: vb. *be.* Following is a paradigm of its present and preterite conjugations. Two different present forms derive from the two distinct verbs but they substitute for one another freely. Present tense of **bēon**

may be used to carry either an implicit future sense (**wel bið ðām ðe wyrcð willan þīnne**, *it shall be well for the one who does thy will*) or an eternal truth (**hēr bið frēond lǣne**, *here are friends transitory*).

Indicative	*Present*	*Present*	*Preterite*
1sg	eom = *am*	bēo = *am, (shall) be*	wæs = *was*
2sg	eart = *art (are)*	bist = *are, (shall) be*	wǣre = *were*
3sg	is, ys = *is*	bið, byð = *is, (shall) be*	wæs = *was*
1,2,3pl	sind/synd, sindon/syndon, sint/synt = *are*	bēoð, bīoð = *are, (shall) be*	wǣron = *were*
Subjunctive			
1,2,3sg	sīe, sīo = *were, should be*	bēo = *were, should be*	wǣre = *had been, should have been*
1,2,3pl	sīen, sȳn = *were, should be*	bēon = *were, should be*	wǣren = *had been, should have been*
Imperative			
1,2,3sg	wes = *be*	bēo = *be*	
1,2,3pl	wesað = *be*	bēoð = *be*	

beorg: noun, masc. *mountain, hill.* asg VR[32] **beorge** dsg VR[50]
beorht: adj. *bright, radiant.* **beorhta** nsg ABL[8] **beorhtan** dsg VR[66] **beorhtost** superl CLP[12] VR[6]
beorhtny(/e)s: noun, fem. *brightness, splendour.* **beorhtnysse** asg CLP[35]
beorn: noun, masc. *warrior, man.* **beornas** npl VR[32, 66] **beornum** dpl ABL[47]
(ge)beran: vb. *bear, carry, give birth (to).* **bereð** 3sg pres VR[118] 3sg pret **gebær** KGM[68] **bǣron** 3pl pret VR[32]
bernelāc, bærnelāc: noun, neut. *burnt offering.* asg KGM[140]
berstan: vb. *break, burst (apart).* VR[36]
bescerwan: vb. *deprive.* **bescerwe** imp sg KGM[110]
bestēman: vb. *drench, make wet.* **bestēmed** p ptc VR[22, 48]
beswīcan: vb. *deceive, seduce.* CLP[116]
beswillan: vb. *drench, soak.* **beswyled** p ptc VR[23]
besyrian, besierwan: vb. *deceive, entrap, deprive.* **beserode** 3sg pret KGM[22]
(ge)bētan: vb. *atone for.* **gebētte** 3sg pret KGM[171]

betǣcan: vb. *show forth* CLP[91]
betera: adj. *better.* **betere** apl CLP[102]
Bethleem: proper name. *Bethlehem.* asg BC[25] dsg ABL[47]
beþurfan: vb. *have need of.* **beþurfon** 1pl pres CLP[126]
bewindan: vb. *wind, entwine.* **bewunden** p ptc VR[5]
bewrēon: vb. *cover.* **bewrigen** p ptc VR[17, 53]
bewyrcan: vb. *enclose, construct.* **bewyrc** imp sg CLP[88]
Bezabe: proper name. *Bathsheba (wife first to Uriah, then to David, and mother of King Solomon).* asg KGM[23]
(ge)bīdan: vb. *experience, endure.* **gebād** 3sg pret VR[125] **gebiden** p ptc VR[50, 79]
(ge)biddan: vb. *ask for, request, pray* [often w gen/acc of thing asked for and dat/acc of person it is asked of]. KGM[75] **(ge)bidde, bydde** 1sg pres JLP[2] ABL[23, 68] **(ge)biddað** 1pl pres CLP[4, 121] 3pl pres CLP[60] VR[83] **gebæd** 1sg pret VR[122] 3sg pret KGM[27]
bifian: vb. *tremble, shake.* VR[36] **bifode** 1sg pret VR[42]
(ge)big: see **(ge)bycgan**
bilewit, bilwit: adj. *merciful, gracious, innocent.* KGM[90, 112] **bilewitne** asg KHP[8]
bist: see **bēon**
biter: adj. *bitter.* **biteres** gsg VR[114]
bið: see **bēon**
blǣd: noun, masc. *bounty, abundance, blessing.* asg ELP[6] **blēdum** dpl VR[149]
blēo: noun, neut. *colour.* **blēom** dpl VR[22]
(ge)bletsian: vb. *bless, consecrate.* **blætsiað** 1pl pres KHP[8] **gebletsod** p ptc DOX[14]
blis(s): noun, fem. *bliss, joy, grace.* VR[139] **bliðse** asg KGM[112] **blisse** dsg BC[21] VR[149, 153] KGM[50] ?dsg (see note) KGM[88] **blissa** gpl CLP[12]
(ge)blissian: vb. *gladden, rejoice, exult;* with **ge-**, *make happy, gladden.* **blissast** 2sg pres CLP[38]
blīðe: adj. *joyful, happy.* KGM[80] isg VR[122]
bliðsian, blissian: vb. *rejoice.* **bliðse** ?3sg pres (see note) KGM[88] **blissað** 3sg pres KGM[129]
blōd: noun, neut. *blood.* **blōde** dsg VR[48] KHP[26]
blōdgete, blōdgyte: noun, masc. *bloodshed.* dsg KGM[126]
bōc: noun, fem/neut. *book, Bible.* **bēc** dsg DOX[41] npl CLP[24] **bōca** gpl DOX[14]
(ge)bod: noun, neut. *command, order.* asg DOX[32] **bodu** apl CLP[121]

(ge)bodian: vb. *proclaim, announce.* **gebodode** 3sg pret BC[15] **bodedan** 3pl pret BC[25]

(ge)bohtest: see **(ge)bycgan**

bōsm: noun, masc. *breast, womb.* BC[21]

(ge)brecan: vb. *break, shatter.* **brǣcon** 1pl pret CLP[121]

brȩga, breogo: noun, masc. *ruler.* KGM[2]

brengan: see **bringan**

brēost: noun, neut. *breast.* **brēostum** dpl (with singular sense) VR[118]

brēostcofa: noun, masc. *affection, heart.* **brēostcofan** dsg BC[18]

bretta, brytta: noun, masc. *prince, one who dispenses [treasure].* KGM[139]

(ge)bringan: vb. *bring.* **brengan** KGM[140] **gebringe** sg pres subj VR[139] **brōhte** 3sg pret KGM[23] sg pret subj KGM[137]

(ge)brocian: vb. *crush, break.* **gebrocenan** p ptc npl KGM[90]

(ge)brosnian: vb. *crumble, decay.* **gebrosnodon** p ptc *decayed, decomposed.* CLP[98]

brūcan: vb w gen. *enjoy, partake [of].* VR[145]

bryne: noun, masc. *burning, fire.* asg VR[149]

būgan: vb. *bend, bow.* VR[36, 42]

burg: noun, fem. *walled city.* **byrig** dsg ABL[47]

būta: see **bēgen**

būtan: prep w dat. *without.* ABL[79]

būton, būte: conj. *unless.* CLP[8]

būtū: see **bēgen**

(ge)bycgan: vb. *acquire, buy, ransom.* **gebig** imp sg CLP[86] **gebohtest** 2sg pret KHP[26]

bydde: see **(ge)biddan**

byrig: see **burg**

(ge)byrgan: vb. *bury, inter.* **byrigde** 3sg pret BC[32] see also note to VR[101]

byrigan: vb. *taste.* **byrigde** 3sg pret VR[101]

bysmerian: vb. *revile, insult.* **bysmeredon** 3pl pret VR[48]

byð: see **beon**

campian: vb w dat. *fight on behalf of, campaign for.* **campað** 3sg pres ABL[12]

canst: see **(ge)cunnan**

cāsere: noun, masc. *emperor, caesar.* CLP[66] KGM[11]

cealf: noun, masc/neut. *calf.* asg KGM[157]

ceaster: noun, fem. *castle, town, "heaven."* **ceastre** dsg KHP[19]

(ge)cennan: vb. *acknowledge, conceive, bring forth.* **gecenne** 1sg pres BC[5] **cende** 3sg pret BC[22]

ceorfan: vb. *carve (out).* **curfon** 3pl pret VR[66]

(ge)cēosan: vb. *choose, elect.* **gecorene** p ptc pl. *chosen, precious, dear* CLP[59] **gecorenan** p ptc pl. DOX[47]

(ge)cierran: vb. *convert, turn, return.* **gecerre** sg pres subj KGM[70] **gecerdan** 3pl pret KGM[120] **cerrende** pres ptc KGM[61]

clǣne, clęne: adj. *pure, free from sin, innocent, hallowed.* DOX[19, 59] asg DOX[13] npl CLP[59] **clęne** asg KGM[99] **clǣna** nsg JLP[23] **clǣnre** dsg DOX[41]

(ge)clǣnsian, (ge)clansian: vb. at times + gen. *purify, purge, cleanse.* **geclansa** imp sg KGM[42, 127] **geclænsod, geclansod** p ptc KGM[82, 145]

clipian: vb. *cry out, call out.* **clypiað** 3pl pres CLP[14, 27] **clypast** 2sg pres CLP[50] *etc*

cnyssan: vb w acc of person. *beat, strike, knock.* ELP[9]

cōlian: vb. *grow cold.* **cōlode** 3sg pret VR[72]

cōm: see **cuman**

(ge)coren: see **(ge)cēosan**

costung: noun, fem. *temptation.* **costunge** dsg JLP[36] **costunga** apl ELP[9] CLP[117]

cræft: noun, masc. *courage, virtue, excellence.* **cræftas** apl DOX[37, 63]

cræftig, creaftig: adj. *powerful, wise.* DOX[19, 59] KGM[11]

Crīst: noun, masc. *anointed one, Christ.* JLP[6, 23, 36] *etc* **criste** dsg CLP[14, 59] KGM[61]

crīsten: adj. *Christian.* **crīstene** dsg DOX[41] apl DOX[31]

cuman: vb. *come, approach, become.* **cyme** sg pres subj ELP[4] **cume** imp sg JLP[9] CLP[31] *etc* **cymð** 3sg pres CLP[7] **cōm, cwōm** 3sg pret VR[151, 155] **cumen** p ptc VR[80]

cumbolgebrec: noun, neut. *crash of banners.* npl KGM[11]

(ge)cunnan: vb. *know, be aware of.* **canst** 2sg pres BC[9] **cunnon** 3pl pres DOX[31]

curfon: see **ceorfan**

cūðlice: adv. *clearly, certainly.* BC[22]

cwæð, gecweden: see **(ge)cweðan**

cwellan: vb. *kill, murder.* CLP[117]

(ge)cwēman: vb w dat. *be pleasing to, please.* **gecwēmað** 3sg/pl pres BC[68]

(ge)cweðan: vb. *say, proclaim.* VR[116] **cwyð** 3sg pres VR[111] **cweþað** 1pl pres DOX[42] 3pl pres CLP[14] **cwæð** 3sg pret BC[42] **gecweden** p ptc BC[47]

cwic: adj. *living, alive.* **cwicera, cwucra** gpl as subst *living thing* KHP[15, 39] **cwicum** dpl CLP[130]

cwīðan: vb. *bewail, lament.* **cwīðdon** 3pl pret VR[56]

cwōm: see **cuman**

cwuc: see **cwic**

cwyð: see **(ge)cweðan**

(ge)cydd(est): see **(ge)cȳðan**

(ge)cynd: noun, fem/neut. *generation, people, race, quality, conception.* CLP[27, 48] *etc*; asg DOX[13, 59, 62] erron. dsg CLP[73]

cȳne, cēne: adj. *brave, daring.* **cȳnost** superl KGM[3]

cynebearn: noun, neut. *royal child, Christ.* CLP[130]

cynedōm: noun, masc. *royal dignity, kingdom.* **cynedōmes** gsg KGM[169]

cyning, cyninc, cyningc, kyning: noun, masc. *king* CLP[3, 15, 62] ABL[42] *etc* asg BC[12] VR[133] **kyninga, cyninga** gpl ABL[42] KHP[15] KGM[3]

cynn: noun, fem/neut. *race, people, kind.* asg VR[94] KGM[64] **cynnes** gsg JLP[22] **cynne** dsg KHP[32] **cynna** gpl DOX[23]

cȳnost: see **cȳne**

cyst: noun, fem. *choicest of [something].* asg VR[1]

(ge)cȳðan: vb. *make known, make manifest, reveal.* KGM[18] **gecȳddest** 2sg pret DOX[19, 59] **cȳddest** DOX[63] **cȳðað** 3pl pres DOX[37] **gecȳdd** p ptc CLP[130]

daga: see **dæg**

Dauid: proper name. *(King) David.* KGM[1, 9, 27]

dǣd: noun, fem. *deed, action.* **dēda** gpl KGM[167] **dǣdum** dpl CLP[26]

dæg, dæig: noun, masc. *day.* **dæge** dsg BC[37] **daga** gpl BC[39] VR[136] **tō dæge** dsg *today* ELP[6] JLP[19] but **tō dæg** CLP[85] **dæges** gsg *by day* CLP[119] **dæiges and nihtes** gsg *by day and by night* ABL[12, 17, 63]

dæghwāmlice: adv. *daily.* CLP[77]

dǣlan: vb. *share out, divide.* **dǣlest** 2sg pres CLP[78] BC[67]

dēad: adj. *dead, unliving.* **dēadra** gpl KGM[141] (as subst) KHP[39] **dēadum** dpl CLP[130]

dēað: noun, masc. *death.* asg BC[30] VR[101] KGM[59] **dēaðes** gsg VR[113]

dēda: see **dǣd**

dēma: noun, masc. *judge.* JLP[10] CLP[32, 41] *etc*

dēman: vb. *judge.* VR[107]

dēofol: noun, masc/neut. *devil, evil one.* **dēofles** gsg CLP[108]

dēop: adj. *deep.* **dēopan** dsg VR[75]

dēopnes: noun, fem. *profund nature, mystery.* **dēopnesse** asg ABL[53]

deorc: adj. *dark.* **deorcan** dpl VR[46]

dēore: adj. *dear, beloved.* BC[30]

derne, dierne: adj. *hidden, secret.* apl KGM[77]

(ge)deð: see **dōn**

didon: see **dōn**

dīormōd, dēormōd: adj. *courageous, brave-hearted.* KGM[1]
disig, dysig: noun, neut. *error, foolishness.* **disige** dsg CLP[119]
dolg: noun, neut. *wound.* npl VR[46]
dōm, doom: noun, masc. *judgement, doom, justice.* DOX[5] possibly *doomsday* asg KGM[63] **doom** asg KGM[19] **dōmes** gsg VR[107] **dōme** dsg CLP[95] **dōmas** npl CLP[16] apl KGM[102] **dōma** gpl BC[29]
dōmdæg: noun, masc. *Judgement Day, Doomsday.* **dōmdæge** dsg VR[105]
dōmfæst: adj. *just, famous, illustrious.* **dōmfæstne** asg ELP[6]
dominus: Lat. noun. *Lord.* KGM[17, 90, 112, 160] **domine** vocative Latin form (i.e. OE nom) KGM[109]
(ge)dōn: vb. *do, make.* **dō** 1sg pres ABL[63] **gedō** imp s KHP[34] **gedoo** KGM[149] **gedeð** 3sg pres KGM[13] **dyde** 3sg pret VR[114] **didon** 1pl pret CLP[119] **dydest** 2sg pret DOX[61]
doom: see **dōm**
drēam: noun, masc. *pleasure, joy.* VR[140] **drēames** gsg VR[145] **drēame** dsg ELP[2] **drēamas** *choirs, celebrations.* DOX[40] apl KGM[176] **drēamum** dpl VR[133]
(ge)drēfan: vb. *afflict, trouble.* **gedrēfed** p ptc VR[20, 59]
(ge)drēogan: vb. *perform, suffer, endure.* **gedrēogeð** 3sg pres ABL[20]
drihten, dryhten: noun, masc. *lord.* JLP[2, 19, 23] CLP[16] *etc*; **drihtne** asg ABL[17] dsg KGM[27, 30] **drihtenes** gsg CLP[108] DOX[33] **dryhtnes** VR[9, 75] *etc* **dryhtne tō willan** *at the lord's will.* KGM[141]
duguð: noun, fem. *body of retainers, men, people, followers.* **duguðe** dsg CLP[77] fig *strength of all hosts* **ealra dugeþa duguð** ABL[44]
dūn: noun, fem/masc. *mountain, hill.* KGM[151]
durran: vb. *dare.* **dorste** 1sg pret VR[35, 42, 45, 147]
dyde, dydest: see **dōn**
dyrnan: vb. *hide, conceal.* CLP[103]
dysig: see **disig**

ēac: adv. *also, and, moreover.* **ēac þon** *besides, also* ELP[5]
(ge)ēacnian: vb. *become pregnant, bring forth.* **geēacnod** p ptc KGM[67]
ēadig: adj. *blessed, fortunate.* ABL[16]
(ge)ēadmēdan: vb. *humble (oneself), make humble.* **geēadmēded** p ptc KGM[146]
ēadmōd, ēaðmōd: adj. *benevolent, gracious, humble.* CLP[63] **ēaðmōd** VR[60] **ēadmōda** subst ABL[59]
ēage: noun, neut. *eye.* **ēagena** gpl CLP[35] **ēagum** dpl KGM[47]
eal(l): adj. *all, whole, entire, all (men).* CLP[55] **ealne** asg BC[4] **ealle** asg CLP[35] **ealles** gsg KHP[41] CLP[2] DOX[4] **ealre** dsg DOX[18] **ealle** npl VR[9] apl CLP[131]

DOX[13, 22] VR[37] npl CLP[14] DOX[3] **ealra** gpl JLP[37] ABL[43, 44, 47] KGM[64]. See also **ealle**

ealdgewyrht: noun, neut. *ancient deed.* **ealdgewyrhtum** dpl VR[100]

(e)aldor, ældor: noun, masc/neut. *lord, prince, king; life, vitality.* VR[90] ABL[5, 40] KGM[26, 166] asg BC[56] **ældran** asg KGM[71] **aldre** dsg KGM[21, 43]

(e)aldorlice: adv. *nobly, excellently.* KGM[116]

ealle: adv. *wholly, entirely.* CLP[24] DOX[40] VR[74] **eall** VR[48] see also **eal(l)**

ealne, ealre: see **eal(l)**

ealtēawe, æltǣwe: adj. *complete, whole, true.* **ealtēawne** asg ABL[20]

eard: noun, masc. *country, homeland, condition, fate.* **eardas** npl CLP[107] apl DOX[22] **earda** gpl CLP[33, 82]

eardian: vb. *inhabit, dwell.* **eardast** 2sg pres ELP[1]

eardung: noun, fem. *dwelling, habitation.* **eardunge** dsg JLP[15]

ēare: noun, neut. *ear*, **ēarna** gpl KGM[86]

earm: adj. *wretched, pitiful.* **earme** npl VR[68] **earmra** gpl subst VR[19] **earmon (-on = -um)** dpl CLP[114]

earming: noun, masc. *wretched one.* ABL[11] **earminge** dsg ABL[10]

(ge)earnian: vb. *earn, merit.* KGM[176] **geearnaþ** 3sg pres VR[109] **geearniað** 1pl pres CLP[109]

earning: noun, fem. *merit.* **earnunge** dsg JLP[33]

eart: see **bēon**

ēaðe: adv. *easily, without doubt, unquestionably.* ABL[24]

ēaðmōd, ēaðmed: adj. *humble-minded, obedient.* **ēaðmēde** dsg KGM[172]

eaxl: noun, fem. *shoulder.* **eaxlum** dpl VR[32]

eaxlgespann: noun, neut. *crossbeam.* **eaxlgespanne** dsg VR[9]

ēce: adj. *eternal.* ABL[2] **ǣce** KHP[37] asg ABL[24] **ēcne** asg BC[5] **ēcan** gsg JLP[33] CLP[33] **ǣce** apl KGM[176]

ēce: adv. *eternally.* CLP[41] DOX[38]

efenēadig: adj. *equally blessed.* KHP[21]

efne: adv. *indeed, fully, exactly.* **emne** BC[47]

efstan: vb. *hasten.* VR[34]

eft: adv. *again, afterwards*

efter: see **æfter**

eg(e)sa: noun, masc. *fear, horror, terror, awe.* CLP[106] VR[86]

egeslic: adj. *terrifying, horrible.* VR[74]

ellen: noun, neut. *courage, zeal.* **elne** isg VR[34, 60, 123]

elmehtig: **see** ælmihtig

emne: see **efne**

ende: noun, masc. *end, edge, conclusion.* asg ABL[20] dsg VR[29] ABL[79]

endedæg: noun, masc. *last day, doomsday.* **endedæge** dsg CLP[124]

engel, angel, ængel: noun, masc. *angel.* asg VR[9] **englas** npl DOX[49] VR[106] **engla, angla** gpl JLP[42] CLP[8] ABL[35] KHP[17] **englum, ænglum** dpl VR[153] KHP[5]

ēode: see **gān**

eorre, ierre: noun, neut. *anger.* asg KGM[24]

eorðbūend, eorðbūgend: noun, masc. *earth-dweller.* **eorðbūgende** dsg ABL[28] **eorðbūendra** gpl ABL[52] **eorðbūendum** dpl BC[23]

eorðe: noun, fem. *earth.* **eorðan** asg DOX[21] gsg JLP[15] DOX[7] dsg JLP[30] VR[74] KHP[5]

eorðwaru: noun, fem. *dwellers on the earth, humanity.* CLP[105]

eorðweg: noun, masc. *earthly way.* **eorðwege** dsg VR[120]

ēþel, ēðel: noun, masc/neut. *homeland, country.* VR[156] asg BC[35, 41]

ēðest: see **ȳþost**

fāh: adj. *stained.* VR[13]

fæder, fęder: noun, masc, uninfl in sg. *father.* ELP[1] JLP[2] CLP[2] *etc* gsg CLP[80] KHP[43]

fæger: adj. *lovely, fair.* CLP[45] VR[73] **fægran** dsg VR[21] **fægere** DOX[27] npl subst VR[8, 10] *etc*

fægere, fegere: adv. *well, justly.* CLP[52, 81] TAD[2] ABL[46] KHP[43]

fǣmne, fēmne: noun, fem. *maid, virgin, bride.* **fǣmnan** gsg BC[21] **fēmnena** gpl ABL[46]

fǣr: see **fēr**

fæst: adj. *steadfast.* JLP[5] **fæstum** dsg BC[44]

fæste: adv. *firmly.* JLP[7] CLP[89] VR[38, 43] **feste** KGM[104]

(ge)fæstnian: vb. *fasten, fix in place.* **gefæstnodon** 3pl pret VR[33]

(ge)fēa: noun, masc. *joy.* **gefēan** gsg/dsg (see note) KGM[88]

fēa: adv. *little.* VR[115]

feallan: vb. *fall.* VR[43]

fęder: see **fæder**

fegere: see **fægere**

fe(o)la: adj uninfl w gen. *many.* CLP[54, 118] DOX[23] **feala** take as gpl VR[50, 131] take as apl VR[125] KGM[53]

(ge)fēlan: vb. *perceive, be aware of.* **gefelde** 1sg pret KGM[58]

(ge)fellan: see **(ge)fyllan**

fēmne: see **fǣmne**

fēond, fīond: noun, masc. *enemy.* **fīond** asg KHP[25] **fēondas** npl VR[30] **fēonda** gpl JLP[41]

fēondscip: noun, masc. *hostility.* **fēondscipe** dsg JLP[38]

feorgbold: noun, neut. *life-house, body.* VR[73]
feorh: noun, masc/neut. *life, soul, spirit.* **(his) feores sceldig** *responsible for his soul, on peril of his soul* gsg. KGM[20] **tō wīdan feore** *for eternity, forever* ELP[11]
feorhhyrde: noun, masc. *guardian of the spirit, protector of life.* DOX[10]
feorran: adv. *from a distance.* VR[57]
fēr, fǣr: noun, masc. *sudden attack.* **fēre** dsg KGM[22]
feran: vb. *bring.* **mē . . . feran mōte** *be permitted to bring myself* KGM[57]
ferdrinc: noun, masc. *warrior.* asg KGM[22]
ferhð, ferð: noun, masc/neut. *spirit, soul.* **ferðe** dsg KGM[104, 125, 173]
ferhðloca: noun, masc. *enclosure of the spirit*, so *thoughts.* **ferhðlocan** dsg JLP[7, 41]
feste: see **fæste**
(ge)fetian: vb. *fetch, obtain, bring.* **gefetige** sg pres subj VR[138] **gefette** 3sg pret BC[33]
fīf: numerical adj. *five.* **fīfe** npl VR[8]
fīond: see **fēond**
firen: noun, fem. *transgression, sin.* BC[19]
firendēd, firendǣd: noun, fem. *evil deed.* **firendēda** gpl KGM[48]
(ge)flǣman: see **(ge)flīeman**
flǣsc: noun, neut. *body.* **flǣsces** gsg BC[65] **flǣsce** dsg CLP[6, 98]
flǣschama: noun, masc. *body.* **flǣschaman** dsg KGM[163]
(ge)flīeman, (ge)flǣman: vb. *put to flight, drive away.* **geflǣmdest** 2sg pret KHP[25]
folc, folk, follc: noun, neut. *folk, people.* VR[140] **follc** asg KHP[25] **folkes** gsg ABL[8] **folca** gpl ELP[10] KHP[20] **folcum** dpl KGM[5]
foldbūend: noun, masc. *mankind, earth-dweller.* **foldbūendum** dpl BC[24]
folde: noun, fem. *earth, ground, land.* **foldan** gsg VR[8, 43] dsg ELP[5] BC[65] DOX[23] *etc*
folgere: noun, masc. *follower.* **folgeras** apl BC[39]
folk, follc: see **folc**
for: prep w dat/acc/inst. *on account of, for, because of*
forgefnes, forgiefnes: noun, fem. *forgiveness, remission, pardon.* **forgefenesse** dsg KGM[39]
forgīefan: vb. *give.* **forgēaf** 3sg pret VR[147]
forgyfan: vb. *forgive, pardon.* **forgyf**, **forgif, forgef** imp sg JLP[25] CLP[94] KGM[49, 69, 159, 174] **forgifað** 1pl pres CLP[113] **forgefene** p. ptc asg KGM[56] **forgeofene** dsg KGM[165]
forht: adj. *frightening, terrible.* **forhtan** asg BC[65] *afraid* VR[21]

forhtian: vb. *fear, be afraid.* **forhtiað** 3pl pres VR[115]
forlǣtan: vb. *overlook, surrender, abandon, lose, let go.* BC[42] **forlǣtað** 1pl pres JLP[30] **forlēton** 3pl pret VR[61]
forð: adv. *(hence)forth* JLP[17] VR[132] KGM[116] **ā on worlda forð** *world without end* CLP[137]
forðām, forðān: conj/adv. developing from **for ðǣm ðe** ('for that [reason] which') *because* (conj), *therefore* (adv) CLP[3] KGM[171] VR[84]
forðgesceaft: noun, fem. *eternal decree, future.* asg VR[10] KGM[57]
(ge)forðian: vb. *send forth, put forth.* **geforðad** *accomplished, carried out* p ptc DOX[27]
forðsīð: noun, masc. *going forth, journey of death.* **forðsīðe** dsg CLP[80]
forðweard: adj. *progressing, moving towards.* KGM[88]
forðweg: noun, masc. *departure.* **forðwege** dsg VR[125]
forweornan: vb. *refuse, deny.* **forweorn** imp sg ABL[74]
forwundian: vb. *wound grieviously.* **forwunded, forwundod** p ptc VR[14, 62] ABL[3]
forwurðan, forweorðan: vb. *perish, pass away.* CLP[124]
fracod: adj. *wicked.* **fracodes** gsg [as a substantive collective] VR[10]
fram: see **from**
frēa: noun, masc. *ruler, lord.* BC[6, 30] DOX[17] ABL[8] KHP[20]
fremde: adj w gen of thing. *devoid, bereft of.* JLP[38]
(ge)fremman: vb. *bring about, accomplish, commit.* **gefræmmað** 3sg pres KGM[14] **gefremede, gefræmede** 1sg pret KGM[43, 53] **gefremmed** p ptc BC[19] **gefrę̄med** KGM[163, 173]
fremsume, fræmsume: adv. *graciously.* KGM[149]
frēobearn: noun, neut. *child of gentle birth.* BC[48]
frēod: noun, fem. *peace, friendship.* **frēode** dsg BC[44]
frēodōn, corrupt form of **frēodōm** (likely because of levelling **-m** > **-n**): noun, masc. *freedom, liberty.* asg ELP[10]
frēolice: adv. *freely, readily.* BC[17]
(ge)frēon, (ge)frēogan: vb. *liberate, free.* **gefrēo** imp sg JLP[40]
frēond: noun, masc. *friend.* VR[144] **frēondas** npl VR[76] **frēonda** gpl VR[132]
(ge)frignan: vb. *ask, find out, learn by inquiry.* **frīneð** 3sg pres VR[112] **gefrūnon** 3pl pret VR[76] **gefrigen** p ptc KGM[5]
friðian: vb. *keep, observe.* **friðiað** 3pl pres DOX[30]
frōfor: noun, fem. *consolation.* **frōfre** DOX[18] asg KGM[149] dsg CLP[37] BC[24] ABL[47] **frōfres** gsg JLP[2] **frōfra** gpl DOX[10]
from, also **fram**: prep w dat/inst. *from* ELP[10]
from: adj. *active, strong, bold.* **fromne** asg KGM[22]

fruma: noun, masc. *origin, beginning, cause.* KGM[20] **fruman** dsg CLP[81] DOX[17] KHP[20]
gefrūnon: see **(ge)frignan**
ful: adv. ***very***
full: adj. *filled with, full.* **fulle** npl DOX[53]
fultum: noun, masc. *help, support.* asg CLP[89]
fundian: vb. *set out.* **fundaþ** 3sg pres VR[103]
fūs: adj. *eager, brilliant (?).* **fūse** asg VR[21] npl subst VR[57]
fylian: vb. *follow.* BC[43]
fyl(l): noun, masc. *fall, death.* asg VR[56]
(ge)fyllan: vb. *fill up, replenish; fell, strike down.* VR[38, 73] **fylde** 3sg pret BC[21] **(ge)felled** p ptc KHP[43]
(ge)fylstan: vb w dat. *aid, support, protect.* **gefylste** sg pres subj ABL[71]
fyrd: noun, fem. *national army, troop.* **fyrde** dsg CLP[52]

galan: vb. *sing.* VR[67]
(ge)gān: vb. *go, walk, happen, occur.* **ēode** 3sg pret VR[54] **geīode** 3sg pret KGM[13]
gang: noun, masc. *flow.* **gange** dsg VR[23]
gārsecg: noun, masc. *ocean.* **gārsecges** gsg BC[8]
gāst: noun, masc. *spirit, soul.* asg CLP[88] VR[49] KGM[103] **gāstes** gsg KHP[12] KGM[56] **gāste** dsg TAD[3] **gāstæ** dsg KGM[165] **gāstas** npl VR[11] **gāsta** gpl CLP[13] VR[152] KGM[42]
gealga: noun, masc. *gallows.* VR[10] **gealgan** asg VR[40] dsg BC[31]
gealgtrēow: noun, neut. *gallows, cross.* **gealgtrēowe** dsg VR[146]
gēara: adv. *formerly, long ago, in earlier days.* CLP[102] VR[28]
(ge)gearwian: vb. *make ready, prepare, equip.* **geara** imp sg ABL[2] **gegearwod** p ptc CLP[81]
gelt: see **gylt**
gēo: adv. *formerly, once.* **iū** VR[28, 87]
geoguð, gioguð: noun, fem. *youth.* **gioguðe** dsg KGM[162]
gēomormōd: adj. *sorrowful.* BC[32]
geond: prep w acc. *throughout.* CLP[29]
geong: adj. *young.* VR[39]
georne: adv. *eagerly, sincerely, earnestly.* JLP[43] KGM[27, 29]
giefan: vb. *give, allow, grant.* **gief** imp sg ELP[10]
gīet: adv. *yet, still.* **gȳta** VR[28]
gif: conj. *if, whether.* ABL[40]
gifnes: noun, fem. *grace, favour.* **gifnesse** asg/gsg CLP[61, 127]

gift: noun, neut. *nuptials, gift, marriage gift, dowry*. **giftum** dpl BC[19]

gimm: noun, masc. *gemstone*. **gimmas** npl VR[7, 16]

gioguð: see **geoguð**

gītsung: noun, fem. *desire, covetousness, lust*. **gītsunge** dsg KGM[24]

glīdan: vb. *vanish, glide away*. KGM[165]

God, god: noun, neut. *God, god*. JLP[23] **Godes** gsg CLP[127] **Gode** dsg JLP[28] BC[55] **goda** gpl ABL[59]

gōd: adj. *good*. **goodes** gsg KHP[6] **gōdan** dsg KGM[150] **gōde (hwīle)** dsg (*a good while*) VR[70]

gōd: noun, neut. *advantage, virtue, goodness*. **gōde** dsg ABL[11]

godfæder: noun, masc. *father who is God*. KHP[31]

godferhtu, godfyrhtu: noun, fem. *fear of God*. **godferhte** asg KGM[14]

gold: noun, neut. *gold*. **golde** dsg VR[7] isg VR[77]

gramhēgdig, gramhȳdig: adj. *hostile*. see note to KGM[54]

grōwan: vb. *increase, flourish*. **grōweð** 3sg pres DOX[39]

grund: noun, masc. *ground, foundation*. asg CLP[43] ABL[31] **grunde** dsg DOX[43] **grundas** apl BC[8]

guma: noun, masc. *man*. **guman** gsg VR[146] dsg VR[49] **gumena** gpl JLP[19] BC[31] KHP[6]

gylt, gelt: noun, masc. *sin, guilt*. KGM[14] **gyltas, geltas** apl KGM[29, 43] **gelta, gylta** gpl KGM[54, 94, 127]

(ge)gyrwan: vb. *adorn, dress*. **gyredon** 3pl pret VR[77] **gegyred, gegyrwed** p ptc VR[16, 23]

gȳta: see **gīet**

habban: vb. *have, possess*. **hæbbe** 1sg pres VR[50, 79] KGM[163] **habbað** 1pl pres CLP[127] **hæfst, hafest** 2sg pres ABL[25] KHP[13] **hafað** 3sg pres BC[50] ABL[14, 19] **hæbben** pl pres subj KGM[5] **hæfde** 3sg pret VR[49] **hæfdon** 3pl pret VR[52]

hād: noun, masc. *rank, office*. **hādes** gsg ABL[54]

hāl: adj. *healthy, whole, hale*. **hāle** npl KHP[34]

(ge)hālgian: vb, wk 2. *hallow, make holy*. **hālgodest** 2sg pret DOX[28] **hālgad, (ge)hālgod** p ptc ELP[2] JLP[5] CLP[21] *etc*

hālig: adj. *holy [saint, as subst]*. ELP[1] JLP[3] CLP[15, 69] *etc* **hālige** KHP[22] asg DOX[21, 32] **hāligne** asg CLP[88] KGM[108] **hāliges** gsg DOX[48] **hāligum** dsg ABL[78] **hālige** npl DOX[40] VR[11] apl KGM[102] **hāligra** gpl BC[59] **hālgum, hālgan** dpl VR[144, 154] KHP[2, 7]

hāligdōm: noun, masc. *holiness, sanctity*. **hāligdōmes** gsg DOX[52]

hālsian: vb. *implore, entreat, adjure*. **hālsige** 1sg pres ABL[67]

hām: noun, masc. *home.* asg VR[148]
hand: noun, fem. *hand.* asg CLP[6, 92] **handa** gpl VR[59]
handgeweorc: noun, neut. *handiwork, word of your hand.* DOX[39] asg CLP[123] **handgeweorces** gsg KGM[33]
handgyft: noun, fem. *wedding present.* asg BC[20]
handlēan: noun, neut. *recompense, retribution.* apl ABL[14]
(ge)hātan: vb. *promise, order, command, call, name.* **hāte** 1sg pres VR[95] **gehǣtst** 2sg pres CLP[79] **hēt** 3sg pret BC[35] KGM[18] **hēte** 2sg pret DOX[39] **hēton** 3pl pret VR[31] **hāten** p ptc KGM[1]
hǣahsetl: see **hēahsetl**
hæfst, hæbben, hæfde, hæfdon: see **habban**
hæftnȳd, hæftnīed: noun, fem. *bondage.* **hæftnȳde** dsg JLP[45]
(ge)hǣlan: vb. *heal, save.* VR[85] **gehǣl** imp sg ABL[4]
hǣlend, hęlend: noun, masc. *lord, king, Christ.* ABL[29] KHP[16] **hǣlendne** asg BC[12]
hæleð, heleð: noun, masc. *hero, warrior, man.* VR[39, 78, 95] KGM[1] **hæleða** gpl ABL[30] **heleða** KHP[34]
(ge)hǣlig: see **hālig**
hǣlu, hēlu: noun, fem. *salvation, health.* **helo** KGM[128] **hǣlo** gsg KGM[113] **tō hǣle** dsg *as salvation* JLP[21]
hǣnðu, henðu: noun, fem. *humiliation.* **hǣnðum** dpl KGM[91]
gehǣtst: see **(ge)hātan**
hē: personal pronoun. Following is the paradigm for the third-person personal pronoun, singular and plural. These replace nouns of the same grammatical gender, although because many of our texts are later, we are seeing the start of the shift from grammatical to natural gender taking place in this process.

	Masc	*Fem*	*Neut*	*Plural*
Nom	hē	hēo, hīo	hit	hīe, hī, hȳ, hig, hīo
Acc	hine	hīe, hȳ, hī, hig	hit	hīe, hī, hȳ, hig, hīo
Gen	his	hire	his	hīra, heora
Dat	him, hiom	hire	him, hiom	him, hiom

heafen: see **heofon**
hēafod: noun, neut. *leader, head.* CLP[69] **hēafdum** dpl (with sg meaning) VR[63]

hēah: adj. *high, exalted.* CLP[21, 44, 66] *etc* **hēahan** asg DOX[30] **hēanne** asg VR[40] **hēhstan** superl (as subst) gsg DOX[32]

hēahcyning, hēahcyninc, hēahkyning: noun, masc. *high king.* JLP[20] ABL[70] KHP[42] asg BC[57]

hēahfæder: noun, masc. *high-father, God the Father.* **hēahfædere** dsg VR[134]

hēahnes, hēanes: noun, fem. *excellence, sublime nature.* **hēahnisse** asg ABL[55]

hēahsetl, hǣahsetl: noun, neut. *throne.* CLP[44] **hǣahsetle** dsg KHP[29]

hēahþrymnes: noun, fem. *great glory.* **hahþrymnesse** dsg CLP[57] DOX[48]

healdan: vb. *keep, hold, observe, grasp.* **healdað** 3pl pres DOX[30] **tō healdenne** infl inf KGM[102]

healf: noun, fem. *side, half.* **healfe** dsg CLP[47] VR[20]

hēanes, hēahnisse: see **hēahnes**

hēanlice: adv. *miserably, pathetically.* CLP[123]

hēanne: see **hēah**

heard: adj. *hard, difficult.* **heardost** superl. VR[87]

hearpera: noun, masc. *harper.* KGM[4]

hebban: vb. *raise, heave up, lift.* VR[31]

hefig: adj. *heavy.* **hefian** dsg VR[61]

hegelēas, hygelēas: adj. *thoughtless, unbridled.* **hegelēasra** gpl KGM[164]

hēhsta: see **hēah**

heht: see **hyht**

hehtful: see **hyhtful**

heleð: see **hæleð**

hell: noun, fem. *hell.* **helle** dsg BC[33]

hellewīte: noun, neut. *hell-torment.* **hellewītes** gsg JLP[45]

helm: noun, masc. *protector, defence.* KGM[113]

help: noun, fem/masc. *aid, help.* CLP[69] **helpe** dsg VR[102]

helpan: vb w gen/dat. *aid, support.* **help** imp sg KGM[33] **helpst** 2sg pres CLP[49]

helpend: noun, masc. *helper.* ELP[7] KGM[128]

hel(l)waru: noun, fem. *dwellers in hell.* CLP[105]

hēlu: see **hǣlu**

heofon, heafen, hiofen: noun, masc. *heaven.* **heofenes** gsg VR[64] **heofonas** npl DOX[52] apl DOX[21] VR[103] **heofena, heafena, hiofena** gpl JLP[20] BC[57] KHP[29, 42] **heofonum, hiofenum** dpl ELP[1] JLP[3] VR[85, 134, 140] KGM[4]

heofonengel: noun, masc. *angel of heaven.* **heofonengla** gpl CLP[15]

heofonlic: adj. *heavenly.* KHP[22] **heofonlicne** asg VR[148]

heofonrīc, hiofenrīc: noun, neut. *kingdom of heaven.* **heofonrīces, hiofenrīces** gsg VR[91] KHP[2, 128] **heofonrīce** dsg CLP[66]

heofonware: noun, masc/fem. *dwellers in heaven.* **heofonwaru** npl CLP[105]

heofonwuldor: noun neut. *heavenly glory.* **heofonwuldre** dsg JLP[16]

heonon: adv. *away from here, hence.* VR[132]

heorte: noun, fem. *heart, soul, mind, desire.* **hiorte** KGM[145] **hiortan** asg KGM[99]

heortlufu: noun, fem. *committed love, love from the heart.* **heortlufan** asg DOX[32]

hēr: adv. *here.* **hēr for līfe** *forever* BC[57, 60]

(ge)herdan, (ge)hyrdan: vb. *brace up, "harden."* **herdon** 3pl pres (subj?) with a sense of reflexivity KGM[61]

here: noun, masc. *army, multitude.* **herige** dsg CLP[53]

herian: vb. *praise, glorify.* **hero** 1sg pres KGM[82] **heriað** 1pl pres KHP[7] 3pl pres CLP[27, 129] BC[56] *etc*

herige: see **here**

(ge)hērnes, (ge)hīernes: noun, fem. *hearing.* KGM[87]

hēt(e): see **(ge)hātan**

hider: adv. *thither, here*

hīe, hig, hī: see **hē**

(ge)hīeran: vb. *hear, obey.* **gehȳran** VR[78] **hȳræð** 3sg pres ABL[17] **gehȳrde** 1sg pret VR[26] **gehȳred** p. ptc CLP[36, 51]

hierde, hiorde: noun, masc. *guardian, pastor.* KGM[114, 121]

hīenðu: see **hǣnðu**

(ge)hīernes: see **(ge)hērnes**

Hierusolimę: proper name. *Jerusalem.* KGM[153]

higefrōfer: noun, fem. *consolation.* DOX[15]

hiht: see **hyht**

hilderinc: noun, masc. *warrior.* **hilderincas** npl VR[61] **hilderinca** gpl VR[72]

him: see **he**

hīo: see **hē**

hiofen: see **heofon**

hiofenrīc: see **heofonrīc**

hiom: see **hē**

hiorte: see **heorte**

hlāf: noun, masc. *bread.* asg ELP[7] JLP[20] CLP[76]

hlǣnan: see **lǣn**

hlēoðor: noun, neut. *hearing*. asg KGM[86]
hlēoðrian: vb. *make utterance, speak*. **hlēoðrode** 3sg pret VR[26]
hlīfian: vb. *tower.* **hlīfige** 1sg pres VR[85]
hlīoðorcwide, hlēoðorcwide: noun, masc. *harmonious song, speech*. **hlīoðorcwidum** dpl KHP[2]
hlūttor: adj. *pure, clear*. JLP[16]
hnīgan: vb. *bow down*. **hnāg** 1sg pret VR[59]
(ge)hnyst: adj. *contrite*. **gehnysta** KGM[145]
holt: noun, neut. *forest, wood*. **holtes** gsg VR[29]
holtwudu: noun, neut. *trees of the wood*. asg VR[91]
hord: noun, neut. *hoard*. asg KGM[28, 171] apl KGM[78]
hrǣw: noun, neut. *corpse, body*. VR[72] asg VR[53]
hrēowcearig: adj. *sorrowful, troubled*. VR[25]
hrōf: noun, masc. *roof, ceiling, sky*. **hrōfe** dsg ELP[5]
hū: adv. *how*
hundseofontig: numerical adj. *seventy*. See **twā**
hūru: adv. *certainly, indeed*
hūð: noun, fem. *plunder*. **hūðe** asg BC[33]
(ge)hwā: pro, masc/fem **(ge)hwæt** neut. each *one, everyone, anyone/thing*. asg VR[116] **gehwæs** gsg KHP[20] **gehwām** dsg ELP[11] CLP[17] **hwæt** nsg, almost as a rel pro, *which* VR[2]
hwār, hwǣr: adv or conj. *where*. CLP[7] VR[112]
hwænne: conj. *until*. VR[136]
(ge)hwǣr: adv. *everywhere*. KGM[47]
hwæt: interj. *lo behold* VR[1, 90] see also **hwā**
hwæðre, hwęðere: adv or conj. *however, nevertheless*
(ge)hweorfan: vb. *depart*. **gehweorfe** 1sg pres ABL[73]
hwīl: noun, fem. *time, while*. **þā hwīle þe** conj. *while* CLP[110] **hwīle** dsg VR[24, 64, 84] **hwīle** dsg **(ge)hwilc**: pro or adj. *each*. **gehwylces** gsg JLP[41] BC[62] KHP[15] **gehwilcum** dsg KHP[6] **gehwylcum** dpl VR[108] **gehwylce** isg VR[136] **hwīlum**: dpl *at times* ABL[64, 65] VR[22, 23]
hȳ: see **hē**
hygecræft: noun, masc. *wisdom*. **hygecræftum** dpl JLP[5]
hygelēas: see **hegelēas**
hyht, hiht: noun, masc/fem. *hope, trust, comfort*. VR[126, 148] CLP[11] **heht** asg KGM[113] **hihte** dsg BC[46]
hyhtful: adj. *full of joy*. KGM[87]
hyldan: vb. *bow, bend*. VR[45]

(ge)hȳran: see **(ge)hīeran**
(ge)hyrdan: see **(ge)herdan**
hys: see **hē**

ic: personal pronoun. Following is the paradigm for the first- and second-person pronouns in singular, dual and plural form. Possessive adjectives are formed when the genitive picks up adjectival endings which then agree with those of the noun that they modify: **þinum** dpl ELP[2] **mīnre** dsg ABL[23] **ūserne** asg ELP[7]

	Singular		*Dual*		*Plural*	
	1st	*2nd*	*1st*	*2nd*	*1st*	*2nd*
Nom.	**ic** = *I*	**þū** = *thou*	**wit** = *we two*	**git** = *you two*	**wē** = *we*	**gē** = *you*
Acc.	**mē** = *me*	**þē** = *thee*	**unc** = *us two*	**inc** = *you two*	**ūs, ūsic** = *us*	**ēow** = *you*
Gen.	**mīn** = *my*	**þīn, þȳn** = *thy*	**uncer** = *our, of the two of us*	**incer** = *your, of the two of you*	**ūre, ūser** = *our*	**ēower** = *your*
Dat.	**mē** = *me*	**þē** = *thee*	**unc** = *us two*	**inc** = *you two*	**ūs** = *us*	**ēow** = *you*

īdel: adj. *vain, empty, worthless.* **īdele** npl CLP[120]
ides: noun, fem. *woman, virgin, lady.* BC[16]
īecan: see **ǣcan**
ieldo: noun, fem. *old age.* **ælde** dsg KGM[162]
ierre: see **eorre**
īeþost: see **ȳþost**
in: prep w acc after verbs implying motion: *into, onto*; w dat after verbs implying no motion: *in, on*
ingeðanc: noun, masc/neut. *conscience, thought.* **ingeðance** dsg KGM[172] **ingeðancum** dpl KGM[146]
innan: prep w acc/gen/dat. *within, in, into*
inwidhlemm: noun, masc. *malicious wound.* **inwidhlemmas** npl VR[47]
inwitnīð: noun, masc. *cunning, maliciousness.* **inwitnīðas** apl ABL[66]
(ge)īode: see **(ge)gān**
Iōsēp: proper name. *Joseph (of Arimathea, see Matthew 27: 57–59).* BC[32]
Israēl: proper name. *Israel.* **Israēla** gsg KHP[26] KGM[2]
iū: see **gēo**

kyning: see **cyning**

lāc: noun, masc/neut. *sacrifice, offering.* asg KGM[156]
(ge)lācnian: vb. *cure, heal.* **gelacna** imp sg ABL[5]
lamb: noun, neut. *lamb.* KHP[22]
(ge)lamp: see **(ge)limpan**
land: noun, neut. *earth, land.* **landes** gsg KGM[177]
lang: adj. *long.* **lange** dsg VR[24]
langsum: adj. *lasting.* asg KGM[62]
langunghwīl: noun, fem. *time of longing.* **langunghwīla** gpl VR[126]
lārēow: noun, masc. *teacher, master.* DOX[14]
lāttēow: noun, masc. *leader, guide.* DOX[11]
lāð: adj. *hateful, evil, malignant.* **lāðe** npl *evil (ones)* CLP[116] **lēdre** comp, see note for KGM[44] **lāðost** superl VR[88]
lǣce: noun, masc. *physician.* CLP[69] **lǣca** gpl ABL[6]
lǣdan: vb. *lead, guide, bring forth, lift.* VR[5] **lǣdað** 3pl pres CLP [28] **lǣd** imp sg JLP[35]
lǣn, lēne: adj. *transitory, impermanent, sinful.* **lǣnum, lǣnan** dsg VR[109, 138] **hlǣnan** ABL[73] **lēne** apl KGM[15]
(ge)lǣran: vb. *convert, persuade, guide, teach.* **lǣrde** 1sg pret KGM[119] **lǣrdes** 2sg pret KGM[60]
lǣs: adv and as subst adj. *less.* **þȳ lǣs (þe)** conj w subj. *lest.* JLP[37]
(ge)lǣstan: vb. *accomplish, accompany, serve, carry out.* BC[44] **gelǣstað** 1pl pres CLP[83] **gelǣsted** p ptc JLP[14]
(ge)lǣtan: vb. *permit, allow.* **lǣt** imp sg ELP[9] CLP[116, 123] ABL[76]
(ge)lēafa: noun, masc. *belief, faith.* JLP[11]
leahtor: noun, masc. *sin, crime.* **leahtras** apl JLP[26, 30] BC[62] **leahtra** gpl KGM[164] **leahtrum** dpl KHP[33]
lēne: see **lǣn**
lēode, līode: noun, masc/fem (pl). *people.* **līoda** gpl KGM[156] **lēodum** dpl VR[88]
lēof, līof: adj. *dear, beloved.* **lēofa** VR[78] ABL[57] **līofan** asg KHP[33] **lēofe** npl subst BC[55] **līofost** superl KGM[3]
lēofwende: see **līofwende**
lēoht, līoht: noun, neut. *light.* ABL[21] KHP[22] asg ABL[50] **lēohtes, līohtes** gsg DOX[11] ABL[21] KGM[114] **lēohte** dsg VR[5]
lēðre: see **lāð**
libban: vb. *live.* **lifiaþ** 3pl pres VR[134]
līc: noun, neut. *body.* **līces** gsg JLP[26] VR[63]

licgan: vb. *lie*. **licgende** pres ptc VR[24]
līchama: noun, masc. *body*. **līchaman** gsg KGM[15] see note for KGM[44]
(ge)līefan: vb. *believe, trust in*. **gelȳfe** 1sg pres BC[6, 11, 55, 62] ABL[57]
gelȳfað 3pl pres ABL[49]
līf, lȳf: noun, neut. *life*. asg VR[147] **līfes** gsg JLP[33] CLP[33] VR[126] KHP[3] *etc*
lȳfes ABL[21] **līfe, lȳfe** dsg VR[109, 138] ABL[73]
līfdæg: noun, masc. *lifetime*. **līfdæge** dsg JLP[11]
lifiaþ: see **libban**
lifiende: adj from pres ptc of **libban** (vb. *live*). *that which is living*. CLP[112] ABL[42] **lyfiendne** asg ABL[49] **lifigend(r)a** gpl CLP[28] KGM[177]
liicwerðe, līcwyrðe: adj. *pleasing, acceptable*. KGM[144]
(ge)limpan: vb. *happen*. **gelamp** 3sg pret KGM[16]
limwērig: adj. *limb-weary, tired out*. **limwērigne** asg VR[63]
līode: see **lēode**
līof: see **lēof**
līofwende, lēofwende: adj. *acceptable, loving*. apl KGM[156]
līofwendum, lēofwendum: adv. *fervently, ardently*. KHP[3]
līoht: see **lēoht**
līohtfruma, lēohtfruma: noun, masc. *source of light*. KGM[50]
liss: noun, fem. *joy, peace*. **lisse** gsg KGM[76] isg BC[62]
lof: noun, neut. *praise, glory*. asg CLP[28] KGM[134]
lofian: vb. *praise, extol*. **lofiað** 1pl pres CLP[129]
(ge)lōme: adv. *often*. **oft and gelōme** *frequently* ABL[66]
lufian: vb. *cherish, show love towards*. KHP[3] **lufast** 2sg pres KGM[74]
lufedest 2sg pret KGM[139]
lufu: noun, fem. *love, favour*. CLP[34] DOX[4] **lufan** asg KGM[84,123] gsg KGM[50]
lustum: adv. *gladly*. BC[6]
lȳf: see **līf**
(ge)lȳfe: see **(ge)līefan**
lyft: noun, fem. *air, sky* asg. VR[5]
lȳsan: vb. *ransom, redeem*. VR[41]
lȳtel, lītel: adj. *small, unimportant*. **lȳtla** subst ABL[61]
lȳðre: adj. *corrupt, wretched*. **lȳðra** ABL[61]

mā: indecl substantive. *more*. KGM[143]
magan: vb w inf. *have authority [to do]*. **mæg** 1sg pres VR[85] 3sg pres VR[110] ABL[30] **miht** 2sg pres CLP[4, 132] DOX[6] VR[78] ABL[6] **magon, mage** 1pl pres CLP[103] ABL[33] **magon** 3pl pres ABL[37]
man, mon: indefinite pro, often used to translate a passive into Old English. *someone, one*. CLP[107] VR[73] asg KGM[16]

māndǣd: noun, fem. *sin, crime*. **māndǣda** apl JLP[27]

manig: adj. *many*. **manega** apl CLP[72] BC[34] DOX[24] **manigra** gpl VR[41] **manegum** dpl CLP[22] DOX[29, 36] VR[99] **monegum** dpl CLP[49] see also **menigu**

mann: noun, masc. *person, mankind*. **men** dsg CLP[18] **men(n)** npl VR[12, 82] **manna** gpl JLP[22] KHP[17, 32] KGM[8, 32] **mannum** dpl JLP[9] CLP[37] VR[96, 103] **menn** dpl VR[93]

manncyn(n): noun, neut. *mankind, humanity*. asg VR[41,104] **manncynnes** gsg JLP[2] VR[97] *etc*

mānscild: noun, fem. *sin, fault*. **mānscilde** apl KHP[23]

māre: adj (comp of **micel**). *more*. asg CLP[79]

Maria: proper name. *Mary*. **Marian** asg VR[92] dsg BC[15]

mæge: see **magan**

mæga, maga: adj. *powerful*. **mægena** gpl KHP[11]

mægen: noun, neut. *power, might, valour*. DOX[4] asg DOX[7]

mægenstrang: adj. *of mighty power, of great virtue*. ABL[41] **mægenstranga** subst ABL[58]

mæhtig, mæhte: see **mihtig, miht**

(ge)mǣne: adj. *universal*. TAD[2]

mænige: see **menigu**

(ge)mǣnscipe: noun, masc. *fellowship, community*. asg BC[59]

mǣre: adj. *glorious, famous*. JLP[12] CLP[44, 133] VR[12, 82] *etc* **mǣrne, mǣran** asg BC[22, 59] VR[69] **mǣrra** gpl BC[9] **mǣrost** superl KGM[4]

mǣrlice: adv. *splendidly, gloriously*. CLP[22]

(ge)mǣrsian: *proclaim, make famous*. **mǣrsodest** 2sg pret DOX[29] **gemǣrsod** p ptc CLP[49]

mǣst: adj (superl of **micel**). *most, greatest*. **mǣste** nsg DOX[51] npl CLP[110]

(ge)mǣtan: impersonal vb. (+ dat. of person) *dream* **gemǣtte** 3sg pret VR[2]

mǣte: adj. *small*. isg VR[69, 124]

meahte: 1sg pret VR[18] **mæge** sg pres subj ABL[72]

meahta: see **miht**

meahtig, mehtig: see **mihtig**

men(n): see **man**

menigu, menio: noun, fem. *multitude, company*. asg BC[9] **mænige** dsg VR[112] **manigeo** dsg VR[151] **menio** dsg KGM[37]

meotod: see **me(o)tod**

(ge)mētan: vb. *fall in with, encounter, meet*. **gemēte** 1sg pres KGM[84] **gemētað** 3pl pres CLP[34]

mete: noun, masc. *food.* asg CLP[79]

me(o)tod: noun, masc. *fate, creator, God.* ELP[8] ABL[27] **meotod** KGM[160] **metode** dsg BC[67]

mēðe: adj. *weary.* VR[65, 69]

micel(e): adj. *great, mighty, much.* CLP[37] VR[130] **mycel** VR[139] ABL[39] **micle** KGM[143] **miccla** (as substantive) ABL[58] **micele** asg DOX[36] **micclum** dsg CLP[53] **miclan** dsg VR[65, 102] gsg for gpl KHP[11] **mycle** isg VR[34, 60, 123] see also **māre, mǣst**

micel, micclum: adv. *greatly.* CLP[49]

mid: prep w dat/acc/inst. *(in company) with*

midd: adj. *middle.* **midre** dsg VR[2]

middan(g)eard: noun, neut. *the world, earth.* **middaneard** DOX[42] asg JLP[22] CLP[133] VR[104] ABL[32] **middangeardes** gsg KHP[23]

miht, meaht, mæht: noun, fem. *power, authority, miracle, virtue.* asg CLP[9, 53] DOX[21, 36] **mæhte** asg KGM[133] **mihte** dsg VR[102] **mihta** npl CLP[110] DOX[54] apl CLP[86] gpl JLP[9] CLP[31] ABL[53] **meahta** gpl KGM[32, 96] **mihtum** dpl JLP[44] **mæhtum** KHP[12] see also **magan**

mihtig: adj. *powerful.* VR[151] **meahtig** subst KHP[32] **mæhtig, mæahtig, mehtig** KGM[68, 100, 143, 174]

milde: adj. *merciful, generous.* JLP[44] KGM[80] **mildum** dsg JLP[27] **mildostan** superl asg KGM[8]

milds, milts: noun, fem. *favour, benevolence.* **mildse** asg CLP[74, 86] dsg CLP[64] DOX[51] npl DOX[4] **mildsa** gpl JLP[37]

mildsa: see either **mild(/t)s** or **miltsian**

(ge)miltsian: vb w dat. *show mercy.* **mildsa, miltsa** imp sg CLP[31] KHP[32] KGM[32] **gemilsa** imp sg ABL[9] **gemilsige** sg pres subj ABL[69]

(ge)miltsung: noun, fem. *mercy, pity, compassion.* **miltsunga** apl KGM[96]

mīnre: see **ic**

mirhð, myrgð, mirigð: noun, fem. *mirth, pleasure.* **mirhðe** asg CLP[35] **mirigðe** dsg ABL[13]

misdǣd: noun, fem. *transgression, evil deed.* **misdēdum** dpl KGM[94]

mōd: noun, neut. *mind, spirit.* asg CLP[86] **mōdes** gsg DOX[4, 51] **mōde** dsg JLP[12] VR[122, 130]

mōdig: adj. *brave, resolute.* VR[41]

mōdor: noun, fem. *mother.* asg VR[92]

mōdsefa: noun, masc. *mind, heart, spirit.* VR[124]

mōdswīð: adj. *resolute.* **mōdswīðne** asg KGM[100]

moldærn: noun, neut. *sepulchre.* asg VR[65]

molde: noun, fem. *earth, mould, dust, world.* **moldan** dsg VR[12, 82] ABL[32] BC[38]

mon: see **man**
monegum: see **manig**
mōtan: vb (modal auxiliary). *be allowed, have opportunity.* **mōt** 1sg pres VR[142] **mōton** 1pl pres CLP[90] **mōte** sg pres subj VR[127] KGM[57, 117] read as pl pres subj (see note) KGM[165] **mōste** sg pret subj KGM[140]
(ge)munan: vb. *remember.* **geman** 1sg pres VR[28]
mund: noun, fem. *protection.* asg CLP[53]
mundbyrd, mundberd: noun, fem. *protection.* VR[130] KGM[122]
mundian: vb. *protect, guard.* **munde** sg pres subj KGM[170]
mūð: noun, masc. *mouth.* KGM[133]
mycle, mycel: see **micel**
(ge)myndig: adj w gen. *mindful.* KHP[31] KGM[167]
myrgð: see **mirhð**

nā: adv. *never, not, no.* CLP[116]
nā: conj. *neither, nor*
nama, also **noma**: noun, masc. *name.* JLP[6] ELP[6] **naman** gsg KHP[35] dsg DOX[33] VR[113]
(ge)nāman, (ge)nāmon: see **(ge)niman**
nǣfre: adv. *never*
nægl: noun, masc. *nail.* **næglum** dpl VR[46]
nǣnne: adj/pro. see **ne** + **ǣnne.** *none.* BC[42] **nǣnigum** dpl VR[47]
næs: vb. see **ne** and **bēon.** *not be.* **ne** + **wæs**: **næs** 3sg pret BC[19]
ne: adv. *not, no*
ne: conj. *nor, neither*
nēat: noun, neut. *beast, ox.* **nēata** gpl KGM[141]
(ge)ne(a)hhe: adv. *frequently, often.* ABL[62]
nellan: vb. see **ne** and **willan**. *not desire.* **ne** + **wolde**: **nolde** 3sg pret BC[42]
(ge)nemnan: vb. *name, call.* **genemned** p ptc BC[49]
nergend, neriend: noun, masc. *redeemer, saviour.* ELP[3] KHP[35] KGM[16, 64] *etc*
(ge)nerian: vb. *rescue, liberate.* **generedes** 2sg pret KHP[25] **neri(g)ende** pres ptc JLP[6, 36]
niht: noun, fem. *night.* **nihtes** gsg *by night* CLP[119] **dæiges and nihtes** gsg *by day and by night* ABL[12, 17, 63] **nihte** dsg VR[2]
(ge)niman: vb. *take, seize.* **genāman, genāmon** 3pl pret VR[30, 60]
(ge)niowan: see **nīwian**
nīð: noun, masc. *evil, strife.* **nīða** gpl KHP[35]
niððas: noun, masc (pl only: used in verse): *men, people.* **niþþa** gpl ELP[3]
nīwian: vb. *restore, renew.* **genīowa** imp sg KGM[104] **genīwad** p ptc VR[148]

(ge)nōg: adj. *enough.* **genōge** npl VR[33]
noma: see **nama**
nū: adv. *now*

of: prep w dat. *from*
ofer: prep w acc or dat. *upon, on, against; above (*sc. *more than)* KGM[83]
oferswīðan: vb. *overcome, vanquish.* **oferswīddest** KGM[63]
oferwinnan: vb. *overcome, conquer.* KGM[175]
oft: adv. *often.* comp **oftor** VR[128] **oft and gelōme** *frequently* ABL[66]
on, an: prep w acc after verbs implying motion: *into, onto*; w dat after verbs implying no motion: *in, on, within, in accordance with* CLP[87]
onbyrgan: vb w gen. *taste.* VR[114]
oncnāwan: vb. *understand, acknowledge.* **oncnāwe** 1sg pres KGM[46] **oncnāwað** 1pl pres CLP[100]
onfindan, anfindan: vb. *feel, discover, suffer.* **anfunde** 3sg pret KGM[25]
onfōn: vb. *receive, accept.* **anfehst** 2sg pres KGM[155] **onfeng** 3sg pret BC[17]
onginnan: vb. *begin.* **onginnen** pl pres subj VR[116] **ongan** 3sg pret VR[19, 27, 73] **ongunnon** 3pl pret VR[65, 67] perhaps w subj sense ABL[37]
ongyrwan: vb. *strip, unclothe.* **ongyrede** 3sg pret VR[39]
ongytan, ongietan: vb. *perceive, see.* VR[18]
onlȳsan: vb. *redeem.* **onlȳsde** 3sg pret VR[147]
onsægednes, onsegednes: noun, fem. *sacrifice, burnt offering.* **onsegednesse** asg KGM[137]
onsendan: vb. *send forth.* **onsendest** 2sg pres JLP[21] **onsende** 3sg pret KGM[16] **onsended** p ptc VR[49]
onsittan: vb. *occupy.* **onsittest** 2sg pres CLP[46]
ontēnan, ontȳnan: vb. *reveal, display.* **ontēndes** 2sg pret KGM[78] **ontēnde** 3sg pret KGM[28] **ontȳn** imp sg *open* KGM[86, 132]
onwrēon: vb. *reveal.* **onwrēoh** imp sg VR[97]
open: adj. *open.* **opene** npl VR[47]
(ge)openian: vb. *declare, reveal, make manifest.* **geopenod** p ptc CLP[41] DOX[2]
ordfruma: noun, masc. *point of origin, source.* BC[7]
oruð: noun, neut. *breath.* asg DOX[61]
oððæt (sometimes **oð ðæt**): conj. *until*
oððe: conj. *or*

Pilatus: proper name. *Pilate.* BC[28]
pontisca: noun from Latin, elsewhere in the canon **Pontisc** translating

Pontius Pilate; here, BC[28], perhaps being taken as a weak masc noun since it has acquired the demonstrative **sē**, and meaning *pontifex, ruler*?

rǣcan: vb. *reach, extend to*. **rǣcað** 3pl pres CLP[17]
rǣdbora: noun, masc. *counsellor.* CLP[43]
rǣdfæst: adj. *resolute, wise*. ELP[4]
recen: adj. *prompt, quick, swift*. BC[38]
(ge)rēne: see **(ge)rȳne**
(ge)reord: noun, fem/neut. *voice, language*. **reorde** dsg ABL[78] **gereordum** dpl CLP[22] BC[48]
reordberend: noun, masc. *voice-bearer* i.e. *human being.* VR[3] **reordberendum** dpl VR[89]
rēotan: vb. *weep*. **rēotende** pres ptc VR[70]
rest: noun, fem. *rest, bed, resting-place*. **reste** either asg or dsg (see note) VR[3]
(ge)restan: vb. *rest, be still, take repose.* **gerestest** 2sg pret DOX[26] **reste (hine)** 3sg pret (w reflexive) VR[64, 69]
reðe: adj. *righteous, just.* CLP[70]
rīce: noun, neut. *power, rule, reign*. ELP[4] JLP[10] *etc* asg VR[119,152] **rīces** gsg BC[29] JLP[15] KHP[29] **rīce** dsg BC[13]
rīce: adj. *powerful.* CLP[43] KGM[2] **rīcra** gpl VR[131]
rīcsian: vb. *reign, rule.* **rīcsast** 2sg pres KHP[40] **rīxað** 3pl pres DOX[46]
riht: adj. *fair, lawful*. **rihtne** asg VR[89] KGM[103] **rihte** npl CLP[17]
riht: noun, neut. *justice, righteousness*. asg CLP[83] **on riht** *correctly, properly* DOX[8]
(ge)rihtan: vb. *direct, correct.* **geriht** p ptc VR[131]
rihtwīs: adj. *righteous*. JLP[10] CLP[70]
(ge)rīm: noun, neut. *number, total.* asg ABL[37]
rīxað: see **rīcsian**
rōd: noun, fem. *cross, rood.* VR[44, 136] asg **rōde** VR[119] dsg VR[56, 131]
rodor: noun, masc. *heaven, sky*. **rodores** gsg ELP[5] **rodore** dsg BC[2] **rodera** gpl KGM[103] **roderum** dpl ABL[50]
Rōmware: noun, fem/masc. **Rōm** + **-ware**: *Rome-dwellers, citizens of Rome*. **Rōmwarum** dpl BC[29]
rūm: adj. *wide, spacious, noble.* **rūmne** asg CLP[43] **rūmre** dsg ELP[5] **rūme** npl CLP[17]
rūmheort: adj. *generous*. CLP[70]
rūn: noun, fem. *mystery, secret, counsel*. **rūnum** dpl BC[40]

(ge)rȳman: vb. *open (a path).* **gerȳmde** 1sg pret VR[89]
(ge)rȳne, (ge)rēne: noun, neut. *mystery, sacrament.* **gerēna** gpl KHP[11] **gerȳnum** dpl BC[51]

(ge)samnian: see **(ge)somnian**
samod: adv. *together, at the same time.* CLP[34]
sancta: adj. from Latin (OE **hālig**): **sanctan**: *holy, saint* dsg BC[15]
sangere: noun, masc. *singer, poet.* KGM[6]
sār: adj. *sore.* **sārra** gpl VR[80]
sāre: adv. *grievously.* VR[59]
(ge)sāwe: see **(ge)sēon**
sāwol, sāul: noun, fem. *soul.* **sāwl** VR[120] **sāule** asg ABL[3] KGM[41] **sāwle** asg CLP[5, 9] DOX[61] **sāule** gsg KGM[161] **sāwle** dsg ABL[23] apl CLP[92,113] **sāwla, sāula** gpl BC[34] DOX[50] KGM[16, 64] **sāwlum** dpl JLP[21]
sæcgan: see **secgan**
sǣl: noun, masc/fem. *time.* VR[80]
sæle: see **sellan**
sændan: see **sendan**
scamian: vb. *be ashamed.* **scamige** sg pres subj CLP[94]
scamu: noun, fem. *shame, dishonour.* **scame** dsg KGM[69]
sceadu: noun, fem. *shadow, shade.* VR[54]
(ge)sceaft, (ge)scęft: noun, masc/fem/neut. *creation, existence.* VR[12, 55, 82] asg BC[3] KHP[17, 33] **gesceafta** apl CLP[71] gpl ABL[27, 60]
scēat: noun, masc. *region, surface.* **scēatas** VR[37] **scēatum** dpl VR[8, 43]
scēawian: vb. *behold, look at.* **scēawað** 3sg pres ABL[14, 19] **scēawode** 1sg pret VR[137]
sceld: see **scyld**
sceldig: see **sculan**
sceolde: see **sculan**
scepe: see **(ge)scieppan**
sceppen(d): see **scieppend**
sceððan: vb. *injure.* VR[47]
(ge)scieppan: vb. *create, make, shape.* **sceōpe** 2sg pret BC[3]
scieppend, scyppend, scippend, sceppen(d): noun, masc. *creator, God.* ABL[8, 43] KHP[34] *etc* **sceppend** asg KGM[8] BC[23]
scīma: noun, masc. *light, brilliance.* **scīman** asg VR[54]
scīnan: vb. *shine, be visible.* VR[15] **scīnað** 3pl pres KGM[49] **scīnende** pres ptc KGM[83]
scippend: see **scieppend**

scīr: adj. *bright, shining.* **scīran** asg BC[3] **scīrne** asg VR[54]
sculan: vb. *be obliged to, have to, must.* **sceolde** 1sg pret VR[43] ABL[63] **scoldan** 3pl pret KGM[12, 123]
(ge)scyld: noun, masc/fem. *transgression, fault, sin.* **scelda** npl KGM[49] **sceldum** dpl KGM[69]
scyldi(g): adj. *guilty, responsible (for)* + gen. ABL[65] **sceldig** KGM[20]
scyppend: see **scieppend**
se, sēo, þæt: demonstrative (adj or pro). *the, that, that [one]:*

	Masc	*Fem*	*Neut*	*Plural*
Nom	**sē**	**sēo**	**þæt**	**þā**
Acc	**þone**	**þā**	**þæt**	**þā**
Gen	**þæs**	**þǣre**	**þæs**	**þāra, þǣra**
Dat	**þǣm, þām (þān)**	**þǣre**	**þǣm þām (þān)**	**þǣm, þām**
Inst	**þȳ, þon (þan)**		**þȳ, þon (þan)**	

(ge)seah: see **(ge)sēon**
searocyne, searocene: adj. *cleverly bold, very bold.* KGM[10]
sēaþ: noun, masc. *pit.* **sēaþe** dsg VR[75]
(ge)sē(o)can: vb. *seek out, desire, strive for.* KGM[123] BC[35] VR[104, 119, 127] **sōhton** 3pl pret VR[133]
secg: noun, masc. *warrior, man.* **secgum** dpl VR[59]
secgan, sæcgan: vb. *declare, tell.* VR[1] ABL[36] KGM[18] **secge** sg pres subj VR[96] **secgað** 1pl pres JLP[43] 3pl pres CLP[23] *etc*
sefa: noun, masc. *mind, heart.* **sefan** dsg BC[44]
sēl: adj. *good.* **sēlost, sēlest**: superl *great(est), excellent.* CLP[33, 82] ABL[67] **sēlesta** nsg VR[27] asg VR[118]
self, silf: pro. *self.* adj. *own, proper, appropriate.* CLP[135] DOX[55] *etc* **sylfa** VR[105] **selfa** KGM[28, 78] **sylfe** asg *herself* VR[92] **selfes** gsg KGM[25, 130] **sylfes** gsg CLP[92] DOX[5] **sylfan** dsg TAD[3] **selfum** dsg KGM[18, 47]
(ge)sellan: vb (w dat of person and acc of thing). *give, supply, lend, entrust.* **syle, sile, sæle** imp sg ELP[6] JLP[19] CLP[85] KGM[112] *etc* **sylest** 2sg pres CLP[53] **sealdest** 2sg pret CLP[73] DOX[62]
sendan, sændan: vb. *send forth, despatch.* **sændest** 2sg pres CLP[5] **sænst** 2sg pres CLP[76]
senn: see **synn**
sēo: see **se**

seofoða: numerical adj. *seventh.* **seofoðan** asg/gsg, adverbially DOX[26]

seolfor: noun, neut. *silver* **seolfre** isg VR[77]

(ge)sēon: vb. *see, perceive.* **gesāwe** sg pret subj VR[4] **geseah** 1sg pret VR[14, 21, etc]

(ge)settan: vb. *set out, set down, assign, ordain, create.* **gesettest** 2sg pres CLP[24] BC[4] **settest** 2sg pret DOX[23] **gesetton** 3pl pret VR[67] **geseted** p ptc VR[141]

sī: see **sīe**

sibb: noun, fem. *peace, friendship, relationship.* **sib** DOX[5] **sibbe** asg CLP[34] KGM[84, 123] dsg CLP[76] **sibbe** DOX[50]

sīd, sȳd: adj. *wide, broad.* **sīdne** asg ABL[31] **sīde** dsg BC[52] **sȳddra** gpl ABL[27] **wīde and sīde** adv. *far and wide* VR[81]

sīd: noun, fem. *side.* **sīdan** dsg VR[49]

sīe: see **beon**

(ge)siene: adj. *visible.* npl VR[46]

sigebēam: noun, masc. *tree of victory.* VR[13] asg VR[127]

sigecempa: noun, masc. *victorious champion.* KGM[10]

sigedrihten: noun, masc. *victory lord, God.* JLP[43]

sigefæst, sigefest: adj. *victorious, triumphant.* BC[52] KHP[16] KGM[151] **sigorfæst** VR[150] **sigefęst** KHP[4]

sigehrǣmig, sigehrēmig: adj. *rejoicing in victory.* KHP[30]

sigor: noun, masc. *victory.* **sigores** gsg ABL[40] **sigora** gpl VR[67]

sile: see **sellan**

silf: see **self**

simle: see **sym(b)le**

sīn: poss pro. *his, her, its, their.* **sīne** apl BC[39] **sīnum** dpl KGM[7]

sinc: noun, neut. *treasure.* **since** dsg VR[23]

singāl: adj. *perpetual, everlasting, daily.* VR[141] **singālan** asg ELP[8]

singan: vb. *sing.* **singað** 3pl pres CLP[60]

(ge)singod: see **(ge)syngian**

sīo: see **beon**

sioððan: see **siððan**

sittan: vb. *sit, be seated.* **sitst** 2sg pres CLP[95]

sīðfæt: noun, masc. *expedition, journey.* **sīðfate** dsg VR[150]

sīðian: vb. *journey.* VR[68]

siððan: adv. *afterwards.* CLP[72, 100] VR[142] **sioððan** KGM[72, 116]

siððan: conj. *after.* VR[3]

six, sex: numerical adj. *six.* DOX[26]

snāw: noun, masc. *snow.* **snāwe** dsg KGM[83]

snotor: adj. *wise, clever.* **snotra** gpl ABL[36]

(ge)snyttru, (ge)snettru: noun, fem. *wisdom.* **snetera** (with a collective sense) gpl KGM[78]

sōdan: see **sōð**

sōhton: see **(ge)sēcan**

(ge)somnian, (ge)samnian: vb. *assemble, unite, join.* **gesomnie** pl pres subj ABL[31]

sōna: adv. *straightway, immediately.*

sorg: noun, fem. *sorrow.* **sorge** dsg JLP[35] **sorga** gpl VR[80] **sorgum** dpl VR[20, 59]

sorgful, sorhful: adj. *sorrowful, miserable.* **sorhfullan** npl KGM[161]

sorhlēoð: noun, neut. *dirge.* asg VR[67]

sōð: adj. *true.* JLP[43] ABL[27] KHP[16] KGM[9] **sōðan** asg CLP[9] **sōðne** asg BC[11] **sōðum** dsg TAD[3] **sōðe** dsg DOX[50] **soðan** npl DOX[35]

sōð: noun, neut. *truth.* asg CLP[83] KGM[74]

sōðe: adv. *truly, accurately.* ABL[33]

sōðfæst: adj. *trustworthy, righteous, best.* ELP[8] CLP[42] **sōðfæstra** comp *more righteous* DOX[5] **sōðfæstest** superl KGM[6]

sōðfæstnes: noun, fem. *truthfulness, justice.* **sōðfæstnesse** dsg KGM[130]

sōðlice: adv. *truly, in fact, amen*

sp(r)ecan: vb. *speak.* VR[27] **spæc** 3sg pret KGM[30]

spēdig: adj. *successful.* VR[151]

sprǣc: noun, fem. *talk, speech.* **sprǣce** npl CLP[120]

stān: noun, masc. *stone.* **stāne** dsg VR[66]

(ge)standan: vb. *stand, stand up.* VR[62] **standeþ** 3sg pres DOX[38] KGM[48] **stōd** 1sg pret VR[38] **(ge)stōdon** 3pl pret VR[7, 63, 71]

(ge)stāh: see **(ge)stīgan**

(ge)staðelian: vb. *establish, make steadfast.* **gestaðelod** p ptc JLP[7]

staðol: noun, masc. *place, station.* **staðole** dsg VR[71]

stæfn, stefn: noun, fem. *voice.* VR[71] **stæfne** dsg CLP[13, 55] DOX[41] **stefnum** dpl KHP[7]

stēam: noun, masc. *wetness, moisture.* **stēame** dsg VR[62]

stefn: noun, neut. *trunk, root.* **stefne** dsg VR[30] see also **stæfn**

(ge)stīgan: vb. *mount, ascend.* VR[34] **stāh** 3sg pret BC[31] **gestāh** 3sg pret VR[40]

stīðmōd: adj. *brave, determined.* VR[40]

(ge)stōd: see **(ge)standan**

strang: adj. *powerful, strong.* VR[40] **strange** npl VR[30]

strǣl: noun, masc/fem. *arrow.* **strǣlum** dpl VR[62]

sunne/sunna: noun, fem/masc. *sun* (often punned against **sunu** by Anglo-Saxon writers). **sunnan** gsg DOX[28]

sunu: noun, masc. *son*. CLP[47] DOX[12] VR[150] KHP[16] asg BC[11] asg or dsg (see note in TAD Introduction) TAD[3]

suslhof: noun, neut. *place of torment*. **suslhofe** dsg BC[34]

swā, swǣ: adv. *thus*. DOX[6] KGM[166] *etc*

swā, swǣ: conj. *so, such that, so that*. CLP[28] **swā swā** conj. *as, just as* JLP[30] DOX[12] KGM[13] **swā hwaðer** pron/conj *whatever, just as* CLP[109]

swāt: noun, masc. *sweat, blood*. **swātes** gsg VR[23]

swǣtan: vb. *bleed, sweat*. VR[20]

swefn: noun, neut. *dream*. **swefna** gpl VR[1]

swegl: noun, neut. *sky, heavens*. **swegles** gsg ABL[23] **swegle** dsg ABL[77]

sweotol, sweotollice: see **swutol, swutollice**

sweotolian: vb. *become manifest*. **swutelað** 3pl pres DOX[36]

swilc: pro. *such*. DOX[63]

swilce, swylce: conj. *just as, such that;* adv. *likewise*. ABL[29] VR[8] KGM[63] **swylce swā** *just as* VR[92]

swīð: adj. *powerful, strong*. **swīðre** comp *stronger*, so *right* (as in *hand, side, etc*) CLP[47] **swiðran** *right* dsg VR[20] KHP[30]

swīðe, swȳðe: adv. *greatly, very, exceedingly, very much, fiercely*. ELP[9] CLP[22] *etc*

swutelian: see **sweotolian**

swutol, sweotol: adj. *clear, manifest*. **swutole** npl DOX[55]

swutollice, sweotollice: adv. *plainly, clearly, manifestly*. CLP[100]

(ge)swȳcan: vb w gen. *cease (from), abandon*. **geswȳce** 3sg pres subj ABL[15]

sȳ: see **bēon**

sȳd: see **sīd**

(ge)syhð, (ge)sihð: noun, fem. *sight, vision*. **gesyhðe** asg VR[96] dsg VR[21, 41, 66]

syle, sylest: see **sellan**

sylf: see **self**

syllic: adj. *rare, marvellous*. VR[13] **syllicre** comp *more marvellous, rarer* asg VR[4]

symbel: noun, neut. *feast*. **symle** dsg VR[141]

sym(b)le: adv. *always*

sȳn: see **bēon**

synd: see **bēon**

(ge)syne: adj. *visible*. npl DOX[55]

syn(n)ful: adj. *wicked, sinful.* **synfulle** apl subst KGM[60]
(ge)syngian: vb. *sin, offend, transgress.* **syngige** 3sg pres ABL[62] **syngode** 1sg pret KGM[52] **gesingod** p ptc CLP[128]
synn, senn: noun, fem. *sin.* **synna, sinna** apl JLP[25] CLP[94] KHP[28] (see note) KGM[47] gpl CLP[118] KGM[28] **synnum** dpl CLP[9] DOX[12] VR[13, 99, 146] *etc* **sennum** dpl KGM[41]
syððan: see **siððan**

teohhian: vb. *settle, determine.* **tyhhað** 3sg pres CLP[107]
tīd: noun, fem. *time, hour.* asg BC[65]
tīrēadig: see **tȳrēadig**
(ge)tīðian, (ge)tȳðian: vb. *grant, bestow.* **tīðast** 2sg pres CLP[62] **getiþa, getȳþa** imp sg ABL[22, 75]
tō: prep w dat. *to, towards, for, as, at,* expressing purpose with noun, infl inf or gerund; *for* VR[129;]
tō: adv. *too* (?JLP[9]), *also, besides, however*
tōsomne: adv. *together.* ABL[36]
tōsyndrian: vb. *sunder, divide.* **tōsyndrodest** 2sg pret CLP[72] DOX[24]
tōweorpan: vb. *cast down, destroy.* **tōwurpe** 2sg pret KHP[24]
(ge)treme(d): see **(ge)trymman**
trēow, trīow: noun, neut. *tree.* asg VR[4, 14] **trīow** asg KHP[27]
(ge)trēowan: vb. *believe in, trust in, rely on.* **getrēowe** 1sg pres BC[59, 64]
trēowfæst, trīofest: adj. *faithful, honest.* KGM[129]
(ge)trymman: vb. *strengthen.* **getreme** imp sg KGM[115] **getremed** p ptc KGM[152]
tunge: noun, fem. *tongue.* KGM[129]
tungol: noun, masc/neut. *star, planet.* **tungla** gpl BC[9]
twā: numerical adj. *two.* **twā and hundseofontig** uninfl *seventy-two* CLP[23]
twēgen: numerical adj. *two.* CLP[107]
tyhhað: see **teohhian**
tȳrēadig, tīrēadig: adj. *glorious, honour-blessed.* CLP[62, 91] ABL[22, 75]
(ge)tȳðian: see **(ge)tīðian**

þā: adv. *then*; conj. *when*; demonstrative adj/pro, see **se**
þām, þǣm: see **se**
þān: see **se**
þan: see **se**

(ge)þanc, þonc: noun, masc. *thought, will, thanks, gratitude.* DOX[3, 43] asg JLP[42] CLP[87] BC[56] KGM[100]

þancian: vb. *give thanks.* **þanciað** 1pl pres KHP[9] 3pl pres CLP[54, 58]

(ge)þancol: adj. *desirous, wise, thoughtful.* KGM[6]

þancung: noun, fem. *thanksgiving, gratitude.* DOX[50]

þane: see **þone**

þanne: adv. *then*

þār, þǣr: adv. *there.* CLP[36] DOX[51]

þār, þǣr: conj. *where.* CLP[34, 100] VR[139, 142] **ðēr ðū wolde swā** *where thou might wish so* KGM[138]

þāra: see **se**

þās: see **þes**

þǣre: see **se**

þǣron: adv. *therein*

þæs: see **se**

þǣs þe: conj. *after* JLP[44]

þǣs þe: rel pro phrase. *of which.* CLP[23]

þæt(te): conj. *that.* see also **se**

þe: rel particle uninfl. *that, which, who*

þē: see **ic**

þēah, þēh: conj. *although*

þearf: noun, fem. *need.* VR[117]

þearle: adv. *severely, violently, grievously.* VR[52] ABL[65]

þēaw: noun, masc. *custom, habit.* asg CLP[25] **þēawas** apl CLP[87] DOX[31]

þegn: noun, masc. *follower, servant.* **þegnas** npl CLP[59] VR[75]

þēh: see **þēah**

þencean: vb. *think, intend.* **þenceð** 3sg pres VR[121] **þencað** 1pl pres JLP[32] 3pl pres VR[115]

þenian: vb. *stretch out.* VR[52]

þēod, þīod: noun, fem. *nation, people.* **þīode** gsg KGM[166] **þēode** dsg CLP[25, 61] **þēoda** apl DOX[3] gpl BC[37] **þīoda** KHP[9] KGM[26] **þīodum** dpl KGM[7]

þēoden: noun, masc. *lord, prince.* JLP[42] **þēodne** dsg VR[69]

þēos: see **þes**

þēoster: adj. *gloomy, dark.* **þrīostre** see note to KHP[28]

þēowa, þīowa: noun, masc. *servant.* KGM[9]

þēowet, þēowot: noun, neut. *bondage, service. asg* CLP[108]

þēr: see **þār**

þes: demonstrative (pronoun or adjective). *this, this one*:

	Masc	*Fem*	*Neut*	*Plural*
Nom	**þes**	**þēos**	**þis**	**þās**
Acc	**þisne**	**þās**	**þis**	**þās**
Gen	**þisses**	**þisse, þisre**	**þisses**	**þissa, þisra**
Dat	**þissum**	**þisse**	**þissum**	**þissum**
Inst	**þȳs**		**þȳs**	

þīn: see **ic**

þing(c): noun, neut. *creation, creature, thing.* apl CLP[131] DOX[22] **þinga** gpl BC[51]

þingian: vb w dat. *intercede for, pray.* **ðingode** 3sg pret KGM[26, 166] **tō þingienne** infl inf KGM[7]

þīnra: see **ic**

þīod: see **þēod**

þīowa: see **þēowa**

(ge)þōht: noun, masc/neut. *thought.* **geþōhte** dsg ABL[65] **geðohtas** apl KGM[15, 32, 44]

þolian: vb. *suffer, allow, endure.* **þolodan** 3pl pret VR[149] **tō þolienne** infl inf KGM[101]

þon: see **se**; **for þon (þe)** adv/conj. *therefore, because.* see also **þonne**

þonc: see **þanc**

þone: see **se**; rel pro. *whom.* BC[32]

þonne, þon, þan: adv. *then.* CLP[106] VR[107, 115] KGM[66, 77]

þonne, þon, þan: conj. *when.* CLP[52, 95]

(ge)þrec, (ge)þræc: noun, neut. *throng.* KGM[48]

þrēo: see **þrīe**

þridda: numeral *third.* CLP[105]

þrīe, þrȳ: numeral. *three.* BC[49] asg BC[51] **þriddan** dsg BC[37]

þrīnes: noun, fem. *trinity, three-ness.* **ðrȳnesse** dsg KHP[40]

þrīostre: see **þēoster**

þriwa: adv. *thrice, three times.* BC[49]

(ge)þrōwian: vb. *suffer.* **þrōwade, þrōwode** 3sg pret BC[30] VR[84, 97, 145]

þrōwung: noun, fem. *passion, suffering.* **ðrōwunga** gsg or gpl (see note) KHP[28]

þrym(m): noun, masc. *troop, host, army, glory, splendour.* CLP[13, 50, 55] *etc* **þrymme** dsg KHP[40]
þrymfæst: adj. *glorious.* VR[84]
þū: see **ic**
þurh: prep w dat/acc/gen. *through, by means of, throughout*
þurhdrīfan: vb. *drive through.* **þurhdrifan** 3pl pret VR[46]
þurhwunian: vb. *remain, endure.* **þurhwunige** sg pres subj JLP[12]
þus: adv. *thus*
þūsend: numerical adj. *thousand.* gpl **þūsenda** CLP[54]
þȳ: see **se**
þȳn: see **ic**
þyncan: impersonal vb. *seem, appear.* **þūhte** 3sg pret VR[4]
þysne: see **þes**
þysson: levelled form of **þyssum**
þȳstro: noun, fem *shadow, shade.* npl VR[52]
þys(s)um: see **þes**

unc: see **ic**
uncuð: adj. *unknown.* **uncuðe** asg KGM[77]
under: prep w dat or acc. *under, beneath, by*
unforht: adj. *fearless, without fear.* VR[110]
unmǣne: adj. *honest, innocent.* BC[16]
unriht: adj. *wicked, unlawful.* **unrihte** npl CLP[120]
unriht: noun, neut. *sin, wrong, wickedness.* asg KGM[46, 97] **unrihtum** dpl KGM[66]
ūp(pe): adv. *up*
ūplic: adj. *upper, supreme, celestial.* **ūplicne** asg BC[35] **ūplican, ūpplican** dsg BC[13] KHP[19]
ūplyft: noun, fem. *upper air.* asg DOX[22] **ūplyfte** gsg DOX[7]
ūre: see **ic**
ūrne: asg CLP[76] see **ic**
Ūria: proper name. *Uriah (husband of Bathsheba and champion of King David).* **Ūriam** asg KGM[21]
ūs, ūsig: see **ic**
ūser: see **ic**

wā: noun, masc. *misery, woe.* ABL[13]
waldest: see **wealdan**
walden(d): see **wealdend**

wamdǣd: see **womdǣd**
wamm: see **womm**
wang: noun, masc. *field, plain, place*. asg BC[4]
wanhoga: noun, masc. *fool, thoughtless one.* **wanhogan** dsg KGM[119]
wann: adj. *dark.* VR[55]
wāst: see **(ge)witan**
wāt: see **(ge)witan**
(ge)wāt: see **(ge)wītan**
wǣd: noun, fem. *covering, clothing, shrouding (of cross)* **wǣdum** dpl VR[15, 22]
wǣfersȳn: noun, fem. *spectacle.* **wǣfersȳne** dsg VR[31]
wǣre, wǣron: see **bēon**
wæs: see **bēon**
wæstm: noun, masc/neut. *stature, offspring, produce, fruit.* **wæstma** gpl DOX[62]
wǣta: noun, masc. *blood, moisture.* **wǣtan** dsg VR[22]
wē: see **ic**
wēa: noun, masc. *woe, evil.* **wēan** gsg JLP[35]
(ge)weald: noun, neut. *control, authority, command, dominion.* asg VR[107] **gewealdum** dpl KHP[13]
wealdan: vb w gen. *rule, determine, control* w gen. **waldest** 2sg pres ABL[25] **weold** 3sg pret BC[28] **wealdende** pres ptc KGM[170]
w(e)aldend: noun, masc. *leader, ruler, lord.* ELP[10] CLP[31] **walden(d)** KHP[9, 41] *etc* **waldendes** gsg KGM[19] **wealdende** dsg VR[121]
weall: noun, masc. *wall.* **weallas** npl KGM[152]
weard: noun, masc. *guardian.* VR[91] KGM[128] asg KHP[2]
wearg: noun, masc. *criminal.* **wergas** apl VR[31]
weg, weog: noun, masc. *way.* asg VR[88] **weogas** apl KGM[119]
we(o)ler: noun, masc. *lip.* **weoloras** apl KGM[132]
wel(l): adv. *well.* In ABL[18] and CLP[19] the inclusion of **wel** in each clause may be related to **wela**: noun, masc. *prosperity, joy, happiness*
wēnan: vb. *think, expect.* **wēne (mē)** *anticipate, look forward to* 1sg pres VR[135]
wendan: vb. *change.* VR[22]
wenn, wynn: noun, fem. *joy, rapture.* **wynn** ABL[21] **wyn** ABL[46] **wenne** dsg KGM[89, 177] **wynnum** dpl JLP[17] VR[15]
weorc, weork: noun, neut. *labour, work.* CLP[26] DOX[27] CLP[120] asg VR[79] KGM[25] **weorkes** gsg ABL[18] **weorc** npl DOX[35] **weorcum** dpl ELP[2]
weorod: see **werod**

weorð: adj. *worthy, valued, noble.* **weorðne** asg KGM[170]
wergas: see **wearg**
(ge)weorðan: vb. *become, be.* KGM[12, 58] **weorðan** likely pl pres subj JLP[38] **weorðe** sg pres subj JLP[14, 46] KGM[151] **geweарð** 3sg pret BC[24] **gewurðe** sg pres subj CLP[40] **wurde** 3sg pret ABL[7] **wurdon** 3pl pret CLP[97] **geworden** p ptc CLP[99]
(ge)weorðian: vb. *honour, make famous.* VR[129] **wurþiað, weorðiað** 3pl pres CLP[26] VR[81] **geweorðode** 3sg pret VR[90, 94] **geweorðad, geweorðod, gewurðod** p ptc ELP[2] CLP[65, 137] DOX[33] VR[15] *etc*
weorðlic: adj. *splendid, valuable.* **wurðlic** CLP[45] **weorðlican** gsg KHP[10]
weorðlice: adv. *splendidly*
wēpan: vb. *weep, bewail, mourn.* **wēop** 3sg pret VR[55]
wer: noun, masc. *human, person.* **were** dsg (*men, male person*) CLP[97] **wera, weora** gpl ELP[3,7] KGM[59]
wered: see **werod**
werod: noun, neut. *company, throng, host.* ABL[35] **weorode, werede** isg VR[69, 124, 152] **wereda, weruda, weoruda, weorada** gpl BC[53] TAD[1] VR[51] KHP[1] KGM[17, 30]
wesan: see **bēon**
wīde: adv. *widely.* CLP[51] DOX[2, 37] **wīde and sīde** adv. *far and wide* VR[81]
wīf: noun, neut. *woman.* **wīfe** dsg CLP[97] KGM[23] **wīfa** gpl VR[94]
wīg: noun, masc. *strife, battle.* **wīge** dsg KGM[9]
wīgbed: noun, masc/neut. *altar.* asg KGM[158]
(ge)wil(l): noun, neut. *desire, wish.* asg CLP[87]
willa: noun. masc. *will, mind, purpose, delight, desire, love.* ELP[4] JLP[14] **willan** asg CLP[19] ABL[13, 18, 72] gsg KHP[6] dsg KGM[150] **willum** dpl KGM[158]
willan: vb. *desire, intend, wish.* **wylle, wille** 1sg pres VR[1] KGM[75] **wile** 3sg pres VR[107] **wolde** 3sg pret VR[34] sg pret subj KGM[138] **woldon** 3pl pret VR[68]
wilnian: vb. *desire.* **wilnast** 2sg pres KGM[59]
wind: noun, masc. *wind.* gsg DOX[8] (see note)
(ge)winn: noun, neuter. *strife, battle.* **gewinne** dsg VR[65]
(ge)winndæg: noun, masc. *battle-day.* **gewinndagum** dpl KGM[12]
wīse: noun, fem. *custom, habit.* **wīsan** apl CLP[25, 73]
(ge)wītan: vb. *depart.* **gewāt** 3sg pret VR[71] **gewiton** 3pl pret VR[133] **wītan** *consider, hold against.* JLP[32] **wūton** pl pres subj *let us* + inf KHP[1]
(ge)witan: vb. *know, be aware of.* ABL[33, 37] **wāt** 1sg pres ABL[3] 3sg pres CLP[103] ABL[52, 54] **wāst** 2sg pres ABL[40] KGM[32, 67]

wīte: noun, neut. *torment, punishment.* **wīte** dsg JLP[35] VR[61] **wīta** gpl VR[87]
wītega, wītga: noun, masc. *prophet, wise man.* **witgan** asg KGM[17]
(ge)witnes: noun, fem. *witness* **gewitnesse** npl CLP[104]
(ge)witt: noun, neut. *understanding, wit, consciousness. asg* DOX[62]
wið: prep w dat. *against, in conflict with*; prep w acc. *near, beside, with*
wlanc: adj. *stately, magnificent.* BC[53]
wlite: noun, masc. *splendour, beauty.* DOX[18]
wlitig: adj. *glorious, beautiful.* npl DOX[49]
(ge)wlitigian: vb. *become beautiful.* **gewlitegod** p ptc JLP[17] DOX[6]
wolcen: noun, masc/neut. *cloud.* **wolcna** gpl DOX[8] **wolcnum** dpl VR[53, 55]
womdǣd, wamdǣd: noun, fem. *deed of shame, sin.* **womdǣde** apl JLP[32] **womdēda** KGM[19]
womm, wamm: noun, masc. *sin, iniquity.* **wommum** dpl VR[14] **wammum** dpl KGM[41]
word: noun, neut. *word, command, speech.* asg DOX[53, 62] **worde** dsg VR[111] apl VR[27] **wordum** dpl CLP[26] VR[97] KGM[17, 30]
(ge)worden: see **weorðan**
(ge)worhte, (ge)worhton: see **wyrcan**
woruld: noun, fem. *world, age, life.* asg DOX[38] **world** asg CLP[29] **worulde** dsg JLP[17] DOX[6, 18] VR[133] **worulda** gpl ABL[43] **ā on worlda forð** *world without end* CLP[137] **on woruld a woruld** *for ever and ever*
woruldrīce: noun, neut. *earthly kingdom.* dsg CLP[101]
wrāð: adj. *cruel, violent.* **wrāðra** gpl VR[51]
wudu: noun, masc. *wood.* VR[27]
wuldor: noun, neut. *glory.* DOX[2] TAD[1] KHP[4] asg JLP[42] **wuldres** gsg ELP[2] VR[14, 90, 97, 133] **wuldre** dsg CLP[3] DOX[47] VR[135, 143] KHP[43]
wuldordrēam: noun, masc. *heavenly rapture.* **wuldordrēames** gsg KHP[10]
wuldorgifu: noun, fem. *glorious gift, grace.* **wuldorgyfa** npl BC[53] **wuldorgyfe** npl DOX[49]
wuldormicel: adj. *gloriously great.* **wuldormicele** npl CLP[104]
wuldorword: noun, neut. *glorious word.* CLP[51]
wuldrian: vb. *glorify.* KHP[1]
wund: noun, fem. *wound.* **wunde** npl KGM[56, 161, 174] **wunda** apl JLP[26]
wundor, wunder: noun, neut. *miracle, wonder.* ABL[39]
wunian: vb. *dwell, exist, occupy, be occupied with.* VR[121, 143] **wunað, wuniaþ** 3pl pres DOX[46] VR[135] **wunedon** 3pl pret (see note to VR[3]) VR[155]
wurdon: see **weorðan**
wurðlic: see **weorðlic**

wurðmynt, weorðmynt: noun, fem/masc/neut. *honour, glory, dignity*. TAD[1]
wuton: see **(ge)witan**
wȳde: see **wīde**
wylle: see **willan**
wyn(n): see **wenn**
wynfęst, wynfæst: adj. *joyful.* **wynfęste** npl KGM[152]
(ge)wyrc(e)an: vb. *perform, do, make.* VR[65] **gewyrcean** ABL[72] **worhtest** 2sg pret BC[3] **geworhtest** 2sg pret BC[8] DOX[20, 25, 60] **wyrcð** 3sg pres CLP[19] ABL[13] **worhte** 3sg pret CLP[45] **geworhton** 1pl pret CLP[101] 3pl pret VR[31] **geworden** p ptc VR[87]
wyrd: noun, fem. *fate, that which happens.* VR[74] **wyrda** gpl VR[51]
(ge)wyrht: noun, fem/neut. *deed, merit.* **gewyrhta** npl CLP[18]
wyrsa, wiersa: adj. *worse.* **wyrse** apl CLP[102]
wytan: see **witan**

xl: Roman number. *forty.* BC[39]

yfel: noun, neut. *evil.* y**fele** dsg JLP[40] CLP[126] **yfla, yfela** gpl ELP[11] KGM[53]
yld, ild: noun, fem. *age, generation.* **ylda** gpl ABL[48]
ymb(e): prep w acc or dat. *around, about*
ymbclippan: vb. *embrace.* **ymbclypte** 3sg pret VR[42]
ys: see **bēon**
ysope: noun, fem (borrowed). *hyssop.* **ysopon** dsg KGM[81]
ȳþost, īeþost, ēðest: adv. *most easily* (from **īeð**, adv. *easily*). CLP[4] ABL[6]

FSC

Mixed Sources
Product group from well-managed forests, controlled sources and recycled wood or fibre

Cert no. SW-COC-003438
www.fsc.org
© 1996 Forest Stewardship Council